Word Identification Techniques

Josephine P. Ives
New York University

Laura Z. Bursuk
York College, City University of New York

Sumner A. Ives
New York University

D1301658

Rand McNally College Publishing Company   **Chicago**

Dedicated to All Our Students
Who Nagged Us into Writing This Book

Sponsoring editor: Louise Waller
Project editor: Maribeth Allen
Illustrator: Jack Stockman
Designer: Randall Antonson

79 80 81   10 9 8 7 6 5 4 3 2 1
Printed in U.S.A.
Library of Congress Catalog Card Number   78-66441

Preface

Word identification is the foundation on which comprehension and other aspects of reading depends. Because reading textbooks typically include a wide variety of topics related to reading and reading instruction, many teachers do not acquire the depth of understanding essential for the effective instruction of word identification.

Our intention is to describe a linguistically coherent basis for teaching word identification and to present all possible word identification techniques in detail. We became aware of the need for a book that would help teachers understand how written English words are identified in reading, and to give them information about how pupils learn to identify written words, from our own experiences in pre-service and in-service training courses. Prospective teachers, regular classroom teachers, specialized teachers of reading, and teachers of children with specialized needs all need the information this book provides.

The book is prerequisite or corequisite to any course in reading instruction. It is intended for those teachers who have or who expect to have responsibility for teaching reading at any level. It should also be useful to those preparing regular classroom teachers, reading specialists, and teachers of both gifted children and children with learning disabilities.

We have limited this book to a discussion of word identification in order to develop the topic in depth. Chapter 1 provides the theoretical basis of the book, while Chapter 2 develops an understanding of word identification in the total reading process and presents an overview of the various word identification techniques.

Techniques developed in this book include whole word techniques that are linguistically based as well as those that are not. Chapters 3, 4, 5, and 6 present the whole word techniques: clues available from visual configurations, pictures, semantic context, and syntactic context. Chapters 7–10 describe morphemic and phonic word-structure techniques. The technique involving pronunciation spelling is developed in Chapter 11. (This chapter sequence is not to be interpreted as prescriptive of the order in which these techniques should be taught to pupils.) Chapter 12 summarizes the techniques and examines effective and efficient ways to integrate them and personalize them for individual pupils.

The pattern of organization for presenting the various techniques is identical, so that equivalent information about each is available. Thus a comprehensive analysis of each technique can be given without bias. The organization also enables the reader to make comparisons among various techniques. *All* teachers need to be knowledgeable about *all* the techniques if they are to meet the instructional needs of *all* of their pupils. Specifically, each word identification technique is discussed in respect to its characteristics, its strengths, and its weaknesses. Each presentation ends with two sets of exercises, one for teachers and one for pupils.

Suggestions for Using This Book

Before you begin reading this book, you should familiarize yourself with the pronunciation key that appears on pp. vi–vii. The symbols in this key are used throughout the textbook to represent the sounds of English. Like the symbols in dictionary pronunciation keys, they are not intended to differentiate precise phonetic values.

The particular set of symbols included in this key was compiled by correlating the symbols found in the pronunciation keys of commonly used school dictionaries. Adaptations were made to emphasize the one-to-one correspondence between sound symbol and speech sound. For example, the symbols /ȯ/ and /č/ represent the sounds frequently represented in pronunciation keys by the two-letter symbols /oi/ and /ch/. Thus each sound is represented by a symbol that consists of a single letter, with or without an accompanying diacritical mark.

In order to distinguish between spelling patterns and pronunciation patterns, different typographic devices are used. Angle brackets are consistently used to denote letters of spelling patterns, slashes to denote sounds or pronunciation patterns. For example, statements about spelling-sound correspondences are set up as follows: initial ⟨e⟩ in an accented syllable represents /ē/, ⟨cat⟩ = /kāt/. A great deal of misunderstanding and confusion can be avoided by keeping a clear distinction between letters and sounds.

Since terms are used that may be unfamiliar to you or that may be used differently from what you are used to, a glossary is provided at the end of the book. Key terms essential to the understanding of language-reading concepts are defined there. You may wish to consult it as you read to clarify unfamiliar or confusing terms.

The chapters are presented according to a specific rationale; however, they need not all be read or studied in sequence. Chapters 1 and 2 should be read first since they provide the foundation for understanding all the techniques. Chapters 3 through 11 are independent of each other and may be read in any sequence. Chapter 12, which summarizes the techniques, logically appears at the end of the book; however, it may also be read profitably before the individual word identification techniques are studied.

Chapters 3 through 11 conclude with two different sets of exercises. The first has been designed to give the user an opportunity to experience how particular word identification clues function. It is often difficult for proficient, mature readers, who identify words without conscious attention in their own reading, to understand the kinds of clues required by readers at lower levels of reading development. These exercises are not necessarily appropriate for use by pupils in reading instruction.

The purpose of the second set of exercises (Suggested Activities for Pupil Practice) is to illustrate how the various word identification clues can be presented to and practiced by pupils at various stages of development. The number of these activities in each chapter is limited since our intent was primarily to develop the principles and strategies of teaching the several techniques, not to develop a workbook. The directions for these activities, however, are both specific and comprehensive. Since the same principles and strategies can be applied in teaching the use of all of the clues related to a given technique, teachers who understand these principles and strategies should be able to develop additional exercises as needed.

Suggestions for further reading are listed at the end of the book. References have been restricted to texts that are readily available to teachers and have been selected to reflect a variety of viewpoints. The references are provided for those readers who are interested in extending their knowledge and in learning what a sampling of authors have written on the topics of the particular chapters. The list is not intended to be exhaustive.

Acknowledgements

We want to express our appreciation to Dr. James Shepherd of Queensborough Community College of the City University of New York for his careful reading of the manuscript and for his thoughtful commentary and helpful suggestions.

Pronunciation Key—Vowel Phonemes

Pronunciation Symbols	Common Names for Phonemes	Key Words
/ă/	short a	act, cat, back
/ā/	long a	ape, bait, day
/â/	circumflex a	air, pair, there
/ä/	two dot a	art, father, cart
/ĕ/	short e	elk, bet, deck
/ē/	long e	eat, beat, see
/ĭ/	short i	is, hit, pick
/ī/	long i	ice, light, buy
/î/	circumflex i	ear, pier
/ŏ/	short o	ox, cot, dock
/ō/	long o	own, coat, toe
/ô/	circumflex o	order, ball, saw
/ȯ/	diphthong oi	oil, coin, boy
/ŭ/	short u	up, cut, love
/ū/	long u	use, cute, few
/û/	circumflex u	poor, sure
/ u̇/	short double o	book, put
/ü/	long double o	soon, move, you
/ö/	diphthong ou	out, cloud, cow
/3/	r vowel	earn, bird, fur
/ɝ/	unaccented r vowel	urbane, perhaps, advisor
/ə/	schwa	above, succeed, gallop

Pronunciation Key—Consonant Phonemes

Pronunciation Symbols	Common Letter Names for Phonemes	Key Words
/b/	b sound	bad, baby, rob
/č/	ch sound	child, hatchet, much
/d/	d sound	dog, ladder, red
/f/	f sound	fat, wafer, if
/g/	g sound	go, legal, bag
/h/	h sound	hat, aha
/j/	j sound	jam, gem, ledger, hedge
/k/	k sound	cat, kite, acorn, rock
/l/	l sound	land, valley, coal
/m/	m sound	me, rumor, am
/n/	n sound	not, diner, in
/ŋ/	ng sound	long, link, sing
/p/	p sound	page, paper, cup
/r/	r sound	red, sorry, fear
/s/	s sound	so, sister, rice
/š/	sh sound	she, fissure, dish
/t/	t sound	tell, later, it
/o/	th sound (voiceless)	thick, ether, cloth
/đ/	th sound (voiced)	that, father, bathe
/v/	v sound	vine, save, of
/w/	w sound	wet, will
/y/	y sound	yet, loyal, you
/z/	z sound	zip, scissors, rise
/ž/	zh sound	measure, seizure, mirage

Contents

PART ONE

1

Theoretical Considerations

This part consists of two chapters that develop the rationale of the book. Chapter 1 defines reading as a linguistic process and relates reading to the deep and surface structures of language. The differences between beginning and proficient reading are discussed. Implications for reading instruction are presented, and particular attention is directed toward dialectal considerations.

Chapter 2 examines words, word units, and the process of word identification. It also contains an overview of the seven word identification techniques that are presented and explained in this book.

Chapter 1

Reading as a Linguistic Process

reading as a
linguistic process

Any discussion of reading must consider it within the framework of the
entire process of verbal communication since reading is a part of this larger
process. Verbal communication, the transmission of meaning by words in
grammatical arrangements (sentences), involves language. Thus, it is a
linguistic process. Reading is one aspect of that linguistic process; the
other aspects are writing, listening, and speaking.

Oral and written communication are parallel processes. Writing and
reading are related in the same way as speaking and listening. As Figure
1.1 illustrates, speaking and writing are equivalent productive or *encoding*
processes. Similarly, listening and reading are equivalent receptive or
decoding processes. Listeners decode verbal information conveyed through
sound; readers decode verbal information conveyed through writing.
Decoding is not a passive process; it requires active participation. If
listeners and readers fail to carry out their portion of the process,

communication does not take place despite the efforts of speakers and writers.

Figure 1.1

Verbal Communication

	Oral Communication	**Written Communication**
(production) encoding	Speaking	Writing
(reception) decoding	Listening	Reading

When speakers or writers wish to transmit information, they begin with general concepts. These general concepts are fragmented according to the vocabulary and the grammatical rules of a particular language. Exactly how this is done is not fully known. According to some theorists of verbal communication, there is a kind of *deep structure* common to *all* languages. The initial fragmentation takes place according to the rules of this universal deep structure. Next, the concepts are more specifically formulated according to the deep structure rules of the *particular* language. The concepts are then encoded into the surface structure of the *particular* language in two stages. Words are first selected and arranged in sentences according to the rules of a specific *dialect*. These grammatical arrangements of words are then manifested in sound or letter patterns, depending on whether spoken or written language is being used. Thus, the sound or letter patterns constitute the overt means of verbal communication.

Listeners and readers use the overt sound and letter patterns as clues to infer or decode the concepts encoded by speakers and writers. The process of decoding is the reverse of the process of encoding. If the processes of encoding and decoding are successful, the message received is the message intended, and communication occurs.

Other theorists claim that since we know so little about any part of the communication process, speculation about it, at present, is unprofitable. All theorists, however, agree that the portion of the communication process involving deep structure is intuitive and is probably outside the conscious awareness of both the producers and receivers of a message.

Surface and Deep Structure

The actual words and sentence patterns that are heard or seen by listeners and readers are called the surface structure of language. The surface structure of language varies from language to language and also from dialect to dialect. Moreover, at the surface level, the written and spoken forms of a language or dialect are not wholly equivalent; that is, neither duplicates the other. Although both use lexical and grammatical units from the same language system, there often are differences in the specific units used in speech and in writing. An example of a vocabulary difference is the use of slang in speech but not in formal writing. An example of a grammatical difference is apparent in the use of passive sentences, which appear frequently in writing but which are seldom used in speech. However, writing does operate within the range of the vocabulary and the grammatical possibilities of speech.

Two major sources of linguistic information are always available to readers in the surface structure that they see. One is the syntactic format, which tells them by the arrangement and position of the words, which are nouns, which are verbs, and so on. The syntactic format also tells them which words or groups of words are subjects, predicates, objects, etc. For example, the syntactic format (word arrangement) of the sentence "The children wanted a piñata" indicates that the word *children* is a noun functioning as a subject, that the word *wanted* is a verb functioning as a predicate, and that the word *piñata* is a noun functioning as an object.

The other source of information is in the semantic meanings of the words themselves. For example, the word *piñata,* according to Webster, refers to "a decorated pottery jar filled with candies, fruits, and gifts that is hung from the ceiling to be broken as part of Mexican festivities." Both the syntactic and the semantic information are essential to an understanding of the sentence. Neither source by itself is sufficient.

The syntactic and semantic information in one part of a sentence may affect or restrict the meaning (the possible deep structure represented) of other parts of the same sentence. Thus, the different meanings of *see* in the following sentences are not entirely clear until the complete sentences are read.

I see the doctor *now* (or any final adverb of present time).
I see the doctor *tomorrow* (or any final adverb of future time).

Likewise, the syntactic and semantic information in one or more sentences in a passage may be useful in inferring the deep structure of other sentences in the same passage. For example, the meaning of the sentence "Ingrid is fair" is ambiguous without additional information. Its deep structure depends on its context, for example "She sunburns easily," or, "She listens to both sides of the argument."

Sometimes readers must cut through the surface structure to find a logical meaning. An example is the sentence "The treaty is ready to sign." We know that there is an implied passive, "ready to be signed," because treaties are inanimate objects and are thus not capable of doing any signing themselves. The subject in this sentence is obviously not the doer of the action. In a passive sentence, the doer of the action is never the subject; it is either specified in a prepositional phrase or merely implied. The sentence "Smoking is prohibited" is an example of an implied passive construction since the "doer" of the prohibiting is not specified. "Henri was baptized by the priest" is an example of a direct passive construction because the doer (the priest) of the action (baptized) is explicitly stated. The structural arrangements that would make these matters explicit, that would display them in diagrammatical form as worked out by a grammarian, are included in the term *deep structure.*

We do not know just how language users derive deep structure from the surface structure of the sentences they hear and see. It is assumed that they somehow relate the surface structure to more abstract grammatical patterns which, when properly filled with words, contain all the information that is necessary. Consider the following:

Growing corn is easy.
Growing corn is green.

In the first sentence, *growing* is a gerund (a verb ending in ⟨-ing⟩ and used as a noun), *corn* is its object, and this sequence of words is the subject of the sentence. In the second sentence, *corn* is not the object of *growing,* but is modified by it; that is, *growing* is used as an adjective. Despite the similarities in surface structure, the functions, and hence the meanings, of *growing* in the two sentences are different. This difference is related to the difference between the possible contexts of *easy* and those of *green.* These possibilities are matters of deep structure. It is possible to say "It is easy to grow corn," but it is not possible to say "It is green to grow corn." "Corn that is growing is green" is a paraphrase of "Growing corn is green." "Corn that is growing is easy" is not a paraphrase of "Growing corn is easy." However, proficient users of English have an intuitive understanding of the two sentences; that is, an immediate understanding, devoid of conscious analysis.

The Reading Process

All reading starts with written surface structure. The goal in reading is to relate the surface structure to the deep structure in order to get the information (meaning) that is being transmitted by writers. Reading, then, is the process of deriving meaning from written language.

A distinction needs to be made between beginning reading and more proficient reading. The reading done in the initial stages of learning to read is a mediated process. That is, beginning readers start with the written display and must recode that into its spoken equivalent in order to infer meaning. The mediation of the spoken equivalent may be overt (vocalized) or covert (unvocalized). When the mediation process is overt, the reading is oral. When it is covert, the reading is silent. As readers acquire proficiency in identifying written word forms within their respective grammatical structures, they gradually eliminate the mediation step of the process (i.e., overt or covert speech) and infer the meaning directly from the written display. Fluent, silent reading is probably accomplished too rapidly to permit recoding of the writing into sound.

For beginning readers, the purpose of oral reading is to practice associating unfamiliar written word forms and unfamiliar written grammatical patterns with familiar spoken words and familiar oral grammatical patterns. The primary function of a teacher at this stage of pupils' reading development is to direct and monitor this recoding process. If readers are unable to infer meaning from the spoken words and word arrangements that they recode, their reading consists of *word calling*.

The oral reading done by more proficient readers usually has a different purpose, that of sharing a written communication with someone else. For example, parents or teachers may read stories to children, judges may read their charges to juries, ministers may read sermons to their congregations, and so on. The purpose of this kind of oral reading is to transmit to someone else information that has been recorded in writing. In this kind of oral reading, readers look at the written display before them, identify the written word forms within their respective grammatical patterns, and infer the meaning represented by the written display. Then they re-encode the meaning into sound and read aloud. The first part of this process (from the written display to the derivation of meaning) is equivalent to proficient silent reading. The whole process of proficient oral reading is so rapid that both listeners and readers are unaware of the sequence of steps involved. The essential differences between oral and silent reading and between beginning oral reading and proficient oral reading need to be understood by teachers since their expectations of pupils should differ depending on the kind of reading pupils do. These differences are illustrated in Figure 1.2.

Figure 1.2

Beginning Oral Reading	**Proficient Oral Reading**	**Proficient Silent Reading**
1. Written Display	1. Written Display	1. Written Display
2. Oral Equivalent	2. Meaning	2. Meaning
3. Meaning	3. Oral Equivalent	

Dialectal Considerations

Children acquire language at a very early age. This means that children usually enter school with an intuitive command of a language. They have acquired their language informally by participating in a human community—by living with others and learning to communicate with them. It is unknown to what extent their language abilities are innate, to what extent they are acquired, and if acquired, how. The fact is, simply, that children's command of language is already well developed by the time their formal language training begins. This makes it possible for children to add literacy to their developing verbal abilities; because children already have language ability, they can learn to read.

It is important for reading teachers to realize that the surface structures (the actual sounds, words, and grammatical patterns) that young children have acquired represent the dialects of the communities in which they live. If the spoken dialect agrees substantially with the dialect used in reading instruction, the children's task in beginning reading is simply that of transferring recognition from oral to corresponding written arrangements of words. In other words, they merely recode from writing to speech. In doing this they can depend on their linguistic intuition to understand the deep structure that the writing represents and, hence, the meaning being communicated. If, however, the children's spoken dialects differ substantially from the dialect used in their beginning reading materials, they may have difficulty recoding from writing to speech since the written and oral surface structures differ. Particular difficulty may be encountered when the pronunciations, vocabularies, and grammatical patterns of the pupils' dialects are nonstandard, since the language of most reading materials is likely to be standard.

Pupils who speak different dialects of standard English seem to learn to read with about equal facility. One reason for this may be that, in any particular area of the country, teachers and pupils tend to speak the same variety of standard English and, hence, tend to understand each other easily and to respond similarly to the instructional materials. In fact, pupils may experience no difficulty in learning to read even if the dialect shared by teachers and pupils is nonstandard.

Moreover, even very young children can learn to understand and use elements of a variety of dialects as they are exposed to them. Familiarity with more than one dialect enables them to process a greater variety of surface structures successfully. This versatility can facilitate the development of their reading skills. There seems to be no conclusive evidence to suggest that children must *speak* standard English in order to learn how to read it.

Implications for Reading Instruction

Inasmuch as reading shares a common basis with the other aspects of verbal communication, reading instruction should reflect the total communication framework. However, teachers need to be aware of the differences between speech and standard English writing. Speech and writing are related in that English writing is alphabetic and operates within the range of vocabulary and grammatical possibilities of speech. Teachers can take advantage of these facts in teaching people how to read English as long as they recognize that writing is not just manually recorded speech.

In order to plan and carry out effective reading instruction, teachers must be aware of their pupils' oral language abilities and must be prepared to develop these abilities to the levels necessary for success in reading. Initial reading instruction, in particular, is highly dependent on (1) the speaking and listening abilities of pupils and (2) the correspondence of these abilities to the teacher's language and to the requirements of the reading materials.

Reading is not a single, unvarying process. There are many different kinds of reading: oral, silent, beginning, and proficient, among others. The purposes and characteristics of each kind of reading differ from the others, although they share common bases in word identification and comprehension. Teachers' expectations of their pupils should be related to these different purposes and characteristics. Teachers should not expect beginning readers to perform like proficient readers. Reading proficiency must be developed along a continuum. Activities should increase in difficulty in conjunction with the pupils' developing linguistic and intellectual abilities.

Because reading is a complex process, it is best taught by dividing the process into component parts and by then presenting the parts in a carefully ordered sequence, from simple to complex. The authors of this book divide the reading process into three major groups of skill components:

Word identification: the association of the written surface structure with oral surface structure

Comprehension: the derivation of the meaning represented by the written surface structure

Fluency and study skills: the efficient use of the reading process for its several purposes

This book is concerned only with the first of these three groups of skill components, those related to *word identification.*

Chapter 2

Word Identification

word identification
word identification
_____ identification

This chapter discusses words and the process of word identification. It also provides an overview of the seven word identification techniques.

What Is a Word?

Understanding what is meant by the term *word* is essential to understanding the process of word identification. Distinguishing between written words and spoken words is also essential since much word identification instruction is dependent on matching written words with spoken words. This is particularly true in the early stages of reading instruction.

Words are commonly described as single or combined units of meaning. An individual word may consist of only one meaningful part, such as *like* or *blue.* It may consist of two or more meaningful parts, such as *like /s, like /ly, un /like /ly,* and *like /li /hood.* (Further discussion of words consisting of more than one meaningful part may be found in Chapter 7.)

Written words in English consist of sequences of letters that represent the meaningful part or parts of the words. They can be distinguished easily since written words are always separated from each other by blank spaces.

Spoken words consist of sequences of speech sounds that represent the meaningful part or parts of the words. It is not always easy, however, to distinguish the boundaries of individual words in normal speech. Often two or more words are run together so that they sound as if they were one long word. For example, the three-word sentence "How are you?" may be pronounced as if it consisted of only one word (/höry ǝ/); it may be pronounced as if it consisted of two words (/hör yü/); or it may be pronounced as three separate words (/hö är yü/).

Generally, children must be able to match written words with their spoken equivalents in order to learn to read. To do this they must be able to distinguish written words from each other and to segment speech into spoken words. Some children enter school able to do both but many need to be taught.

Emphasis on distinguishing individual words should be limited to the initial stage of reading instruction so as not to foster word-by-word reading, or word calling. It is difficult to decode meaning from sentences uttered in a word-by-word manner since meaning is not conveyed by individual words. Oral reading should reconstruct sequences of words according to the rhythms of speech rather than as a series of uniformly spaced and uniformly stressed individual words. Teachers must encourage reading that concerns itself with meaning from the very beginning of reading instruction.

Although beginning readers are usually very concerned with the perception of individual words, proficient readers do not necessarily perceive all the words in the sentences they read. Instead, they are more likely to perceive only enough of the words, word parts, or word and letter features to enable them to infer the meaning of the sentences. Attempting to perceive each word in every sentence would slow down their rate of reading so greatly as to interfere with their fluency and with their comprehension. Proficient readers are able to make efficient use of an array of word identification clues that beginning readers have not yet mastered. Thus, beginning readers are more dependent upon the perception and identification of all of the words. As readers become skillful in using a wider variety of word identification clues, their dependency on the perception of individual words decreases.

What Is Word Identification?

Word identification is an essential first step in the process of deriving meaning from written context. This is because the reading process is dependent on visual items (written words) that are arranged in grammatical patterns (the visible surface structure). The visual items must be identified in order for meaning to be derived through them. Consequently, word identification is the base on which reading proficiency is built and is the point at which formal reading instruction usually begins. However, it is important to recognize that word identification is not the whole reading process; it is only one part of the overall process of deriving meaning from the printed page. Eventually, the word identification process becomes automatic and subconscious.

Word identification involves assigning literal (denotative) and affective (connotative) meanings and functions to words in written sentences; it is not word pronunciation or word naming alone. Word naming can be done by anyone who knows the letter-sound correspondences of the language. It may also be done in the case of particular whole words ("sight words") by anyone who has memorized the names of those whole word configurations.

There are three aspects to word identification: the written form of the word, the word name, and the word meaning. Readers may be familiar with all three, with two, with only one, or even with none in relation to a given word. Word identification is dependent on which of the three aspects readers are familiar with and can associate in relation to given words. If they are familiar with and can associate all three aspects, they can identify and pronounce the words correctly. If they are unfamiliar with and cannot associate any aspect with another, they can neither identify nor pronounce the words correctly. If they can associate only the forms and the names, they will be able to pronounce the words without identifying them correctly. If they can associate only the forms and the meanings, they can identify the words correctly without being able to pronounce them correctly.

Word identification does not necessarily depend upon accuracy of recoding or word naming. Readers may be able to identify words successfully even though they may not be able to pronounce or name them to the teacher's satisfaction. Differences in word pronunciation may be due to speech problems, dialect variations, or to inadequate knowledge of letter-sound correspondences. For example, pupils of Spanish-speaking backgrounds may pronounce the word *big* as /bēg/ in the sentence "I live in a big house." Pupils speaking a particular black dialect may say /plā/ for *plays* in the sentence "He plays in the street." Pupils with immature speech may say /twē/ for *three* in the sentence "I have three cents." In each case, as long as the pupils derive the appropriate meaning from the words, they have identified them successfully. And, of course, proficient word identification in silent reading does not involve word naming at all. Teachers, however, usually depend upon word pronunciation to infer pupils' skill in word identification. They are not always aware that accuracy of recoding does not guarantee successful word identification and that differences in pronunciation may be speech- or language-related and not reading-related.

The dependence of word identification on meaning becomes clear when nonsense words are considered. Nonsense words are artificially constructed words that follow the patterns of English pronunciation and spelling but that do not represent meaning. For example, the nonsense words *klat* and *fim* can be named or pronounced but they cannot be identified because they do not represent any meaning that readers know or can infer. Since meaning is essential to word identification, teachers must continually verify pupils' understanding of the words that they pronounce in reading. The use of words in reading that come from the pupils' speaking vocabularies is one way of ensuring meaningfulness. Through efficient use of contextual clues, proficient readers are frequently able to identify words in their reading that are not familiar to them in their spoken form. Beginning readers are not usually able to do this. They generally can identify only those written words whose meanings they already know through their speaking and listening experiences.

Terms such as *word attack, word analysis, word recognition, word perception,* and *decoding* are frequently used interchangeably with or in place of *word identification.* These terms should be differentiated since they are not all synonymous. Word attack and word analysis usually refer to the oral reconstruction of the printed word form through application of letter-sound correspondences. Word recognition and word perception usually refer to the oral reconstruction of words on the basis of picture and visual feature clues, without recourse to letter-sound correspondences. Of all these terms, decoding is the only one that is synonymous with word identification since it involves meaning as an inherent aspect.

Since word identification involves understanding of the meaning and function of words, and since word forms usually represent specific meanings and functions only in contextual formats, word identification can best be developed through the use of contextual material. For example, structure words such as the preposition *from* represents no clearly perceived meaning or function in isolation. It becomes part of readers' understanding only in context:

I came *from* home.
Please refrain *from* laughing.

Content words can also represent more than one meaning. For example, *bank* cannot be unambiguously identified until it appears in context:

I put my money in the *bank*.
You can *bank* on her telling the truth.
Grass grows on the river *bank*.

In fluent silent reading, readers are usually not even aware of the ongoing process of word identification; it is accomplished so easily and so quickly at this stage of reading development that it is automatic and inconspicuous. Such proficiency results from considerable practice, practice that entails using all the various word identification techniques with contextual materials, not with isolated words. Preoccupation with word identification during reading slows down reading speed and interferes with the acquisition of meaning; it precludes fluent and proficient reading.

What Are the Various Word Identification Techniques?

Word identification techniques are strategies that readers use to distinguish written word forms. There are several techniques, and each utilizes a different kind of information. A combination of techniques may be necessary in a given instance to identify a word or sequence of words.

Seven word identification techniques will be described and discussed in the following chapters. Some techniques are based on linguistic information and some are based on the non-linguistic information that accompanies the text. The techniques discussed in chapters 3 and 4 involve the use of visual configuration clues and picture clues, and are essentially non-linguistic, whole-word identification techniques. The techniques involving the use of semantic and syntactic clues (chapters 5 and 6) are also whole-word identification techniques, but they are language-related and depend on verbal context. These four techniques are classified as whole-word techniques because readers use them to identify whole words, even though they may not be able to analyze the words into their structural components. For example, readers who have a reading vocabulary in which the longest word is *beautiful* may use the configuration clue of the word length to identify the word form ⟨beautiful⟩ even though they may not be able to analyze its semantic and phonic components. Upon encountering the word form ⟨periscope⟩ beneath a picture of a periscope in a chapter describing submarines, readers may use the picture alone as a clue to identify ⟨periscope⟩. Similarly, in the sentence "The shoes were too small; I could not squeeze my _____ into them" readers can identify the missing word as *feet* without reference to word structure at all since *feet* is one of very few words that makes sense and is syntactically (grammatically) appropriate in this context.

Morphemic and phonic analysis, the techniques discussed in chapters 7-10, are not whole-word techniques. Like the semantic- and syntactic-clue techniques, they are language-related techniques. However, they involve the analysis of individual words into their component sub-units and are, therefore, word-structure techniques.

Morphemic analysis is used primarily for the purpose of identifying words by isolating two or more meaning units in them. For example, readers use morphemic analysis when they analyze the word form ⟨churches⟩ into *church* and ⟨-es⟩ to determine that the word denotes more than one place of worship. They also do so when they divide ⟨unhappy⟩ into ⟨un-⟩ and *happy* to determine that the word denotes sadness.

Phonic analysis is used primarily to identify words by determining correspondences between their conventional spelling patterns and their pronunciation. When phonic analysis is applied to one-syllable words, the analysis of structure is restricted to the relationship between letters (or graphemes) and sounds (or phonemes). For example, readers can use their knowledge of the sounds commonly associated with the letters ⟨f⟩, ⟨a⟩, and ⟨t⟩ to identify *fat*. When phonic analysis is applied to multisyllabic words, letter-sound correspondences are used together with principles of syllabication and accent. For example, when readers use phonic analysis to identify the word form ⟨secret⟩, they use their knowledge of the correspondences between graphemes and phonemes together with (1) a principle of syllabication that advises dividing the word between the letters ⟨e⟩ and ⟨c⟩ and (2) a principle of accenting that suggests that the primary accent should be placed on the first syllable.

The several techniques supply overlapping clues to the identification of words. There is never a fixed amount of visual, orthographic, semantic, syntactic, morphemic, or phonic information required to identify a word. The successful identification of a word is always dependent on how much information is available to the reader. If one source provides many clues, fewer clues are necessary from other sources. Therefore, although they may be used singly, the various word identification techniques are usually used by proficient readers in combinations complementary and supplementary to each other. From the very beginning of formal reading instruction pupils should be taught components of all the techniques and should be taught to use them in appropriate combinations. Proficient reading is possible only through their combined use. Having applied all of these whole-word and word-structure techniques, readers may at times still fail to identify a word or be unsure of their identification. When this happens, they must consult another source of information, frequently a more experienced reader such as a teacher. However, it is the purpose of word identification instruction to give readers complete independence. The use of pronunciation-spelling clues in glossaries and dictionaries, which gives readers such independence, is presented in Chapter 11 as a seventh word identification technique.

When children are taught how to use word identification clues, they are very conscious at first of their application of a given technique. They also tend to use only one technique at a time. As they develop skill, they combine clues and techniques in order to identify words more rapidly and successfully. With developing proficiency, they also begin to use them automatically and reflexively. Children who learn to read on their own, without benefit of specific instruction, represent a different situation since they, in some way, evolve their own strategies. They probably read without conscious awareness of how they accomplish the task right from the outset. However, teaching reading to such children is not the focus of this book. The focus of this book is on systematic instruction for children who need such instruction in order to learn to read. Most children fit into this category.

The sequence in which the techniques are presented here is not related to their importance or to their priority in reading or reading instruction. They are presented in the groupings described above. We believe that aspects of all the techniques should be introduced in the beginning stages of reading instruction and that all of the techniques should be used in combination as early as possible. Over-reliance on any one technique should be discouraged. The seven techniques are discussed separately in this book for purposes of clarification only, so that each technique may be comprehensively explained.

Whole-Word Techniques

This part presents the four whole-word techniques of word identification. Each chapter follows the same organizational pattern. The chapters begin with brief introductions, followed by descriptions of the kinds of clues related to each technique. These descriptions are accompanied by discussions of how the particular techniques work, what they depend on, and their advantages and limitations. Each chapter concludes with exercises for teachers and suggested activities for pupils.

Chapter 3 describes visual configuration clues. Picture clues are discussed in Chapter 4. Chapters 5 and 6 distinguish the two kinds of contextual clues, semantic and syntactic.

Chapter 3

Visual Configuration Clues

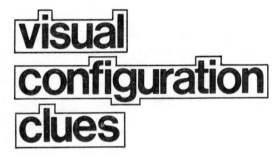

Before a name or meaning can be associated with a particular written word form, that word form must, in some way, be distinguished from all other word forms. One way of doing this is to use configuration clues, distinctive visual features that can be associated with particular word forms.

Visual configuration clues are based on non-linguistic visual information and are frequently called distinctive-feature clues, whole-word clues, visual-feature clues, word-form clues, immediate or direct word-identification clues, sight-word clues, and look-and-say or see-and-say clues. They may be used to identify individual words or groups of words such as phrases and whole clauses.

Since these clues are non-linguistic, some people do not believe that their use should be recognized as a word identification technique. However, it is highly doubtful that the use of visual configuration clues can be discouraged, much less eliminated. It is a natural way of learning that we apply to many things. We use visual configuration clues, for example, to differentiate people's faces and figures, automobile models, and breeds of dogs.

Kinds of Visual Configuration Clues

Whole-Word Features

Word Length. The length of a word can serve as a distinguishing characteristic, particularly if it is much longer or much shorter than most of the words that readers know. If most of the words in pupils' reading vocabularies are four letters long (*come, look, mine*), then an eight-letter word (*sometime*) or a two-letter word (*is*) may be distinguished easily from the others on the basis of its length.

Word Shape. The external configuration or outline of a whole word can serve as a distinguishing characteristic. The tops and bottoms of some words are flat and even (*answer, can*), while others are irregular (*orphan, pilot*). Thus, readers can differentiate words of equivalent length such as *once* and *only* by the difference in their outlines, or shapes. However, word shape does not help differentiate words like *home* and *house* or *come* and *came*. Since the lengths and shapes of these words are similar, other clues are needed to distinguish one from the other.

Upper Coastline. The outline or silhouette of just the top half of a written word can be a clue to its identity. The peaks and valleys in the top halves of words like *elephant* and *bunch*, for example, are quite distinctive.

Lower Coastline. Although usually less distinctive than the upper coastline, the outline of the lower half of a written word can also be used as a clue to its identity. A word like *play* can be readily differentiated from words like *plan* or *slam* on the basis of its bottom coastline.

Word Detail Features

Double Letters. Any internal feature of a word that can be easily remembered can serve as a clue to the identification of the whole word. Double letters are among the most easily remembered features. Words like *look* and *see* are distinguishable because of their double vowel letters. Words like *egg* and *llama* can be identified by their double consonant letters.

Capital Letters. Since the major portion of the words that pupils encounter in reading are written in lower case letters, capital letters can serve as distinguishing features. For example, beginning readers frequently use capital letters to identify the names of the characters in reading materials. The initial letters of these words are capitalized regardless of their position in sentences. Mature readers also use capital letter clues when skimming for names of people and places.

Hyphens, Apostrophes, and Periods. Non-letter marks that are associated with the spellings of words can be used as distinguishing features. For example, *hook-and-ladder* may be identified through its hyphens, *can't* may be identified through the apostrophe, and *Mr.* may be identified through the period.

Position of Letters in Words. Pairs of words like *on* and *no*, or *was* and *saw* share the same length, are similar in shape, and do not have obvious distinguishing features. However, since these pairs of words are spelled with the same letters in different sequences, the position of a letter or letters in each of these words can serve as a distinguishing feature.

Repetition of Letters in Words. Repetition of letters in words can serve as a distinguishing feature. For example, the repetition of the ⟨a⟩ in *banana* or the repetition of both letters in *mama* may be used as clues to their identification.

Characteristics of Individual Letters in Words. Any feature of a letter may be a clue to the identification of the whole word. The following kinds of letter parts may be distinctive:

       1. dots on letters: ⟨*i, j*⟩
       2. crossbars on letters: ⟨*t, e*⟩
       3. ascending lines: ⟨*b, d, f, h, k, l, t*⟩

4. descending lines: ⟨g, j, p, q, y⟩
5. symmetry of letters: ⟨o, s, g, z, v, w, x, m⟩
6. curved, angled, straight, and oblique lines: ⟨c, k, l, v⟩

Features that distinguish words may also help to distinguish whole phrases or clauses. For example, the straightness of ⟨i⟩ and the roundness of ⟨o⟩, which differentiate the words *in* and *on*, may also serve as clues to the identification of whole phrases such as *in the desk* and *on the table*.

How Visual Configuration Clues Work

Configuration clues are really *word recognition clues*. They always depend on the recall of prior associations of written word forms with word names and meanings. It is during the process of learning what word a given word form represents that readers select the specific configuration clues that can be used for that word's subsequent recognition.

The primary problem confronting readers who use visual configuration clues is how to determine the specific feature or features that will enable them to recognize a word successfully. If an association can be made between a particular feature and the word meaning, that feature is likely to be remembered as a clue to the word. For example, the word form ⟨look⟩ can be recognized by recalling that *look* begins with an ascending letter. However, it would be easier for most children to use the double ⟨o⟩ as the clue because the two ⟨o⟩'s resemble eyes, and eyes are used for looking. Similarly, the descender on the ⟨y⟩ can be used as a clue for the recognition of *monkey* if it is associated with a monkey's tail.

Many pupils use configuration clues spontaneously in beginning reading. Teachers can frequently help not only those pupils, but the other pupils as well, by pointing out features in words that might serve successfully as distinguishing clues. Teachers can also help pupils select clues for words by presenting written words in pairs and small groups so that pupils have opportunities to compare them. Comparison encourages the identification of distinctive visual features in words.

Configuration clues are often very personal. A feature that is distinctive for one teacher or pupil may not be for another. Of two pupils who recognize *bed* through configuration clues, for example, one may do so by recalling the mirror imagery of the first and last letters, while the other associates the overall shape of the word with a bed.

The more familiar pupils are with a written word form, the fewer features they require to recognize it, and the more quickly they can recognize it. Although the use of visual configuration clues is usually considered a beginning technique, it is helpful to readers at all stages of development. Beginning readers, however, tend to use them in isolation, while more proficient readers use them in combination with all other word identification strategies.

What Visual Configuration Clues Depend On

The efficient use of configuration clues is based on skill in visual discrimination and on visual memory. In addition, they can be used successfully only to identify written word forms whose spoken counterparts are in readers' oral vocabularies.

The use of visual configuration clues is not dependent on knowledge of letter names or letter-sound correspondences. The visual features function non-linguistically. However, the more acquainted pupils are with the letters and their names, the more easily they will be able to use configuration clues. Familiarity with letter shapes enables them to notice, remember, and recall many more of the distinctive features of words.

Advantages of Visual Configuration Clues

Because visual configuration clues do not require knowledge of letter shapes and names, or of letter-sound correspondences, beginning readers can read meaningful sequences of words as soon as they can recognize the words through configuration clues. The core of words recognized through configuration clues can then form the basis for learning letter-sound correspondences.

This technique can be used to special advantage by pupils who are unable to use auditory clues effectively, as is required in the use of phonics, but who can profit from visual clues. Such pupils include those who are deficient in auditory abilities, those with immature auditory development, and those who process information more easily through their right-brain hemispheres.

Because it is non-linguistic, this technique has the advantage of not being affected by dialect variability. It can be used equally successfully by speakers of standard, nonstandard, and divergent English, as well as by speakers of other languages.

Since this is a natural way of learning many visually identifiable things, it is a relatively easy technique to teach. Many children begin using configuration clues to learn the words on traffic signs, on cereal boxes, and in television commercials before they start school. Thus teachers need only build on the foundation such children already have.

Finally, since visual configuration clues are not related to the linguistic aspects of words, they can be used for the recognition of all kinds of words. They can be used to particular advantage for learning structure words, which tend to have irregular letter-sound correspondences.

Limitations of Visual Configuration Clues

Beginning readers must first be told what a word is or have their guess verified by someone with greater reading skill. Until they have mastered additional word identification techniques, they cannot be sure they have identified a word correctly without external verification.

Many written English words are similar in internal details as well as in general shape; that is, they share many of the same features (*house* and *horse*, or *expect* and *except*). The more features words share, the more difficult they are to differentiate. Since the English alphabet contains only twenty-six letters that can be arranged in different sequences to spell all the words of the language, similarity in appearance of written words cannot be avoided.

Visual configuration clues can be used only to identify word forms whose oral equivalents are familiar to readers. If the words are unfamiliar to readers in their oral forms, the readers must learn the names and the meanings of the words before they can associate them with their visual features.

Using a specific configuration clue to identify a specific word will not enable readers to identify other words with the same clue. For example, when pupils learn to recognize the word *look* by means of its double ⟨o⟩, they cannot apply this knowledge toward identifying any other words. Furthermore, the features that serve as clues for identifying a word always depend on what other words readers must distinguish that word from. The two circles in the middle of the word *look* can serve as a distinctive feature only as long as the pupils do not have to identify words like *book* and *took*. To distinguish *look* from such other words, they must select substitute or additional clues. As readers add more words to their reading vocabularies and are required to discriminate among greater numbers of words, they must keep changing the choice of features they use as clues to words they already know. Unless pupils can take advantage of other kinds of word identification clues, they rapidly become bogged down trying to make, remember, and associate an ever increasing number of visual distinctions.

After the initial stages of reading development, this technique continues to be useful only in conjunction with other word identification techniques. Therefore, teachers should always teach and encourage the use of a combined approach to word identification. Even pupils' initial sight vocabularies are acquired more easily when other techniques are also used.

Exercises

The purpose of the following three exercises is to demonstrate how visual configuration clues may be used in identifying words. Assume that the list of words in the box is the vocabulary from a beginning reading book. Complete Exercises A, B, and C using only the words in the box. (Answers appear at the ends of exercises.)

go	the	said
me	help	stop
on	you	with
us	Bill	Brown
it	can't	funny
too	come	Barbara
and	fast	merry-go-round
can	here	Kathy
Sam	Lois	Mrs.
see	play	grandfather

Exercise A. What are the following words? Through which configuration clue was each word recognizable?

Figure 3.1

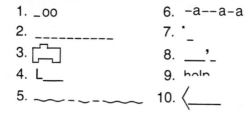

1. _oo   6. –a––a–a
2. _ _ _ _ _ _ _ _ _ _   7. ˙_
3. ⌐‾⌐   8. ___'_
4. L__   9. holp
5. ～～–～–～   10. ‹___

	Answer	Visual Configuration Clues Involved
1.	too	double vowel
2.	grandfather	word length
3.	play	word shape
4.	Lois	capital letter
5.	merry-go-round	hyphens
6.	Barbara	letter repetition
7.	it	dot on individual letter
8.	can't	apostrophe
9.	help	upper silhouette of word
10.	Kathy	oblique lines in individual letter

Exercise B. When two or more words have a common distinguishing feature that can be used as a visual configuration clue, the reader must supplement with additional but dissimilar features to differentiate them successfully. Do this to identify the words below.

Figure 3.2

1. B⸺⸺as opposed to B⸥

2. ⸺⸳ as opposed to ⸺⸳

	Answer	Visual Configuration Clues Involved
1.	Brown / Bill	word outline in addition to capital letter
2.	funny / play	word length in addition to descender on final letter

Exercise C. Complete sentences and stories may be read by identifying each of the component words through visual configuration clues. Do this with the sentences below.

Figure 3.3

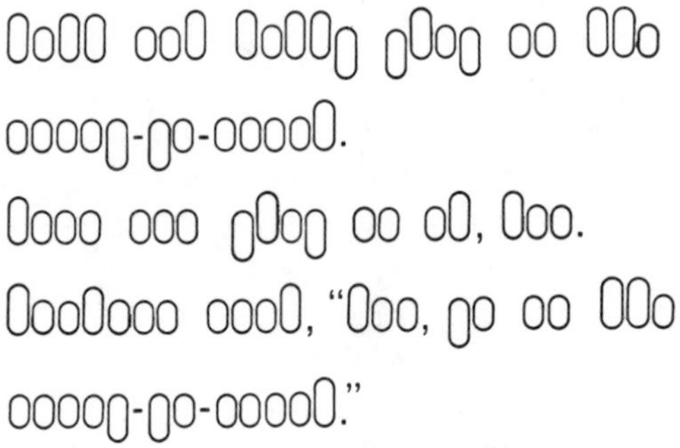

OₒOO ooO OoOOₙ ₙOoₙ oo OOo

ooooₙ-ₙo-ooooO.

Oooo ooo ₙOoₙ oo oO, Ooo.

OooOooo oooO, "Ooo, ₙo oo OOo

ooooₙ-ₙo-ooooO."

Answer
Bill and Kathy play on the
merry-go-round.
Lois can play on it, too.
Barbara said, "Sam, go on the
merry-go-round."

Activities that teachers may use to give pupils practice in using visual configuration clues to identify words follow.

Suggested Activities for Pupil Practice
General Considerations for Teachers

It is important to focus activities on the specific skill(s) you want pupils to practice. Pupils should not be able to get the right answers except by applying the skill(s) you want them to practice. For example, if pictures accompany activities intended to provide practice in the use of word shape as a clue to the identification of words, pupils may be able to identify the words in the activities through picture clues instead. Therefore, if the purpose of the activity is to practice the use of configuration clues (by themselves and not in combination with other kinds of clues), there should be no accompanying pictures or any other kinds of non-configuration clues available to pupils.

Guard against using items in activities that have unintentional common elements, since this might encourage pupils to make unwarranted generalizations. If in teaching word length as a configuration clue, all the short words you present include a common letter such as the ⟨o⟩ in the words *to, go, on, of,* and *no*, pupils may generalize that the ⟨o⟩ is an integral part of short words.

Activities similar to those that are described for pupil practice may be used as diagnostic skills tests or as criterion-referenced tests to analyze pupils' proficiencies and deficiencies in the use of specific configuration clues. Diagnostic test activities may be used before and/or after teaching the skills.

Activity 1

Purpose. To provide practice in using whole-word configuration features (word length and word shape) as clues to identifying written words.

Level. Early primary.

Directions for Teachers. Select words whose meanings pupils already know but whose word forms they have not yet learned to identify. Pronounce each word and then write it on the chalkboard (or easel or large chart paper) while pupils listen and watch so that they can associate the written forms with the spoken forms. After each word is pronounced and written, have it "read" by the pupils. This "reading" can be done in several ways. Individual children can repeat the pronunciation of the word; the whole group can pronounce it in chorus; or the pupils can pronounce it together with you. The words used in this kind of exercise should differ in their lengths and shapes, as in the example below. (When presenting combinations of words that resemble one another in length and shape, other visual configuration clues or other types of word identification techniques should be utilized since length and shape will not help in discriminating among them.)

mother
go
stop

Word Length as Clue. *Ask* pupils if all three words are the same in length. (It is important that the pupils *discover* that the words differ in length, rather than being told that they do. In fact, never tell the pupils anything that they can be led to discover for themselves.) Direct a pupil to point to the longest word as he or she pronounces it. Have another pupil point to the shortest word and pronounce it. Have a third pupil point to the word that is medium in length, that is neither the shortest nor the longest, and pronounce it. If certain pupils are unable to "read" the word, say it for them as they point to it and have them repeat it.

Next, have the pupils practice using the lengths of the words as clues to discriminate among and identify each of the words in the exercise. The following procedure is suggestive of what might be done:

1. Draw three wavy lines of varying lengths, as shown below, and have the pupils pronounce each word as they connect each wavy line to the word form that matches the length of the line. The result would look like this:

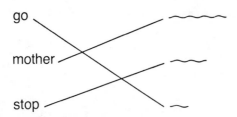

2. Have pupils connect dotted lines of different lengths to the appropriate words. The pupils should pronounce each word as it is associated with its distinguishing length. The result would look like this:

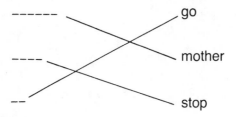

Word Shape as Clue.. Write the target words of the exercise (*mother, go, stop*) on the chalkboard, easel, or chart. Draw the outline around each word as pupils watch. Pronounce each word as you outline it. The result would look like this:

Ask pupils if the shapes or outlines of the words are the same or different. Then have them describe in what ways they differ. For example, the word *mother* is even along the bottom, but it has a tall place on the top; the word *go* is even along the top but it goes down low on the bottom; *stop* is not even either along the top or the bottom. Accept any reasonable descriptions of the shapes or outlines of the written word forms. (It is important that you write the words as they appear in printed form so that the shapes with which pupils practice identifying the words resemble the shapes that the words have in the printed materials that they will be expected to read. Also, having pupils verbalize the observable differences among word forms helps them to focus attention on these differences and to remember them as clues to the identification of the words.)

Next, have pupils practice using the shapes of the words as clues in discriminating among and identifying each of the words in the exercise. The following procedure is suggested:

1. Draw the outline of each word. To the right of the outlines, write each of the target words of the exercise, but in a different sequence (so that the pupils will not be able to match shape to word on the basis of the order in which they are listed).

Have pupils draw lines from the word shapes to the words they match as pupils pronounce them. The result would look like this:

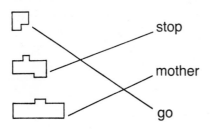

2. If the pupils know how to write the letters that spell the target words, have them fill in the following outlines by copying the spellings of the appropriate words from the chalkboard, easel, or chart as they pronounce the words. The result would look like this:

Activity 2

Purpose. To provide practice in using internal details of word forms (apostrophes, double letters, capital letters) as clues to the identification of words.

Level. Early primary.

Directions for Teachers. Using words whose meanings pupils already know, present the target words of this exercise by pronouncing each word as you print it on the chalkboard, easel, or large chart while pupils listen and watch. After each word is pronounced and written, have it "read" by pupils. Words used in this kind of exercise must differ in their distinguishing details, but may be similar or different in whole-word features such as word length and shape, as in the words below.

> can't
> little
> Kathy

Ask pupils to look at the first word, *can't,* as you pronounce it again. Elicit from them that the apostrophe of *can't* distinguishes it from the other two words. This can be done by asking pupils in what way the word *can't* looks different from the other words. Continue to ask for suggestions until someone mentions the apostrophe by whatever term they use for it (all other reasonable differences mentioned should be positively acknowledged). Then have pupils "read" the word *can't.*

Repeat this procedure for the word *little*, but this time elicit from the pupils that the double ⟨tt⟩ in the middle of the word is its distinguishing feature. Repeat again for the word *Kathy,* but this time establish the large or capital letter ⟨K⟩ at the beginning of the word as the distinguishing feature.

Have pupils practice using the distinguishing details of the target words to identify each of them. The following procedure suggests what might be done:

1. Write on the chalkboard, easel, or chart the distinguishing features that have previously been associated with each of the target words. In a list to the right of them, write the complete words in a different sequence. Have pupils draw a line from each distinguishing feature to the word in which it appears, as they pronounce the word. The result would look like this:

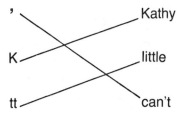

2. Write only the part of each word that is distinctive, leaving a wavy or straight line for the remainder of the word. In an accompanying list, write the complete words. Have pupils draw a line from each incomplete word (in which only the distinguishing detail shows) to its matching complete word. Have them pronounce each word as they do so. The result would look like this:

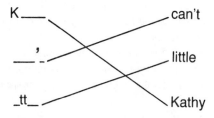

3. Have an oral activity in which you ask pupils to tell you what specific detail will help them to identify the word *can't* whenever they see it. Ask the same question in relation to the words *little* and *Kathy*.

Chapter 4

Picture Clues

picture
clues

Pictures are another source of clues for identifying whole words. Readers can infer the words that specific word forms represent by associating these specific word forms with pictures or aspects of pictures. Like configuration clues, picture clues are non-linguistic in nature and may be used to identify individual words or groups of words such as phrases and sentences. Other terms frequently used in conjunction with this technique are *pictorial aids* and *graphic clues*.

Most instructional materials for beginning readers traditionally include many pictures. Sometimes the pictures serve simply as space fillers to break up long pages of text. At other times they are used to make the pages of books more attractive and appealing to children. More often, the story line of beginning reading materials (pre-primers, primers, and first-readers) is carried by the pictures rather than by the limited text.

Some linguists and teachers are critical of the use of pictures in instructional materials. They argue that pictures are distracting. They also argue that picture clues do not constitute a "viable" means of identifying words since they do not involve the direct association of written word forms with any specific linguistic units. However, there doesn't seem to be any hard evidence to support their claims. Although the so-called "linguistic materials" tend to be free of pictures, thus forcing readers to use other word identification techniques, pictures occur frequently in most other reading materials at all levels of development. Their presence provides a valuable source of clues that should not be overlooked for identifying words.

Kinds of Picture Clues

Some of the elements in pictorial representations that can function, singly or in assorted combinations, as clues to the identification of written word forms include those described below:

Single-Object Pictures

The Object Pictured. If only one object—such as an animal, person, or thing—is represented in a picture, that object may serve as a clue to a written word form. For example, if a picture consisting only of a dog appears with the single word form ⟨dog⟩, readers may assume that the word form represents the word *dog*. Children's alphabet books routinely use this principle, as do many basal pre-primers, for developing sight vocabulary.

If readers already know the names of the characters in a story, pictures that accompany the story may provide clues to these names when they are used. For example:

> *Alice* is skating.
> *Abraham Lincoln* was known for his honesty.
> Everybody loves *Smokey the Bear.*

If an inanimate pictured object has a proper name that is orally familiar to readers, its picture may be a clue to the unfamiliar printed form that appears in the text. For example:

> We visited the *Statue of Liberty.*
> *The Grand Canyon* is beautiful.

Textbooks, dictionaries, encyclopedias, and other reference materials also contain pictures that can serve as clues to the single words or terms that appear beneath them. In a dictionary, for example, one might see a picture of the ornamental top part of a column with the word *capital* printed beneath it.

Details of the Pictured Objects. Even pictures of single objects usually include details, any one of which may serve as a clue to the identification of a specific word form in context. The kinds of details that might appear in a single-object picture are the physical characteristics of the pictured object such as its component parts, size, color, and shape. Thus, in the sentence "The dog has two long _____" (the blank space indicates an unknown word), readers may search the accompanying picture of the dog for a clue to the unfamiliar written word, which in this case is *ears.*

Action Portrayed by the Pictured Object. A picture may depict an action that may be used as a clue to the identification of unfamiliar word forms representing action words. For example, if a picture is designed to be used as a clue to the verb *run*, the individual pictured would be shown in a running posture.

Multiple-Object Pictures

Objects Included in a Picture. Most illustrations that accompany text include more than a single object. For example, a dog might be pictured eating from a dish on the kitchen floor, while a kitten watches him and a family group sits eating at a nearby table. Any of the objects included in the picture might be the clue to an unfamiliar word form. Selecting the appropriate clue from this kind of picture is much more difficult than from a single-object picture. Since these kinds of multiple-object pictures accompany most basal reader selections, successful word identification usually requires the use of supplemental clues.

Details of Pictured Objects. Details associated with the objects in multiple-object pictures may serve as clues to unfamiliar word forms, just as they do in single-object pictures. In addition, words related to number (*three* boys, *five* chairs, etc.) and comparisons (*taller, closer,* etc.) may be clued by such pictures.

Action Portrayed by Pictured Objects. Actions associated with the objects in multiple-object pictures may also serve as clues to unfamiliar word forms, just as they do in single-object pictures ("The dog *is eating*," "Father is *smoking* his pipe.").

Relationships between Pictured Objects. Identification of many structure words through picture clues is made possible by noting the placement of the pictured objects in relation to each other. For example, a ball may be *on* a chair, *under* a chair, *behind* a chair, *in front of* a chair, and so on. A child may be pictured walking *toward* a house, *away from* a house, *into* a house, or *out of* a house.

Attributes of Pictured Objects. Various kinds of traits and characteristics may be associated with pictured objects. Words relating to the senses of touch, smell, taste, and hearing, for example, as well as words relating to emotional states, may frequently be inferred from pictures. For example, word forms such as ⟨frightened⟩, ⟨soft⟩, ⟨sweet⟩, and ⟨happy⟩, among others, may be identified through picture clues.

Clues from Maps, Diagrams, and Picture Graphs

Maps, diagrams, and picture graphs frequently include non-verbal symbols which can be useful in word identification. The sentence "There are large _____ ranges on the east and west coasts of the United States" may be accompanied by a relief map showing the mountain ranges represented by the symbol /\/\. Readers unfamiliar with the word form ⟨mountain⟩ may be able to search the map for pictorial clues to the identification of the unfamiliar word form. Similarly, although readers may not be able to recognize the word form ⟨axle⟩, they may be able to identify it if a diagram accompanies the text they are reading and they recognize the pictured axle.

How Picture Clues Work

In order to use this technique, textual material must be accompanied by pictures, and readers must be aware of the possibilities of using this pictorial information as an aid to word identification. If readers recognize the pictorial representation and know the name for it, they can associate that word name with it and assume that the written word form represents that name and concept.

At times, readers may have a general concept of what a pictorial representation is without knowing its name. In this case, they can associate the word form with the general concept even though they cannot associate it with a specific word name. Their comprehension may lose some precision as a result. At other times, however, readers may not even be able to recognize the pictorial representation. In this case, they will not be able to use picture clues to identify words.

Let us now consider how readers might use a picture clue in a given instance. For example, pupils might encounter the word form ⟨giraffe⟩ in their reading material and not be able to recognize it. They should be able to get clues to the word from the accompanying illustration if they recognize the picture as representing a giraffe and they have the word /jə răf'/ in their oral vocabulary. But if pupils have difficulty recognizing the pictured animal because they do not know what a giraffe is, or do not know what the oral name for the pictured animal is even though they have seen such pictures before, they will not be able to associate a word name with the picture. Nor will they be able to do so even if the word /jə răf'/ is in their oral vocabulary if the illustration is a poor one and is not clearly a giraffe that they can recognize. In both cases, obviously, they will not be able to associate the spoken word /jə răf'/ with the written word form ⟨giraffe⟩. They may, however, be able to grasp that the written word form represents that pictured animal, whatever it may be called, if they have a general concept of the animal or of animals.

The general understanding of picture clues is a generalizable concept, but specific picture clues are always unique to each picture and its accompanying text. Thus, even if readers identify a given word on one page of a book through clues available in an accompanying picture, they may not be able to identify another instance of that word on another page because the picture on that page (if there is one) may be inappropriate for that purpose.

Teachers can encourage the use of picture clues by drawing readers' attention to an accompanying picture when they are unable to identify a given word. At the same time, they should focus pupils' attention on the essential aspects of the picture through leading questions, using the semantic and syntactic context surrounding the unknown word as the source of questions. On a page with a picture of two boys playing ball and the sentence "The two boys played with the _____," teachers might guide readers to the correct identification of the word *ball* by telling them to look at the picture to find out what the boys are playing with.

It is helpful if the word form to be identified is in context. If an illustration is complex and contains many details, the reader may not necessarily know what part of the picture to consult for clues, but context can help narrow down the search if enough of the other words in the context are known. The presence of semantic and syntactic clues in the context help pinpoint or specify what details of the picture may be represented by the written words.

Using picture clues as a means of identifying word forms in the printed text accompanying the picture or pictures is not the same as making inferences about the story line just by looking at the pictures. Very young children or non-readers of any age may be able to "read" a story by orally relating what they see in a sequence of pictures in a book. This practice does not involve using pictures to identify words. Similarly, the story line of comic strips may be inferred by reference to the sequence of frames, but that does not involve word identification either since the "readers" of the comic strip are not using the pictures to get clues to the identification of word forms. In sum, there is a difference between "reading" pictures to get at meaning in a general way and using pictures for clues as to what printed word forms represent.

Picture clues to word identification should also not be confused with "rebus" writing, in which pictures are used in place of some written words in sentences. In rebus, pictures usually substitute for nouns and, less often, for verbs in the sentences. For example, a sentence using rebus might look like this: "The 🐈 jumped up on the 🪑 ." The rebus technique eliminates selected word forms completely. The association is directly between the pictures and the spoken words or the concepts represented by the pictures. Some beginning reading materials use rebus to restrict the number of written words that beginning readers need to identify.

What Picture Clues Depend On

Fundamental to the use of picture clues is the presence of relevant pictures in the reading materials. Readers will be able to make inferences about specific words only if they are able to recognize the pictured representations that are related to them. Equally, readers must be aware that accompanying pictures can contain clues that may help them identify written word forms.

The efficient use of picture clues as a means of identifying written words also depends largely on pupils' stored information and knowledge, on their speaking vocabularies, and on their inferential abilities. Picture clues are useful and usable at all stages of reading development, as are configuration clues. However, they become less useful in narrative materials of a literary type, as the level of difficulty of these kinds of materials increases. They do continue to be useful in materials relating to science, mathematics, history, and geography. These types of materials include pictorial content such as illustrations, photographs, diagrams, maps, graphs, and charts for the specific purpose of enhancing readers' understanding of the written text. In fact, textbooks frequently refer readers to the pictorial material as it is discussed.

Advantages of Picture Clues

Because the use of picture clues is independent of knowledge of letter names and of letter-sound correspondences, it can be used to advantage by beginning readers who do not have this knowledge. Many children, spontaneously or through informal parental guidance, learn to identify some words even before starting school by associating them with pictures on cereal boxes and toys, in television commercials, and so on. Many children also learn words from pictures in alphabet books and picture dictionaries.

Another advantage of this technique is that it is not dialect-dependent in relation to the pronunciation of words. Thus, if pupils identify a picture of a body of running water as /krēk/ or /krĭk/ when the word form in the text is ⟨creek⟩, identification of the word is correct.

Because it is an immediate, non-mediated whole-word technique, the use of picture clues is a fairly rapid means of word identification. It enables readers to follow the flow of a story with a minimum of discontinuity. In fact, if readers examine pictures carefully before they begin to read the accompanying text or when they first use it for clues, they may be able to remember and use the contents of a picture without having to interrupt their reading further.

Limitations of Picture Clues

The picture clue technique has several limitations. One of the most serious is its complete dependence upon the presence of pictures. In addition, the pictures must contain information that will be useful in identifying the written words of the text. This is not always the case. The more objects included in a given picture, the less reliable the inferences based on the picture are, if pictures are the sole source of clues for word identification.

Another limitation is that readers can only be sure that they have correctly identified a word through a picture clue by having someone else who recognizes the word form verify their identification of it. Furthermore, they may identify a word form erroneously since objects and ideas may be represented by different words. A given object may have several different names, and a picture cannot indicate which of the names the written word form represents. For example, a picture cannot indicate whether a written word form is *bunny,* or *rabbit;* it cannot indicate whether a written word is *cat, kitten, pussy, puss, feline, pet, animal,* or some proper noun such as *Felix* or *Daisy.* Thus readers cannot be sure that they have supplied the precise word from their lexical reservoir, even though it fits the picture and makes sense in the context, unless someone else verifies it for them or unless they know other word identification techniques by which they can double-check their inferences. This weakness endures even after repeated encounters with a written word form if pupils rely solely on picture clues—even after someone has told them what the word is.

In order to be more accurate in associating pictures with correct word names (and with correct concepts), pupils must combine their use of picture clues with other word identification techniques. However, once a word has been correctly identified through picture clues, it can thereafter be identified through other kinds of clues if an association is made between some feature or features of the word form and its spoken counterpart. It is not likely that a word form, once identified by some other word identification technique, will thereafter be identified solely through picture clues.

The picture clue technique is dialect-dependent in that the names for things and ideas may differ from one dialect to another. An object that is called a *pail* by some pupils may be called a *bucket* by others; what is called a *river* in one region of the country may be called a *creek* in another. While such differences may interfere with the word-naming aspect of word identification, they do not impair understanding at all, since *pail* and *bucket* have the same referent, as do *river* and *creek*. Of course, the use of phonic clues together with picture clues can help in selecting the correct name, provided that name is in the pupils' oral vocabularies. However, in dialect-difference instances, phonic clues do not help if the word is not in the pupils' oral word stock.

Another shortcoming of this technique is that there are many words in English that are difficult or impossible to picture. Abstract words (*love, kind, ready*) are not generally picturable in a manner that permits written-spoken word association on a one-to-one basis. The concepts of many structure words (*about, to, which*) are also difficult to portray through pictures. Therefore, pupils must acquire a feeling for the kinds of words that are likely to be identifiable through picture clues, so that their use of picture clues is productive. The following kinds of words can frequently be identified through picture clues:

1. Concrete and picturable nouns (*chair, tree, window*)
2. Names of characters in selections (*Sam, Lois, Kate*)
3. Action verbs (*jump, dive, climb*)
4. Adjectives relating to picturable qualities
   a. number (*one, three, ten*)
   b. quantity (*many, few, some*)
   c. color (*red, green, yellow*)
   d. size (*big, little, tall*)
   e. position (*first, last, middle*)
   f. mood (*happy, sad, frightened*)
5. Prepositions representing the relationships, particularly those of position (*under, over, behind,* and so on)

The usefulness of picture clues is also limited if they are used as the sole means of identifying words. However, this technique is not as dependent as the visual configuration clue technique. In the latter, readers must initially be told what a given word form represents. Picture clues at least enable readers to infer what a word form might represent without someone first telling them.

Exercises

Exercise A. The purpose of the following exercise is to illustrate how picture clues may be used for word identification. The words missing from the sentences are to be identified from clues available in Figure 4.1. They are deliberately blanked out to prevent their identification through configuration, phonic, or morphemic clues. However, semantic and syntactic clues derived from the sentence contexts are unavoidable since they are intrinsic to the sentences.

Figure   4.1

1. Kathy is playing with a _____.
2. Sam is _____ his kite.
3. The color of the cat's fur is _____.
4. The wind is blowing Kathy's _____.
5. Kathy is sitting _____ the flowers and the tree.

	Answers	*Picture Clue Involved*
1.	cat	one of the items in a multiple-item picture
2.	flying	the action portrayed by an item in a multiple-item picture
3.	black	an attribute of a pictured object
4.	hair	detail of a pictured item

5. between   relationship of items to each other in a
                  multiple-item picture

The precision with which a word can be identified through picture clues
can vary. For example, in the preceding exercise, each of the blank spaces
could be filled in correctly by only one specific word. However, in the
following sentences, also based on Figure 4.1, any of several words might
be appropriate.

There are _____ flowers. (*five, some, several, pretty*)
It is a _____ day. (*nice, fair, sunny, pleasant, summer, warm*)

Exercise B. If configuration clues are used in conjunction with picture
clues, word identification becomes easier and tends to be more accurate.
Supply the missing words in the following pairs of sentences. Again, clues
to the identification of the blanked out words may be derived from Figure
4.1.

1a. Sam is in the park with his _____.
1b. Sam is in the park with his ⌐_ .   .
2a. Sam likes to play with his _____.
2b. Sam likes to play with his ◌o◌o.
3a. The rabbit is _____ under the flowers.
3b. The rabbit is h____g under the flowers.

Answer(s)
1a. sister, cousin, kite, toy, dog, cat, friend
1b. dog
2a. friend, sister, cousin, kite, dog, cat, sister
2b. kite
3a. playing, sitting, eating, hiding, looking, etc.
3b. hiding

Several different words can appropriately fit the blank spaces in the first
sentence of each pair. But if configuration clues are used in conjunction
with picture clues as in the second sentence of each pair, the identification
of the missing words becomes more exact.

The more kinds of clues readers use to identify unfamiliar word forms,
the greater their accuracy of word identification is likely to be.

Exercise C. The effective use of picture clues in the identification of
unfamiliar word forms depends on the number of such word forms within a

given amount of written text. If the proportion of unknown to known words becomes too large, this technique breaks down. This is illustrated by the following sentence, which again is based on Figure 4.1. Try to supply the missing words.

The _____ and the _____ _____ with Sam to _____ _____
his _____ _____ _____ _____ park.

> *Answer*
> The cat and the dog went with Sam to play with his new kite in the park.

Suggested Activities for Pupil Practice

General Considerations for Teachers

It is important to focus activities on the specific skill(s) you want pupils to practice. Pupils should not be able to get the right answers except by applying the skill(s) you want them to practice. Therefore, activities intended to provide practice in using picture clues should include words that cannot be identified through clues in the sentence context itself. If a picture shows two boys riding their bicycles, for example, and the accompanying sentence is "The two boys were riding their bicycles," the verb form ⟨riding⟩ may be identified through semantic and syntactic clues, without recourse to the picture. On the other hand, picture clues would be needed to identify the words *two, boys,* and *bicycle* if pupils are unfamiliar with phonic clues and have not learned to identify these words through configuration clues. Thus, one of these words, not the word *riding*, should be the target word.

Guard against using items in activities that have unintentional common elements, since this might encourage pupils to make unwarranted generalizations. If, in an activity that focuses on the use of picture clues, all of the target words relate to people pictured in the illustrations, pupils may generalize that picture clues are applicable only to words relating to people. To avoid such erroneous generalizations, different kinds of target words should be used in picture clue activities.

Activities similar to those that are described for pupil practice may also be used as diagnostic skills tests or as criterion-referenced tests to analyze pupils' proficiencies and deficiencies in the use of specific picture clues.

Such diagnostic test activities may be administered before and/or after teaching the skills.

Activity 1

Purpose. To provide practice in using objects portrayed in single-item pictures as clues to the identification of noun words in isolation.

Level. Early primary.

Directions for Teachers. Use (1) words whose meanings pupils already know but whose written word forms they have not yet learned to identify and (2) pictures that can be readily recognized by the pupils. The words used in any one exercise should differ in their configurations. For example, *horse* and *house* or *boy* and *dog* should not be used together in the same single-item picture exercise.

Pictured Objects as Clues. Select words to be identified in this exercise and draw or locate pictures to represent their concepts. Good sources of pictures are magazines, calendars, children's coloring books, and catalogs.

Draw or paste each picture at the top of a piece of oaktag, cardboard, construction paper, or the like. In manuscript, clearly print the appropriate word beneath each picture. Use light-colored paper so that the words stand out. The words may be printed with any dark crayon, felt pen, or lettering pen. Cards similar to those shown in Figure 4.2 should result.

Figure   4.2

| dog | house | flower | girl |

Present one card at a time. Ask pupils what the picture represents, that is, what the illustration is a picture of. If they respond with the word that is printed on the card, tell them that they are correct. If they respond with another word, such as a synonym, continue questioning them until you elicit the desired response. If you present a picture of a dog, for example, and pupils respond with the word *puppy*, you might say: "Yes, this is a picture of a puppy. What kind of animal is a puppy?" (or any similar question that will help pupils arrive at the word *dog*). On occasion you may have to supply the correct answer. For example: "Could we say that a puppy is a young dog, and that this is a picture of a dog?" As soon as pupils identify the pictured item as a dog, ask them what they think the word under the picture is. If pupils do not respond with the word *dog*, you might then ask, "What did we decide that this is a picture of?" Pupils should respond by repeating the word *dog*. Then explain that when a word and a picture appear together, the picture is very often a clue to the word; therefore, they can often figure out what a written word is by looking at the picture that goes with it. (Children who are familiar with alphabet books and picture dictionaries may already know how to do this.)

After presenting each word in this fashion, shuffle the cards so that they can be presented a second time in a different order. Hold up the cards one at a time and ask pupils to tell you what word is written on each card. If any words are identified incorrectly, remind the pupils to use the pictures as clues to the words. If necessary, repeat the questioning described above.

Now determine whether pupils can recognize the written words they have just learned when the words are separated from the pictures. (This implies that pupils will need to use additional word identification clues, such as configuration clues.)

While pupils watch, separate the words from the pictures by cutting the cards into two parts. Better still, have pupils cut the cards. Place the pictures where they can be seen by all the pupils, for example, on the chalkboard ledge or flannel board. Then have one pupil at a time pick a word card at random and match it with the appropriate picture until all the cards have been used. (Alternately, you might hold up the word cards one at a time and have the pupils tell you, as a group, which picture each word card goes with. Assign one pupil to place the word cards next to the pictures.) This procedure may be carried out just as easily in reverse; that is, the word cards are displayed and the pictures are matched to them.

A similar procedure may be used to provide practice in identifying action words, prepositions, and adjectives. Examples of such picture-word correspondences are shown in Figure 4.3.

Figure   4.3

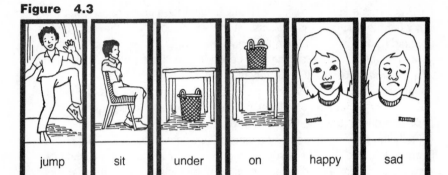

| jump | sit | under | on | happy | sad |

Activity 2

Purpose. To provide practice in using action portrayed in multiple-item pictures as a clue to the identification of verb word forms in context.

Level. Primary.

Directions for Teachers. Prepare a set of sentences containing the action verbs that you want pupils to identify through picture clues. Words may be those whose meanings are familiar to the pupils as well as those whose meanings may need to be derived from the pictures. In any case, the verbs should be those that can be confirmed through reference to the pictures. The other words in the sentences should all be familiar to the pupils so that they present no word identification problems.

Sentences may be independent of each other or they may be sentences from a continuing passage. (Although independent or unrelated sentences have value for practice purposes, pupils also need practice using picture clues with connected text, since that is how picture clues are usually used.) In either case, contextual clues are always available whenever sentences are used, and pupils should be encouraged to combine them with picture clues.

Locate a picture or pictures appropriate to the sentences. If appropriate pictures are not available, try to assemble some by making collages, that is, by putting together parts of pictures to form the scenes you need. You may also draw the pictures to illustrate the sentences. One picture or several pictures may be required, depending on the sentences and the pictures.

Pictured Actions as Clues in Independent Sentences. Select the verbs to be identified in the exercise. Compose sentences using these verbs (one per sentence) and other words that pupils can already recognize in print. Then locate or draw pictures that contain clues to the identification of the verbs.

Figure   4.4

1. Jim is *diving* from the high board.
2. Kate is *splashing* in the water.
3. Lisa is *floating* on the raft.

Prepare a ditto sheet of the picture and the sentences as shown in Figure 4.4 and distribute a copy to each pupil. Discuss the scene depicted in the picture, associating the names in the sentences with the children portrayed. Direct the pupils' attention to the sentences one at a time. Each sentence should first be read silently so that pupils can use contextual clues in conjunction with picture clues to identify the verbs. Then call on pupils individually to read the sentences aloud. As pupils identify the verbs correctly, ask them to explain how they knew what the word was, and elicit both the picture clue as well as the contextual clues that were used. When a verb is misidentified, the next step depends on what word pupils substitute for it. If they substitute a synonym, they are probably using the picture clue and the contextual clues, but they now need to be encouraged to use phonic clues also, particularly initial consonant grapheme-phoneme clues. For example, if they say *jumping* or *falling* instead of *diving* in the first sentence, you should ask them if the word *jumping* or *falling* begins with the same sound as the word in the sentence does. Then ask them to think of a word that fits what the picture shows Jim to be doing, that makes sense in the sentence, and that begins with ⟨d⟩ as does the word in the sentence.

If pupils do not know the appropriate grapheme-phoneme correspondences, however, and they substitute a word that matches the action in the picture and also fits the context of the sentence, their response should be accepted. For example, if pupils read the verb in the third sentence in this exercise as *resting* instead of *floating* (and they do not yet know that initial ⟨fl⟩ represents /fl/), their answer should be positively acknowledged. You should use such an opportunity, though, to extend their vocabulary by saying, "We could also say that Lisa is floating on the raft."

If pupils substitute a word that does not make sense in the sentence but does begin with the same initial consonant as the target verb (*dunking* instead of *diving*), you should direct them to look carefully at what Jim is doing in the picture. Then ask them to think of a word to describe that action, one which will make sense in the sentence. (In this case pupils may be overrelying on initial consonant clues.) If pupils substitute a word that fits in with neither the picture nor the sentence, and that bears no phonic resemblance to the word in print, direct their attention to all three kinds of information-bearing clues, that is, the picture, the sentence context, and the initial consonant grapheme-phoneme correspondence.

Similar strategies may be used to provide pupils with practice in identifying nouns, adjectives, adverbs, and prepositions.

Pictured Actions as Clues in Connected Text. Select the verbs to be identified in this exercise. Compose a paragraph or short story containing these verbs and locate or draw a picture that contains clues to their identification, as in Figure 4.5.

One day, Lisa's cat *jumped* to the roof from the tree. She could not get down. Barbara *climbed* up the ladder to get her. Bill *held* the ladder while Barbara went up it. Lisa *cried* until the cat was on the ground again. The cat was glad to get down.

Follow procedures similar to those described for the immediately preceding activity.

Figure 4.5

Activity 3

Purpose. To provide practice in using map features to identify words in sentences.

Level. Intermediate.

Directions for Teachers. Use words whose meanings pupils already know but whose written word forms they have not yet learned to identify, or use word forms pupils can pronounce but whose meanings they do not know. Select the word(s) to be identified in this exercise, and locate or draw a map or portion of a map that includes the feature(s) related to the word(s).

Prepare a sentence or sentences containing the word(s) and present the sentence(s) together with the appropriate map, as in Figure 4.6. The sentence(s) used should contain contextual clues that can help in the identification of the word(s). The words in the sentence(s), other than the one(s) to be identified through the map clues, should be familiar to the pupils so that they present no word identification problems. Note Figure 4.6 and the accompanying sentences:

Figure 4.6

San Diego Bay is nearly enclosed by two *peninsulas*. The southern one is the Silver Strand, a *sandspit* ten miles long.

Follow procedures similar to those described for the activities above. Instead of preparing ditto sheets for pupils, a number of alternate ways may be used to prepare materials. For example, pictures and sentences may be put on transparencies for use with an overhead projector. Another alternative is to post or draw the picture(s) on the chalkboard and either write the sentence(s) on the board or give pupils a ditto sheet containing only the sentence(s). Of course, you may always use pictures that are already contained in reading materials being used by pupils. In this case, you may use the sentences or text that accompanies the picture(s) for your exercise, or you may write your own sentence(s) to accompany the picture(s). Whichever procedure you use, be sure that the pupils are aware of how they can use picture clues effectively to identify or confirm the identification of words.

Example of Combination Activity

Since picture clues are more effective when used in combination with other kinds of word identification clues, pupils should be given practice in so using them. Activities such as the following one, which combines picture clues with configuration clues, is illustrative.

Figure   4.7

1. The children had a ⅼⅼⅼⅼⅼⅼ .
2. Jim rode on his hike.
3. Laurie rode on her ⌐.
4. Mary rode on her ⌐⊓⊓⌐.
5. And Juan rode on his ⌐oo⌐.

Answer

1. parade   (The picture clue is the display of pictured items;
                the configuration clues are the number and height
                of the letters.)

2. bike   (The picture clue is the pictured item; the
                configuration clues are the word length and the
                upper coastline of the word.)

3. pony   (The picture clue is the pictured item; the
                configuration clues are word length and the final
                descending stroke.)

4. skates   (The picture clue is the pictured object; the
                configuration clue is the word shape.)

5. scooter   (The picture clue is the pictured object; the
                configuration clue is the repeated circle in the
                middle of the word.)

semantic clues- of or relating to meaning in language

Two sources of clues can be used to identify whole words in connected verbal context. One is semantic (lexical) information and the other is syntactic (grammatical) information. Readers make use of semantic clues through their knowledge of the meanings of other words in the context. They make use of syntactic clues through their knowledge of the ways in which sentences are formed.

Semantic and syntactic clues are interdependent. Semantic units carry syntactic information; syntactic units carry semantic information. Thus, readers tend to use the two together to anticipate and confirm the identification of words. It is probably for these reasons that many people who speak or write about the teaching of reading do not distinguish between semantic and syntactic clues, but refer to them together as *meaning clues, sentence clues, story clues,* or *contextual clues.* They are, of course, all of these, but labeling them jointly fails to distinguish between two important divisions of the language system. Failure to differentiate the two systems results in the misrepresentation of language and can lead to confusion in the teaching of the clues.

It is important to note that people who do not consider semantic and syntactic clues distinct from each other may also not regard them as primary means for the identification of written words. They may consider these kinds of clues merely as a means of checking on or supplementing other word identification techniques. They expect readers to identify a given word by means of phonic clues, for example, and then consciously ask themselves, "Does that make sense and does it sound right?" If the inferred identification of the word does make sense and does sound right in the context of the passage being read, readers may then assume that their phonic analysis is correct and has resulted in a correct identification of the word. If the inferred word does not make sense, however, or does not sound right in the sentence, readers must assume that their phonic analysis has not resulted in the correct identification of the written word and that they must try an alternative analysis.

This is an accurate but incomplete theory of the use of semantic and syntactic clues. It is true that semantic and syntactic clues serve as a check on the accuracy of word identification, but they can also serve as a primary means of identifying words by permitting readers to *anticipate* words that appear in written context. When readers use semantic and syntactic clues to anticipate words in context, the result is faster and more efficient word identification than may be achieved by other techniques. Proficient, fluent reading probably depends greatly on the effective use of these kinds of clues since they involve use of the largest units of language—phrases, clauses, sentences, paragraphs, and so on.

Kinds of Semantic Clues

Semantic clues may be either implicit or explicit. Implicit clues are those that are inherent in written context. Explicit clues, on the other hand, are clues that are deliberately included by a writer to provide additional or redundant information. Implicit and explicit clues may be used singly, but they are more likely to be used in combinations. The specific kinds of implicit and explicit clues are described below.

Implicit Clues

The lexical value of individual words and of word combinations provides clues to the identity of other words in a sentence or paragraph. Efficient use of such clues in a particular instance depends upon readers' knowledge relevant to the information being communicated. The following are examples of implicit clues.

The Topic. The topic or subject matter helps determine the sense in which specific words are used. If the topic relates to money, for example, the word form ⟨bank⟩ probably refers to a depository for money; if the topic relates to geology, ⟨bank⟩ may more likely refer to an elevation of ground. If a selection is about boating, the word form ⟨bow⟩ probably represents /bō/; if it is about clothing, it probably represents /bō/. Previewing a selection before reading it enables readers to become oriented to the topic of the selection so that they can use semantic clues as soon as they begin reading. Without preview, readers must gradually acquire information about the topic and are, therefore, less able to use semantic clues as effectively at the beginning of the selection.

Words Preceding and/or Following an Unfamiliar Word in the Same Sentence. Meanings of unfamiliar words can be inferred from the denotative and connotative meanings of words that precede them in the same sentence, depending upon readers' past experiences and acquired concepts, as well as their knowledge of language. For example, in the sentence "Tony found the map of Louisiana in the _____," the unfamiliar word form ⟨atlas⟩ may be anticipated and identified if readers can relate it to the preceding word *map*.

Known words that follow an unknown word in the same sentence can be used in the same way. Consider the identification of the word form ⟨batter⟩ in the following pair of sentences:

> The *batter* hit the ball over the fence for a homerun.
> The *batter* has been mixed and is ready for baking.

The semantic clues to the identification of ⟨batter⟩ in the first sentence are the meanings of the words *ball, hit*, and *homerun*, which are familiar to anyone who knows baseball. In the second sentence the clues are the meanings of the words *mixed* and *baking*, words which are known to anyone familiar with the preparation of baked goods.

Clues to the identity of an unfamiliar word may both precede and follow that word in the same sentence. For example, in the sentence "The puppy found a cozy _____ in which to sleep," the word form ⟨nook⟩ may be identified by anyone familiar with the sleep habits of puppies by relating it to the preceding known word *cozy* and the following known word *sleep*.

Words in Sentences Preceding and/or Following the Sentence in Which an Unfamiliar Word Appears. Clues for identifying a word may be provided by the denotative and connotative meanings of words that appear at intermittent intervals throughout the reading material. If readers are able to accumulate a sufficient number of clues, they may be able to identify a word form that they would not be able to identify on the basis of a single clue. Some readers may require more clues than others, and any one reader may require a different number of clues at different times to identify words, even to identify the same words. The following pairs of sentences are examples in which the semantic clues may be found in a preceding sentence:

> The boys have decided to play baseball. They need a *pitcher.*
> They're going to serve milk. They need a *pitcher.*

The meanings of the words *baseball* and *milk* in the first of each pair of sentences above are the clues to the identification of ⟨pitcher⟩ in each of the second sentences. In other instances the clue(s) may be found in a succeeding sentence:

> The *batter* was not good. He kept striking out.
> The *batter* was not good. She used a spoiled egg.

Here the expressions *striking out* and *spoiled egg* in the second sentences provide the semantic clues to the identification of ⟨batter⟩ in the first sentences. The clues need not be in sentences adjacent to the one containing the word they clarify. They may be separated by one or more sentences as in the following paragraph:

> It was the first baseball game of the season. All the parents had come to watch. Everybody was excited. It was time to start. The *batter* was ready.

The clue to the word *batter* in the last sentence is the expression *baseball game* in the first sentence; three sentences intervene between the clue and the word it helps identify. The word to be identified can, of course, be in the first sentence of a paragraph and its clarifying clue in the last:

> The *batter* was ready. The children came to watch. They were all excited. It was a very special time. Mother was about to put the Christmas cake in the oven to bake.

The clues to the word *batter* in the first sentence are *Christmas cake, oven,* and *bake* in the last sentence; again, three sentences intervene.

Sentences with relevant clues may both precede and follow the sentence containing an unfamiliar word. The following paragraph is an example in which immediately preceding and immediately following sentences provide clues to the identification of the word *batter.*

> Rosa and Jerry went to the ball game. The first *batter* was not good. He struck out.

The following paragraph is an example in which clues to the identification of the word *batter* are in non-adjacent preceding and following sentences.

> Rosa wanted to bake a chocolate cake for Jerry's birthday. He was going to be sixteen years old. She got everything ready. The first *batter* was not good. She had to start all over. This time she mixed in less milk and more flour.

Commonly Used Expressions. If readers are familiar with commonly used expressions—idioms, colloquialisms, figures of speech, proverbs, and other familiar sayings—then whole expressions may function as units for identification purposes. Readers can infer the entire expression from a minimum of clues. For example, if readers encounter the sequence of words "Don't count your chickens," they do not need to look for additional clues to know that the remaining words are "before they hatch."

The same process is applicable to longer sequences of words that are familiar to readers, such as nursery rhymes and other forms of poetry, excerpts from well-known plays, and other forms of familiar prose. If readers encounter the sequence of words "Thirty days hath," they can usually supply from memory the remainder of this poem about the number of days in each month. Obviously, readers can do this only if they are already familiar with the proverb, poem, or expression involved. They can even identify otherwise unfamiliar words if they recognize enough of the other words in an expression. For example, the blanked out word in "Life isn't all beer and _____" is most likely to be *skittles.* Americans who use this British expression may not know what skittles are and, therefore, might have difficulty identifying this word out of this specific context.

Explicit Clues

Writers use a variety of stylistic devices to clarify words and concepts that they assume may be unfamiliar to or difficult for readers. Such devices are explicit semantic clues. Authors and editors who prepare subject matter materials frequently include them. Some of these devices are the following:

Synonyms. Synonyms may be included in context in several different ways. The basic device is to introduce the synonym as a post-appositive addition, usually setting it off with some form of punctuation, and frequently introducing it with *or* or *that is*. In the examples that follow the word being clarified by the writer is italicized:

> He was *reliable,* or dependable, in everything he did.
> A *ferocious*—that is, fierce—dog guarded the gate and snarled loudly.
> The *garrulous* (talkative) man chattered incessantly.

Most of the other stylistic devices used by writers to clarify words and concepts through synonyms are variations of the above. For example:

> He killed the man with his *rapier*—a sword.
> Bishop O'Connor ordered the *miscreant* (or heretic) expelled from the Church.

Post-appositive synonyms may also be introduced by *or* without accompanying punctuation, as in the following sentences:

> While hiking in the mountains, they came to a tarn *or* mountain lake.
> The male sperm fertilizes the ovum *or* egg.

This practice may bewilder inexperienced readers who may incorrectly conclude from the first sentence that the hikers came upon both a tarn and a mountain lake, and in the second, that the male sperm fertilizes two different things.

Antonyms. The contrast of antonyms is a useful explicit clue when one of the antonyms of the pair is in the reading vocabularies of the readers. These contrasts are frequently set up by correlative conjunctions such as *not/but, both/and, neither/nor,* and *not only/but also,* among others. For example:

> *Both* the rich *and* the destitute were welcome in his home.

In this sentence the correlative conjunctions *both/and* suggest that *destitute* is the opposite of *rich.* The same suggestion could have been made had the writer used *not only/but also* as the correlative conjunctions:

> *Not only* the rich *but also* the destitute were welcome in his home.

Antonyms may also appear in separate sentences. The clues in such instances are more difficult to recognize. Consider the following:

> My father was beloved by everyone because he paid no attention to social class. The *rich* were often in his home. Just as frequently

the *destitute* would appear there to enjoy his company. Everyone mourned when he died.

Antonyms need not appear in consecutive sentences to serve as clues to each other; one or more sentences may intervene.

Definitions and explanations. Words used in context may be defined or explained in the context. This is usually done in one of four ways:

1. The definition or explanation appears in the same sentence with the word it clarifies:

The large, colorful bird was a *macaw,* a member of the parrot family.

2. The definition or explanation appears in a preceding or in a succeeding sentence:

The large, colorful bird was a member of the parrot family. It was a *macaw.*
I saw a *macaw.* It is a large, colorful bird that is a member of the parrot family.

3. The definitions or explanations consist of several sentences. The following paragraph illustrates this:

The most impressive sights in Yellowstone National Park are the *geysers.* They are jets of heated water and steam. They shoot up in the air intermittently. They originate in underground springs and look like fountains.

The word *geysers* is defined and explained by the series of sentences that follow it. The definition or explanation may, of course, precede rather than follow the target word in the paragraph.

4. Definitions and explanations are introduced in the same way that synonyms are introduced, as parenthetical remarks set off by commas, dashes, parentheses, or other punctuation. For example:

Dinosaurs (extinct reptiles that lived on earth millions of years ago) were often more than seventy feet long.

The words in parentheses supply the semantic clues to the identification of *dinosaurs.*

Descriptions. At times, descriptive context can be helpful in identifying difficult words. The scene described in the following passage supplies clues to the identification of *hurricane:*

The wind blew furiously and the rain poured down. The thunder and lightning were frightening. We huddled close together in the old barn as we waited for the *hurricane* to end.

Examples. Examples included as clues may be introduced by using any of the devices just described for synonyms, antonyms, definitions, and explanations. In addition, examples may be introduced by the phrases *for example* and *such as* or, simply, by citing them. Consider the following sentences:

Citrus fruits, for example, oranges and grapefruits, should be included in everyone's daily diet.
The identification of *morphemes,* such as prefixes and suffixes, may be used to help identify difficult, technical words.
Some examples of *conifers* are pines, firs, and spruce trees.

How Semantic Clues Work

Semantic clues are the clues that answer the readers' question "Does that make sense?" when they are considering the identification of a given unfamiliar word. The answer to this question involves the integration of the context in which a word appears and the readers' background knowledge. These clues enable readers to infer the meaning of a word form if they are able to identify enough other words to be able to follow the sense of the sentence. The source of information for this technique is the semantic structure of the language.

Since readers apply the total of their past experiences as well as their knowledge of language to their reading, words are most predictable when the two are consistent with the content and language of the written material. The more familiar the content of the reading material, the greater use readers can make of semantic clues. Meaning is not something that suddenly appears at the ends of sentences. Information is available at every point to help readers anticipate what is coming and to amplify what has preceded. Readers accumulate semantic information as they read. They have more semantic information at the end of a sentence than at the beginning, even more at the end of a paragraph, and still more at the end of a selection. Therefore, they are ordinarily in a better position to identify words successfully using this technique towards the ends of these units. At the beginnings they have to rely more heavily on word structure clues. The use of semantic clues, either in the initial or proficient stages of reading, most often takes the form of making inferences on the basis of the literal meaning of the material being read.

Since semantic clues may occur before or after an unidentified word form, meaningful context permits the anticipation of words as well as the successful identification of words when clues follow them. Thus, regressive eye movements are not restricted to beginning readers; they are also common among proficient readers. For example, in the sentence "One should be cautious when using a *pesticide* to kill insects," the critical word *pesticide* may be entirely new to readers. Readers may pass over that unfamiliar word momentarily, searching for clues in the words that follow. The phrase "to kill insects" is a clue to the identification of the word form ⟨pesticide⟩. Readers may or may not have regressive eye movements in using such clues. They do not actually have to look back at a word in order to identify it on the basis of the subsequent semantic information. They may simply hold its identification in abeyance until they process enough of the subsequent content to identify the unfamiliar word. Inexperienced readers often read one word at a time, vocalizing each word before considering the next. Imagine the difficulty such readers have determining whether the italicized word in the sentence "Take a *bow;* they're still clapping" is /bō/ or /bö/.

Semantic clues can be useful only in meaningful contextual settings since they rely on the meanings and ideas represented by words in grammatical patterns. They can be used to recognize or identify word forms readers are *already* familiar with. This is a very rapid process of which readers are not even aware, and is one of the hallmarks of proficient reading. Semantic clues may also be used to identify word forms that readers are *not* familiar with. This is a slower and usually a more conscious process. The greater the number of familiar word forms in the context, the more easily and efficiently readers can use semantic clues for the identification of unfamiliar word forms. Since word identification is always most effective and efficient when various techniques are used in conjunction with each other, the effectiveness of semantic clues is heightened when they are combined with clues from other word identification techniques.

There are times when semantic clues *must* be used to identify words, regardless of what other techniques may be used. Word forms like ⟨close⟩ and ⟨rebel⟩ cannot be identified without semantic or syntactic information. The following sentences are illustrative:

> Please *close* the window.
> Please sit *close* to the window.
> John is a *rebel,* although he has nothing to *rebel* about.

Conversely, words like *quickly, swiftly, speedily,* and *hastily* cannot be identified through semantic and syntactic clues alone. Since these words are synonyms, one can be differentiated from the other only with the assistance of word structure clues. For example, only morphemic or phonic clues will enable readers to determine that the italicized word in the following sentence is *hastily,* and not *quickly* or some other synonym: "He left the room *hastily* after the argument."

Homographs that represent the same part of speech can be differentiated from each other *only* through semantic clues, as in the following pairs of examples:

> He was given the *lead* in the school play.
> He was given the *lead* in the small box.
> She was a *fair* person. She inherited her mother's blondness.
> She was a *fair* person. She listened to both sides of the story.

What Semantic Clues Depend On

The efficient use of semantic clues for word identification depends on a number of conditions. Some of the conditions are related more to readers themselves and some are related more to the written material involved.

Conditions related to readers include the dependence of this technique on their store of background information and knowledge, stock of vocabulary and concepts, grammatical fluency, and reasoning abilities. The larger their vocabularies and their funds of information and knowledge, the more resources readers have to draw on. If readers' experiences cannot be brought to bear on the written material, they will have difficulty in using semantic clues. For example, if readers have never had any direct or indirect experience with fairs as competitive exhibitions, and understand the word *fair* only in connection with weather or an attitude, they are likely not to be able to use semantic clues to identify ⟨fair⟩ in a sentence like "Kathy won a prize at the fair."

Older readers are more likely to be successful in using semantic clues than young, beginning readers. Having lived longer, they have had more experiences, have heard and read more, have stored more information and knowledge in their memories, and have accumulated larger vocabularies and more concepts. This enables them to identify words successfully even when the words are not part of their vocabularies. Beginning readers do not have sufficient background experiences and knowledge of language to be able to identify word forms representing words that are not part of their own vocabularies. Moreover, older readers usually have developed greater reasoning abilities that enable them to make inferences more easily than younger readers can.

Conditions related more to the reading material and readers' interactions with it include the readability (difficulty) level, interest level, and cultural content of the material. Materials that are too difficult for readers present them with a disproportionate number of unknown words. This precludes their use of semantic clues because they cannot accumulate enough semantic information to assist them in their identification of unfamiliar words. This is illustrated by the following sentence, in which the blank spaces represent unknown words:

"_____, the _____, believe in _____, _____ not only with our _____ but with the _____ _____ also."

Level of difficulty may be affected by such factors as word length, sentence length, sentence complexity, frequency of difficult words, and conceptual difficulty.

Reading material must also be significant and interesting to readers to make the use of semantic clues effective. Readers must want to understand what they are reading. Unless they are intent upon getting meaning, they will not be aware of the semantic clues that are available. They will be more likely to concentrate on individual word naming and more likely to use word structure clues. Pupils who overrely on non-contextual, word structure clues are commonly called "word callers." They do not anticipate words and have difficulty determining whether they have identified words correctly or not. Pupils who use semantic clues for word identification are usually not word-by-word readers. They are likely to understand what they read to a greater degree than pupils who limit themselves to clues available only within the words being identified.

When the cultural or subject matter content of the material closely matches the cultural background of readers, they have stronger bases for understanding the material. Therefore, they are better able and more likely to use semantic clues. The degree of match directly affects readability level. The more readers know about the content of what they are reading, the more successfully they will be able to use semantic clues. Thus, readers will be able to use semantic clues more effectively with some materials than with others.

Dialect variations also affect the use of semantic clues. When the language of readers approximates the language of the reading material, the use of semantic clues is easy and natural. When the language of the reading material is unfamiliar to readers, they cannot take advantage of semantic clues because of the disparity between the two language systems. For example, if pupils read the sentence "How about some sugar?" within the context of two people greeting each other, they will be confused if the word *sugar* refers only to a sweetening agent in their dialect and not to a kiss.

The dialect component of English is rich and produces variant meanings that surprise even experienced readers. For example, one needs to know that what is called a *brook* in some parts of the United States is called a *branch* in others in order to know that "He jumped over a branch" may not be referring to a part of a tree.

Slang terminology also affects the use of semantic clues. In recent years, for example, the word *dig* has had, as slang, the meanings "understand" and "approve." If readers see this word in dialogue that was written when one of these slang meanings was current, they should not expect a reference to a shovel. Most editors put quotation marks around slang words and expressions, but in recent years editors have tended to omit the quotation marks if they think the context provides adequate indication of how the word is to be interpreted.

In addition to having difficulty understanding slang meanings they have not encountered previously, many inexperienced readers fail to recognize slang words in print even when the slang words are part of their own vocabularies. This may be because their previous reading experiences have not led them to anticipate that their own slang vocabularies may be used to express ideas in print.

Specialized vocabularies present difficulties that are similar in kind. In an account of a baseball game, for example, one might find the sentence "He doubled against the right field wall and drove in three runs." The verb *double* has a perfectly clear meaning in this context, but one has to know baseball terminology to understand it. Whenever people study a new field or subject, they at first devote a great deal of time to learning the specialized vocabulary. It is impractical, if not impossible, to study a new field or acquire new information without learning new words or learning new meanings for old ones.

Because the materials themselves can play a very significant part in the development of pupils' skill in using semantic clues, teachers should choose instructional materials carefully. All the factors discussed above must be considered.

Advantages of Semantic Clues

Semantic clues permit readers to identify written word forms very rapidly, particularly when the content and the word forms themselves are familiar. Also, since this technique requires only a minimum of orthographic or phonic information, it usually results in rapid and fluent reading.

Another advantage of this technique is that meaningful context facilitates the identification of words. Pupils can often identify words in context that they cannot identify in isolation or in word lists. For instance, they might not be able to identify the word *rhubarb* if it is presented by itself, but might do so if the word is in the context of a sentence like "Mother bought some *rhubarb,* apples, and some other fruit."

The more readers use semantic clues for word identification, the more independent they become. They get continual feedback as they read and are able to monitor their own reading. This procedure is frequently referred to as hypothesis testing and confirmation. Readers predict what a word form represents (hypothesis) and then confirm or reject their hypothesis on the basis of whether or not it makes sense in the context of what they are reading. If their hypothesis is confirmed, they continue reading. If their tentative identification does not make sense, they usually try again. If readers are able to combine semantic clues with other kinds of word identification clues, their hypotheses are strengthened.

Semantic clues are particularly helpful to pupils who may be deficient in spelling and recoding. These clues do not require the close attention to visual details that word structure techniques do. Instead, individual words may be perceived in a generalized way. Thus, use of the semantic clue technique often enables poor spellers and recoders to become proficient readers.

One of the most important advantages of this technique is that its use is highly generalizable and applicable to the identification of all kinds of words and word groups. It works as well in the identification of words that do not follow consistent letter-sound correspondences as in the identification of those that do. Structure words can be identified as easily through this technique as content words. Whole phrases and even clauses can be identified as readily as individual words. Furthermore, semantic clues may be used to identify words that are encountered in written form by readers for the first time. Since these clues are anticipatory in nature, new as well as familiar word forms can be identified with equal facility.

Limitations of Semantic Clues

Several words may have similar or nearly similar meanings in English and, therefore, make sense in a given context. Because of this, semantic clues, when used apart from other word identification techniques, do not necessarily result in an exact identification of words. They are similar to picture clues in this respect. For example, just as a picture cannot differentiate among words such as *cat* and *kitty*, semantic clues may not either in many contexts. If an exact oral reproduction of the written words is required, readers need to bolster semantic clues with other word identification clues.

However, all reading does not require an exact reproduction of writing into speech. One's reading purpose usually determines how close the correspondence between writing and speech must be. Some purposes (reading a light novel for entertainment) can tolerate a considerable amount of variance between writing and speech without negative effects, while other purposes require a great amount of precision (reading a legal document or a medical prescription). Consider the word form ⟨cat⟩, for example, which readers may identify as *pussy* in the sentence "Lois gave the *cat* some milk." The underlying meaning of *cat* and *pussy* is the same as far as readers are concerned. They may even habitually refer to all cats as pussies when speaking. If their purpose is simply to follow the plot in the story about the cat, it really doesn't matter that they identify the word form ⟨cat⟩ as *pussy.* On the other hand, exactness of recoding is required for the word form ⟨on⟩ in the sentence "Put the money *on* the desk." Misreading *on* as *in* would completely alter the meaning of the sentence.

Another limitation of semantic clues is that they are not readily available to beginning readers. Beginning readers must first learn to use other word identification techniques such as picture, configuration, and phonic clues. By doing so, they become able to identify a sufficient number of words that they then can use as a basis for using semantic clues. As their reading vocabulary increases, their proficiency in the use of semantic clues can increase. But as long as their reading vocabulary is limited, their use of semantic clues continues to be limited also.

It should also be recognized that the semantic information in a given context may give an incomplete clue to an unfamiliar word. The following example illustrates this point:

He put on his *prosthesis* (an artificial leg) and walked out.

Though there is a semantic clue for the identification of *prosthesis* in this sentence, the clue gives incomplete information about it. Prostheses include all artificial body parts, not just legs.

Exercises

The purpose of the following exercises is to illustrate how semantic clues may be used for word identification. The words missing from the sentences are to be identified from contextual clues. They are deliberately blanked out to prevent their identification through configuration, phonic, or morphemic clues. Syntactic clues derived from the word order of the sentences, however, are unavoidable since they are intrinsic to the running text.

Exercise A. Supply the missing word in each of the following sentences using the context of the sentences as the source of information for clues.

1. The emblem of the Nazis was the _____.
2. The Mexican wore a _____, a brightly colored woolen blanket.
3. The man put on his best bib and _____ to attend the governor's ball.
4. Some South Americans wear cloaks that look like blankets with slits in the middle for the head to go through. These garments are called _____.
5. The man suspected of the crime agreed to take the _____ (lie detector) test.
6. Inflation is a problem not only in the urban but also in the _____ areas of the country.
7. Beverly had received a letter from her friend in Boston and wanted to answer it. However, she had used up all of her _____. She could not write her letter until she bought some.
8. The boy scouts went out on the lake in a _____ (a long narrow raft of logs).

	Answer	*Semantic Clue Involved*
1.	swastika	intrinsic clue: based on the lexical value of other words in the immediate sentence
2.	serape	extrinsic clue: definition built into immediate sentence
3.	tucker	intrinsic clue: based on commonly used expression

4. ponchos   extrinsic clue: description provided in preceding sentence

5. polygraph   extrinsic clue: post-appositive synonym in parentheses

6. rural   extrinsic clue: antonym relationship set up in immediate sentence using correlative conjunctions

7. stationery   intrinsic clue: based on topic of the paragraph

8. catamaran   extrinsic clue: post-appositive definition enclosed in parentheses

Exercise B. If semantic clues are used in conjunction with other clues, such as configuration or picture clues, word identification becomes easier and tends to be more precise. Supply the missing words in the following exercise by using semantic clues together with visual configuration and/or picture clues from Figure 5.1.

Figure   5.1

1. Mother and the boy were going to the _____.
2. Mother was pushing the | I I I I I I I I I I I, that is, the baby carriage.
3. The _____ was riding on the OoOo.
      (a)   (b)
4. The _ _tt_ _ was sitting in the store _____.
      (a)   (b)

Answer	Kinds of Clues Used for Word Identification
1. store, market, supermarket, etc.	semantic and picture
2. perambulator	semantic, picture, and configuration
3. (a) boy	semantic and picture
(b) bike	semantic, picture, and configuration
4. (a) kitten	semantic, picture, and configuration
(b) window	semantic and picture

Exercise C. The effectiveness of the use of semantic clues in identifying unfamiliar word forms depends on the number of unfamiliar word forms in a given amount of text. If the proportion of unknown word forms becomes too large, the use of this technique is diminished even when it is used with other whole-word identification techniques. The following paragraph, based on Figure 5.1, is an example of this:

Mother, _____, and the _____ were _____ to the _____ to get some [_____] and f_ _t. Bill _____ his _____ and Mother _____ the _____. The _____ laughed when he _____ the --tt-- in the _____.

Answer
Mother, Bill, and the baby were going to the store to get some bread and fruit. Bill rode his bicycle and Mother pushed the carriage. The baby laughed when he saw the kitten in the window.

Suggested Activities for Pupil Practice

General Considerations for Teachers

It is important that activities focus on the specific skill(s) you want pupils to practice. Pupils should not be able to get the right answers except by applying the skill(s) you want them to practice. Target words used for practicing the use of semantic clues should be words that pupils cannot identify through any other clues. For instance, if the written word form ⟨answer⟩ in the sentence "I do not know the answer to that riddle" is really unfamiliar to readers and cannot be identified through configuration, phonic, or syntactic clues, the only other clues available to readers are the semantic clues—the lexical meanings of the words *know* and *riddle*.

Guard against using items that have unintentional common elements since this might encourage pupils to make unwarranted generalizations. If various kinds of synonym clues are the only semantic clues used in practice activities, pupils may conclude that a synonymous relationship is an essential component of semantic clues.

Activities similar to those that are described for pupil practice may be used as diagnostic skills tests or as criterion-referenced tests to analyze pupils' proficiencies and deficiencies in the use of specific semantic clues. Such diagnostic test activities may be administered before and/or after teaching the skills.

Activity 1

Purpose. To provide practice in using the lexical value of words in one or more preceding sentences as intrinsic or implicit clues to the identification of words.

Level. Intermediate.

Directions for Teachers. Use words whose meanings pupils already know but whose written forms they have not yet learned to identify, or use word forms pupils can pronounce but whose meanings they do not know. Prepare or locate paragraphs in which these words are embedded and in which lexical clues to their identification are located in one or more preceding sentences.

Select the word(s) to be identified and write or locate a set of two or more related sentences. (You also may use sentences or passages appearing in pupils' published reading materials since semantic clues are a normal aspect of most writing.) The final sentence in each set should include the target word; the preceding sentence(s) should include lexical information related to that word. The words in the sentence(s) other than the one(s) to be identified through semantic clues should be familiar to pupils so that they present no word identification problems. The more familiar the content is to the pupils, the more successfully they will be able to use the contextual (semantic) clues. Consider the following examples:

> a. Helen finished making the applesauce except for putting in the spice. All she needed to add now was some *cinnamon*.

(The word to be identified is *cinnamon*. The semantic clues are the words *applesauce* and *spice* in the preceding sentence.)

> b. Adam loved flying. He flew his plane, a Piper Cub, every Saturday afternoon. One day, while flying to Atlanta in a rainstorm, his plane was struck by lightning. As the plane started to fall, Adam bailed out and *parachuted* safely to the ground.

(The word to be identified through semantic clues is *parachuted*. The semantic clues are *flying* in the first sentence, *plane* in the second sentence, *rainstorm* and *struck by lightning* in the third sentence, and the semantic information preceding *parachuted* in the final sentence.)

Present sets of sentences one at a time. Sentences may be written on the chalkboard, charts, transparencies, or ditto sheets. Have pupils read the sentences silently. Then have one pupil read the last sentence aloud. If he or she reads the target word correctly, ask what that word means and what clues to its identity are available in the preceding sentence(s). Be sure to elicit all semantic clues available in the context preceding the target word.

If pupils are not able to identify the target word correctly, tell them that the information in the preceding sentence(s) can be useful in predicting what the word might be. Then have them reread the set of sentences silently to see if they can now use the semantic clues in the preceding sentence(s) to identify the target word. If they are successful in doing so, elicit the semantic clues. However, if they are still unable to identify the target word (the meanings of all other words in the sentences should be told to them if pupils don't know them), have them reread the set of sentences again, but this time orally, sentence by sentence. Discuss what each sentence is about, and lead them to the identification of the target word by the accumulation of clues. Then have them identify the specific words that function as semantic clues in each of the preceding sentences. In cases where even this closely guided procedure does not result in correct identification of the target word, point out all of the clues and explain that these preceding words suggest what the unfamiliar word might be. (You might also add that it is not wrong to guess at the identities of unfamiliar words if you have meaning clues to work with; that in fact, it is a good idea.) If this is done whenever pupils are unable to identify words through semantic clues after following the above procedures, they will probably acquire an understanding of how semantic clues function and be able to use them efficiently.

Similar procedures may be used when semantic clues appear in the *same* sentence, as well as when they appear in sentences *following* the one in which the target word appears.

These kinds of exercises may be done by pupils working independently at their desks. On their copies of the sentences, have them underline all the semantic clues that help them identify the target words. However, if pupils have difficulty locating such clues, it is important for you to discuss with them the clues that are available and how they help in the identification of the target word. The procedures described in the preceding paragraphs may be followed. Only if pupils understand how semantic clues function will they be able to use them successfully. (In exercises of this kind, it is less important that pupils identify the target words correctly than that they identify the semantic clues through which they infer what words are.)

Activity 2

Purpose. To provide practice in using synonyms that appear as post-appositive additions set off by commas and introduced by the word *or* as extrinsic or explicit clues to the identification of words.

Level. Intermediate.

Directions for Teachers. Use words whose meanings pupils already know but whose written forms they have not yet learned to identify, or use word forms the pupils can pronounce but whose meanings they do not know. Prepare or locate sentences in which synonyms for the target words are set off by commas and introduced by *or*. (This skill is limited to sentence units. For this reason, single sentences that are unrelated to one another may be used effectively for practice purposes. However, in normal reading situations, the sentences to which this skill would be applied appear in the larger context of paragraphs and whole selections. Therefore, it is advisable to present some sentences in context.)

Select the word(s) to be identified and write or locate a sentence for each target word. Each sentence must contain a synonym for the target word set off by commas immediately following the target word and introduced by *or.* The words in the sentence(s) other than the target word(s) should be familiar to pupils so that they present no word identification problems. It is especially important that the post-appositive synonym be easily recognized by pupils if this kind of clue is to be used successfully. The following are examples:

1. The boys found a tortoise, or turtle, in the field. (The target word is *tortoise;* the synonym for it is *turtle.*)
2. The children were so noisy that they exasperated, or annoyed, the baby sitter. (The target word is *exasperated;* the synonym for it is *annoyed.*)
3. The cows grazed peacefully on the grassy plateau, or plain. (The target word is *plateau;* the synonym for it is *plain.*)

Present one sentence at a time. Sentences may be written on the chalkboard, charts, transparencies, or ditto sheets. Have pupils read each sentence silently. Then have one pupil read the sentence aloud. If he or she pronounces the target word correctly, ask what it means and what clues were in the sentence that helped in identifying the word. Be sure to elicit both the synonym and the word *or* set off by commas.

If pupils are not able to identify the target word, ask them to reread the sentence orally to see if they can find any clues in the sentence that might help them. If they are now able to locate the synonym clue and identify the word, proceed as in the preceding exercise. If they are still unable to find the clue to the identification of the target word, write a demonstration sentence on the chalkboard using a similar format but including a target word that is familiar (for example, "I have one brother who is fat and one who is skinny, or thin."). Cover the post-appositive phrase and have them read the sentence. Then cover the words *skinny* and *or* and have them read the sentence again. Then ask if the sentence means the same thing both times or if it means different things. When you elicit agreement that the sentence means the same thing whether the word *skinny* or *thin* is used, ask what the relationship between the words *skinny* and *thin* is. Then ask why both words are used in the same sentence if they both mean the same thing. Elicit that the second word explains what the first word is. (If pupils are familiar with the term synonym, explain that the word introduced by *or* and set off by the comma(s) is a synonym for the word that precedes it.) Now return to the target sentence. Draw attention to the post-appositive construction. With this kind of help, pupils should be able to identify the target word, unless they don't recognize the synonym itself.

Follow the same procedure with each sentence in the exercise, making sure that the pupils identify the clues each time.

Similar procedures may be followed when synonyms (or antonyms) are built into the context in any of the ways discussed earlier in this chapter.

Since the clues are so explicit in exercises of this kind, pupils might even work in pairs or teams, taking turns playing the role of teacher and pupil.

Example of Combination Activity

Since semantic clues are more effective when used in combination with other kinds of word identification clues, pupils should be given practice in so using them. Activity items such as the following one, which combines semantic clues with configuration clues, is illustrative:

The boys and girls went to the park to play. They took their toys with them. Tony wanted to fly his new kite (1). Pedro and Ed wanted to fly their model ooooOoooo (2). Shirley and Ellie sat on the ⬚ (3) and blew up their ～lloo～ (4).

Answer

1. kite (The semantic clue is the lexical meaning of *fly;* the configuration clue is the upper coastline of the word.)
2. airplanes (The semantic clues are the lexical meanings of *fly* and *model;* the configuration clue is the height of the letters in the word.)
3. grass (The semantic clue is the lexical meaning of *sat;* the configuration clue is the shape of the word.)
4. balloons (The semantic clue is the lexical meaning of *blew up;* the configuration clue is the combination of double letters.)

Chapter 6

Syntactic Clues

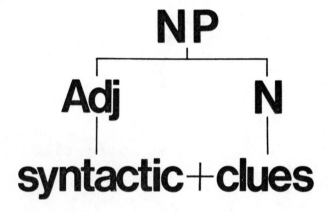

The second whole-word identification technique that relies on connected verbal text uses the clues available from the syntax of the language. Syntactic clues are concerned with the relational rather than the referential (semantic or lexical) aspects of language, that is, with how words are related to each other in sentences.

The different kinds of syntactic structures are limited in number and are used repetitively in English. Moreover, syntactic elements within structures have predictable relationships. For these reasons, syntactic clues are particularly useful in suggesting the kinds of words that belong at given points in sentences. They restrict the number of words that might be appropriate at those points. Readers usually have an intuitive knowledge of syntax that enables them to use syntactic clues to identify word forms in an approximate fashion. However, other types of clues are usually needed for precise identification.

Syntactic and semantic clues are so closely interwoven in sentences that it is difficult to separate them. Both are integral components of context. Successful word identification depends upon using clues from the two systems concurrently. Not only are they interdependent, but syntactic components transmit semantic information and semantic components transmit syntactic information.

The following versions of the same sentence illustrate the effect of separating the two systems:

1. The _____ _____, _____ing _____ _____ at _____, was _____ed by some _____ _____s in _____ of his _____.

2. _____ old man __ return _____ home late _____ night __ _____ mug(g) __ _____ _____ big boy __ _____ front _____ _____ house.

The first version of the sentence includes primarily its syntactic components, the second version its semantic components. Neither version alone supplies sufficient information to reveal what the sentence is communicating. Although people who are familiar with English can make some sense of the second version, they can do so only if they recognize the syntactic structure (in this instance manifested through word order) that relates the words to each other.

While syntactic clues can indicate the kinds of words that fit at a given point in a sentence, there are semantic constraints that help determine what those words can be. For example, in the sentence "The pretty _____ sang a popular song," syntactic clues indicate the presence of a noun. But just any noun is not semantically acceptable. Nouns like *sky, dress, butterfly,* and *stone* would not make sense in light of the other words in the sentence. Even *man* does not fit comfortably in that slot since men are not usually described as being pretty.

Syntactic and semantic clues do not run solely from left to right in a sentence. While the adjective *pretty* in the above example excludes some nouns that could be used to fill the following subject slot *(man, father, policeman),* the phrase "sang a popular song" at the *end* of the sentence excludes still others *(bird, dress, scenery).* The context of the whole sentence must be taken into consideration.

Kinds of Syntactic Clues

The several kinds of syntactic clues are described below. Although they are separated here for discussion purposes, it is important to recognize that they are interdependent and, in reading, are used in conjunction with one another.

Sentence Patterns

Every language has a limited number of common patterns by which the elements of the language may be arranged meaningfully. Readers can use this information for the identification of words. They can anticipate what kinds of words to expect in specific positions in sentences if the sentence patterns are familiar to them. They can also use the same information retrospectively to verify words identified through other techniques.

Statement Sentence Patterns. Commonly used basic sentence patterns are:

> Subject/Verb *(The horse jumped.)*
> Subject/Verb/Direct Object *(The girl hit the ball.)*
> Subject/Verb/Indirect Object/Direct Object *(The boy gave me the book.)*
> Subject/Verb/Direct Object/Objective Noun Complement *(The boy called the girl his friend.)*
> Subject/Verb/Direct Object/Objective Adjective Complement (*They found the baby frightened*.)
> Subject/*be*/Subjective Noun Complement *(Judy was the leader.)*
> Subject/*be*/Subjective Adjective Complement *(Bob is happy.)*
> Subject/*be*/Adverb *(Hattie is outside.)*
> *It*/*be*/Complement *(It was dark.)*
> *There*/*be*/Subject . . . *(There is a white thread on your sleeve.)*

Question Sentence Patterns. The question-making pattern appears in the first part of a sentence, and the sentence may be continued according to any of the statement patterns listed here.

> Auxiliary/Subject/Main Verb . . . *(Is Rita going home?)*
> Interrogative Word/Auxiliary/Subject/Main Verb . . . *(Why is Rita going home?)*
> Interrogative Word as Subject/Auxiliary/Main Verb . . . *(Who is going home?)*
> Interrogative Word as Direct Object/Auxiliary/Subject/Main Verb . . . *(Whom did you see?)*

Other Sentence Patterns. These three also occur frequently.

Command Pattern: Verb . . . *(Stop! Go home!)*
Request Pattern: Polite Word/Verb . . . *(Please leave now.)*
Instruction Pattern: Auxiliary/*not*/Verb . . . *(Do not go there.)*

Exercise

Appropriate words to fill the blank spaces in the following sentences can be inferred from knowledge of sentence patterns. Note that as long as real words are used, semantic information is available concurrently with syntactic information. Complete the following sentences with appropriate words:

1. The baby _____ me a smile.
2. The _____ elected their neighbor president.
3. Why is the cat _____?
4. _____ not walk on the grass.
5. _____ is a full moon tonight.
6. Are you _____ to school?

Examples of acceptable words for the blank spaces are presented below together with designations of the sentence patterns which provide clues to their identification.

Acceptable Words	*Sentence Patterns*
1. gave, offered, beamed	Subject/Verb/Indirect Object/Direct Object
2. people, men, women	Subject/Verb/Direct Object/Objective Noun Complement
3. mewing, scratching, hungry	Interrogative Word/Auxiliary/Subject/rest of verb
4. Do	Auxiliary/*not*/Verb . . .
5. There	*There*/*be*/Subject . . .
6. walking, going, riding	Auxiliary/Subject/rest of verb . . .

This discussion has been restricted to *basic* sentence patterns only, since it is usually these few high frequency patterns that serve as clues to word identification. When sentence patterns become complex, they no longer function reliably as word identification clues, and additional clues and techniques are required for successful word identification.

Word Order Sequences

In addition to whole sentence patterns, various kinds of word sequences within sentences can be used to identify word forms. Knowledge of common word sequences enables readers to predict what kinds of words will most likely precede or follow certain other words. Readers can look for familiar sequences as they read and, as long as they recognize the other words in that sequence, can supply the one they don't know from their background knowledge. For example, word order provides clues as to what words might appear in the following blank spaces:

the _____ teacher
ran home _____
cute _____

The first blank requires an adjective such as *strict, exemplary,* or *knowledgeable;* the second, an adverb such as *quickly, slowly,* or *later;* and the third, a noun such as *child, baby,* or *puppy.* The most predictable English word order sequences include the following:

adjective/noun	*(happy children, tall buildings, charming man)*
verb/adverb	*(walked slowly, talks rapidly, works quietly)*
adverb/verb	*(cheerfully gave, truthfully spoke, lovingly cared)*
article/noun	*(the toy, a top, an egg)*
article/adjective/noun	*(the friendly cow, the handsome lad, the beautiful mountains)*
verb/complement	*(weighed ten pounds, served six years, had many friends)*
preposition/article/noun	*(into the woods, over the hill, inside the tent)*
qualifier/adjective or adverb	*(very tall, rather well, quite late)*
possessive noun/noun	*(dog's tail, Seward's Folly, God's children)*

Exercise

Supply appropriate words to fill the blank spaces in the following phrases.

Infer from knowledge of predictable word sequences. Examples of acceptable answers and clues involved in each phrase are listed below:

1. the _____ clouds
2. cried _____
3. a funny _____
4. _____ the table
5. in a _____

Acceptable Words	Word Order Sequences
1. white, fluffy, dark	Article/Adjective/Noun
2. loudly, quietly, briefly	Verb/Adverb
3. sight, clown, face	Article/Adjective/Noun
4. on, over, under	Preposition/Article/Noun
5. box, bag, room	Preposition/Article/Noun

Mandatory Agreement

The rules of standard English grammar require that certain kinds of words conform to each other in certain ways. The process of such adjustment is called *agreement* or *concord*. For example, the subject and verb of a sentence must agree in number. Singular subjects require singular verbs and plural subjects require plural verbs. Pupils having difficulty in differentiating between the word forms ⟨woman⟩ and ⟨women⟩, or between ⟨child⟩ and ⟨children⟩, need only note the verb forms in the following sequences to identify these words correctly: *the woman works/the women work; the child plays/the children play.* Similarly, the subject and verb must agree in person. For example, the past tense form *was* is associated with the first and third person singular *(I was, it was, Angelo was)* and the past tense form *were* with the plural and the second person singular *(we were, they were, you were).*

Another obligatory agreement exists between pronouns and their referents in English. They must agree in person, number, and gender. Singular referents require singular pronouns and plural referents require plural pronouns. In addition, singular pronouns must agree in gender with their referents. This is illustrated in the following paragraph:

Barbara and Bill went to *their* grandmother's house. *They* had a good time because *she* took *them* for a ride in *her* new car. *She* was proud of *it*.

The pronouns *their, they,* and *them* refer to Barbara and Bill; hence they are plural. Grandmother is a single female and the pronouns *she* and *her* reflect this fact. The new car is singular and neuter so that *it* is third person neuter.

Standard English also requires agreement in number between some noun determiners and the nouns they precede. For instance, we say *an apple* but *some apples, this apple* but *these apples.* Count and mass nouns are also differentiated by their determiners: *a cup* but *some water, fewer cups* but *less water.* These kinds of clues can be very useful to readers in the identification of words.

A more subtle form of agreement is that which exists between adjectives and nouns in relation to their attributes. Adjectives and nouns have attributes such as abstraction/concreteness, humanness/non-humanness, animateness/inanimateness. Nouns are usually modified by adjectives that share the same kinds of attributes. It is appropriate, for example, to refer to a *conscientious man* but not appropriate to refer to a *conscientious chair.* Men are human, chairs are not, and the adjective *conscientious* shares human attributes with *man* but not with *chair.* When attributes between nouns and adjectives are mixed up, metaphors result and agreement cannot be used as a clue to word identification.

Structure Word Markers

The vocabulary of English may be described as consisting of two major divisions of words, *content-oriented words* and *grammar-oriented words*. The content-oriented words include the words traditionally referred to as nouns, verbs, adjectives, and adverbs. They constitute by far the greater portion of the different words of the language. The grammar-oriented words are few and fixed in number. There are only about 300 of them, as opposed to hundreds of thousands of content-oriented words. Grammar-oriented words constitute the most frequently used words of the language and are often called *structure words, function words, functors, service words, empty words, basic sight words,* and *particles.* They include, among others, what are traditionally called prepositions, conjunctions, articles, demonstratives, auxiliaries, and certain qualifiers and pronouns.

Structure words function differently from content-oriented words. Whereas content-oriented words contribute primarily subject matter, content, or lexical meaning to sentences, structure words contribute primarily to the grammatical meaning of sentences by indicating the relationships between content-oriented words. Although the two kinds of words overlap in their functions, content words are primarily referential and the structure words are primarily relational. Structure words, therefore, serve as clues to syntactic meaning. For example, the structure words preceding the blank spaces in the three following incomplete sentences suggest that each sentence would end differently:

I am hot and I want *to* _____. (swim, cool off)
I am hot and I want *a* _____. (drink, shower)
I am hot and I want *some* _____. (water, lemonade)

The first sentence would end with a verb or verb phrase, the second with a count noun, and the last with a mass noun. Structure words serve as markers or signals to various kinds of syntactic structures. Some examples follow:

Noun markers
   predeterminers: all, both, half, double
   determiners:
      articles: a, an, the
      possessive pronouns: his, her, its, my, your, our, their
      demonstratives: this, that, these, those
      others: another, any, each, some which, whose, much
   postdeterminers:
      cardinal numbers: one, two, three . . .
      ordinal numbers: first, second, third . . .
      others: every, few, less, more, most, other, some
Verb markers
   auxiliaries:
      forms of *be*: am, are, been, being, is, was, were
      forms of *have*: had, has, have, having
      forms of *do*: did, do, does
   modals: will, would, shall, should, can, could, may, might, must, ought (to)
Adjective and adverb markers (intensifiers)
   very, rather, too, quite, somewhat, more, most, little, less, least, really, fairly
Phrase markers
   at, by, for, from, in, of, on, to, with, up, down, out, near, off, through
Clause markers
   if, when, why, so, how, until, that, once, now, as, where, who, after, than, while, since
Coordinators and connectives signaling equivalence
   coordinating conjunctions: and, but, for, nor, not, or, so, yet
   correlative conjunctions: either/or, neither/nor, both/and, not/but, whether/or

Derivational Suffixes and Inflectional Endings

Derivational suffixes and inflectional endings transmit syntactic as well as morphemic information. That is, they contain information about the function of words in sentences. Specific suffixes and inflectional endings are associated with nouns (⟨-ness⟩, ⟨-s'⟩), with verbs (⟨-ize⟩, ⟨-ing⟩), with adjectives (⟨-able⟩, ⟨-est⟩), and with adverbs (⟨-ly⟩, ⟨-est⟩). This information can be very useful for word identification.

Syntactic and morphemic elements are closely related in language use. In fact, the term *syntax* is generally used for the linguistic subsystem that involves matters of word structure as well as of word arrangement. They are separated in this book only for discussion purposes, so that the unique characteristics of each set of clues can be clearly brought out. Morphemic units are generally more useful for word structure analysis. Syntactic clues are generally more useful for whole-word identification. In actual practice, however, both sets of clues are used together to ensure faster, more accurate word identification than can be achieved through either set of clues alone. Comprehensive lists of derivational suffixes and inflectional endings appear in Chapter 7.

Punctuation and Typographic Devices

The written forms of most languages use punctuation marks as signals to assist readers to comprehend written material, just as intonational patterns help listeners comprehend spoken material. The punctuation system of written English, however, is far from a complete representation of English intonation. The use of punctuation has developed from and is governed by editorial practice.

Intonation is an important aspect of oral grammar and necessary for the successful transmission of meaning. *Pitch, stress,* and *juncture* comprise the components of intonation. Pitch refers to the rising, falling, and steadiness of the voice as sentences are spoken. Stress refers to the emphasis given syllables and words. Juncture refers to use of pauses of varying lengths to produce syllables, words, phrases, and clauses in sentence arrangements. Punctuation marks and typographic devices provide clues to some aspects of intonation and, therefore, can provide information useful in the identification of word forms. For example, the word forms ⟨where⟩ and ⟨there⟩ resemble each other orthographically and tend to be confused, particularly at beginnings of sentences where little semantic information is available to differentiate them. The punctuation mark at the end of a sentence can be a clue to the identification of these words since a question mark is likely to be the terminal punctuation mark for a sentence beginning with *where* and a period or exclamation point for a sentence beginning with *there (Where is he going? There he goes.).*

The punctuation marks and typographic devices that can function as syntactic clues to word identification include those described below. It should be noted that punctuation marks can serve either as visual configuration clues or as syntactic clues.

Apostrophes ('). May be clues to contractions or to possession, both singular and plural *(The teacher's going home. She went to the teacher's room. She went to the teachers' room.).*

Exclamation points (!). May be clues to words expressing strong emotion *(Wow! Bravo! Ole!).*

Hyphens (-). May be clues to prefix/root combinations and to compound words *(His ex-wife still lives in that God-forsaken town.).*

Question marks (?) and Periods (.). May help differentiate commonly confused pairs of words such as where/there *(Where is she? There she is.),* what/that *(What is the difference? That is the difference.),* and when/then *(When is a good time? Then is a good time.).*

Quotation marks (" "). May be clues to words used in a special way *(She was malnourished and addicted to "horse.").*

Virgules (/). May be clues to alternatives or other kinds of relationships between two or more words *(and/or, cause/effect, price/earnings ratio).*

Brackets ([ ]). May be clues that a synonym, definition, or explanation for the word immediately preceding them is available *(Mother pushed the perambulator [baby carriage] down the street.).*

Colons (:). May be clues to an appositive at the end of a sentence that explains a preceding word *(He bought some tackle and bait: fishing equipment.).*

Commas (,). May be clues that a synonym, definition, or explanation of an immediately preceding word is available *(They promenaded, walked leisurely, down the avenue.).*

Dashes (—). May be clues that a synonym, definition, or explanation of an immediately preceding word is available *(The phonemes /f/ and /v/ are examples of fricatives—consonant sounds characterized by frictional passage of the expired breath.)*.

Parentheses ( ). May be clues that a synonym, definition, or explanation of an immediately preceding word is available *(The genuflecting (kneeling) worshippers were startled by the noise.)*.

Capitalization. May be a clue to names and titles *(He went skiing in the Austrian Alps.)*.

Italicization (underscoring in hand- or typewritten materials). May be a clue that a given word is a name, title, foreign word, or scientific term:

> The *Queen Mary* sailed from Liverpool.
> I enjoyed *Born Free.*
> A wise consumer is aware of *caveat emptor.*
> The flowerless *filicineae* thrive in damp, shady places.

How Syntactic Clues Work

Since syntactic clues involve relational aspects of language, they are the clues that answer the readers' question "Does it sound right?" If the word identified sounds right to readers in the context of the sentence, it probably fits a syntactic structure that is familiar to them. If it does not sound right, the likelihood is that the readers misidentified the word by substituting one of a different part of speech; that is, one serving a different grammatical function in the sentence than the one represented by the written word they were trying to identify. Readers can use their knowledge of syntax to make inferences about the identities of written word forms since words can be inferred from the roles they play in sentences.

For example, assume that the sentence "The cat pulled a feather from the bird's tail" is read by two pupils. One pupil misidentifies *feather* as *father* and the second pupil misidentifies it as *fresh. Father* sounds right but doesn't make sense in the sentence. In other words, the first pupil's misidentification is acceptable syntactically but not semantically. On the other hand, *fresh* neither sounds right nor makes sense. *Fresh,* ordinarily an adjective, has a different grammatical function than *feather* and is unacceptable in this sentence both grammatically and semantically.

Pupils who use syntactic clues are likely to substitute words of the same part of speech when they misidentify words in reading; those who don't are likely to substitute words of different parts of speech. Even when they misidentify a word as a non-word or nonsense syllable, the correct part of speech can frequently be associated with the nonsense word so that it sounds right grammatically even though it doesn't make any sense in the sentence. Consider, for example, the following sentence in which the nonsense word /wē′ bəl/ is used: "We will have a picnic if the /wē′ bəl/ stays fair." Nonsense words in context may be acceptable syntactically although they are never acceptable semantically.

Changing the part of speech of a word does not necessarily make a word sound wrong either semantically or syntactically in the context of a sentence. It may only change the information that readers get from the sentence. For example, consider the sentence "The policeman shouted *directions* to the man trapped in the car." If pupils read it as "The policeman shouted *directly* to the man trapped in the car," the misidentification would be acceptable both semantically and syntactically, even though it is syntactically different from *directions.* When readers make this kind of substitution, they may not even realize they have made an "error" and simply continue reading. They may realize their error only as they accumulate additional semantic information.

If what they read does not sound right and/or make sense, readers tend to reread to try to correct their misidentifications. They usually go back as far as necessary in order to pick up sufficient clues to make corrections and typically reread entire syntactic units, not just individual words. In the example previously cited, in which *feather* was misidentified as *father* and *fresh,* pupils would probably reread the phrase "a feather from the bird's tail," if not the entire sentence.

Pupils who read for meaning and who use syntactic and semantic clues as word identification techniques are usually aware of what doesn't sound right and/or doesn't make sense. On the other hand, pupils who concentrate their attention on within-word clues unrelated to sentence context (configuration, phonic, or morphemic clues), often do not go back to correct their errors even though their reading may not make sense or sound right. They may not even realize it when they misidentify words, since their attention is directed primarily to the naming of words and not to the acquisition of meaning.

There are times, of course, when readers realize that they have made errors, but do not go back to correct them. Instead, they may revise the oncoming syntax to conform to their errors. Consider the following illustration. In reading the sentence "The boy is giving his paper to his teacher," pupils misidentify *boy* as *boys*. They continue reading, changing the remainder of the sentence to conform to the plurality of the subject *boys,* so that their rendition of the sentence is "The boys are giving their papers to their teachers." Pupils who do this are usually good readers; they have a good grasp of syntax and they read for meaning.

The fact that words are arranged in sentences is of considerable assistance in the identification of written words, since the accurate identification of many word forms depends upon their functions in sentences. This is especially true of homographic word forms such as ⟨lead⟩, ⟨wind⟩, and ⟨conflict⟩, whose lexical referents are uncertain until their syntactic roles are established. For example, the identity of the word form ⟨wind⟩ in each of the two following sentences is uncertain until the syntactic role of the word form is known:

> The *wind* blew my clock off the desk.
> I *wind* my clock every night.

Such words do not present identification problems to listeners since they are pronounced differently. Written, however, their spelling is the same, and they must be in syntactic structures to be identified. The more proficient readers are in using syntactic clues, the more easily they can identify such words in writing. Also, the more proficient readers are, the less visual-orthographic information they need and the more they are able to rely on contextual clues, both semantic and syntactic.

Syntactic clues derive largely from the sentence in which a word appears. The syntax of any sentence is usually independent of the syntax of surrounding sentences. There may be times, however, when authors use the same syntactic patterns repetitively. In these instances, syntactic patterns are often predictable from one sentence to another and this knowledge may be used to advantage by readers.

What Syntactic Clues Depend On

The efficient use of syntactic clues for word identification depends on a number of conditions. Some of these conditions are related more to readers themselves and some are related more to the written material.

Conditions related to readers include readers' knowledge of language, their knowledge of how syntactic components of language are represented in writing, and their reasoning abilities. The more they know about the components of language, such as sentence patterns, word order sequences, mandatory agreement, structure-word markers, and word endings, the better prepared they are to use syntactic clues. As an illustration, consider the following sentences:

The pitcher threw the _____.
_____ is a full moon tonight.

Your knowledge of language tells you that the first sentence must be completed with a noun *(ball, glove, game)* because verbs, adjectives, prepositions, and other parts of speech are eliminated by the syntactic relations among the observable elements of the sentence. The second sentence must be completed with the place marker *there.* These expectations derive from your familiarity with the patterns of English sentences.

If pupils are to succeed in learning to read, they also must learn how the various components of language are represented in writing. Unless they know how to interpret various punctuation marks, for example, they will not be able to unravel the syntactic structure of the written material and will not be able to derive appropriate meaning. In the sentence "Sam left Bill, convinced he was wrong," the implication is that Sam was convinced that Bill was wrong. If the comma were omitted ("Sam left Bill convinced he was wrong"), the sentence would imply that Bill thought he himself was wrong. Also note how changing the position of the first set of quotation marks alters who is saying what in the following pair of sentences:

"Bill said Kathy is in school."
Bill said, "Kathy is in school."

In the first sentence someone is reporting what Bill said. In the second sentence Bill himself is doing the talking. The position of the quotation marks helps make this distinction. The comma after *said* in the second sentence is an additional clue that Bill is the person talking.

Older readers are likely to be more successful than young, beginning readers in using syntactic clues. The reason for their superiority is their more extensive experience with both oral and written language. Older readers also have an advantage over beginning readers because, generally, they have greater reasoning abilities. As previously noted, reasoning ability is an important factor in the successful use of contextual clues, either semantic or syntactic.

Conditions related primarily to the reading material and readers' interactions with it include the level of difficulty, the appeal of the material, and the language being used. There are several variables that affect the level of difficulty. Syntactic complexity is one of these variables. For example, basic sentence meaning is expressed in the subject-verb relationship. These two components appear together at the beginning of simple sentences such as "The cat drank the milk." If any word or words intervene between the subject and the verb, understanding the sentence is usually made more difficult. For instance, one or more modifiers can occur between the subject and the verb, as in the sentence "The cat, hungry and thirsty, drank the milk." The insertion of *hungry and thirsty* separates the subject *cat* from the verb *drank,* making the relationship between them less obvious. The same thing happens when phrases or clauses occur between the subject and the verb. The following sentences are illustrative:

> The cat *with the long fluffy tail* drank the milk.
> The cat *who was hungry and thirsty* drank the milk.

Understanding a sentence may also be more difficult if a syntactic structure precedes the subject:

> Being hungry and thirsty, the cat drank the milk.
> While it was in the house, the cat drank the milk.

When more than one of these complications occur in the same sentence, the difficulty is increased, as the following sentence illustrates:

> While it was in the house, the cat, hungry and thirsty, drank the milk.

It should be noted that the syntax of written material is usually more difficult to interpret than comparable syntax in speech. This is due to the fact that speakers can provide more clues to syntax than writers can. Speakers can use intonation, facial expressions, and gestures. That is, they can use suprasegmental and paralinguistic clues that are not available to readers. In writing, an equal amount of space separates words. It becomes the task of readers to group them meaningfully.

Syntactic clues are more likely to be used effectively by readers when they are intent upon getting meaning from what they are reading, that is, when the materials are of interest or importance to them. In turn, the flow of language represented by the syntax facilitates their acquisition of meaning and their identification of words. Thus, the more concerned they are about following the ideas of the selection, the more they rely on syntax to identify words.

As is true in relation to semantic clues, pupils who use syntactic clues are usually not word callers or word-by-word readers. Reading fluency is largely dependent on efficient use of semantic and syntactic clues.

The efficient use of this technique depends heavily on the readers' knowledge of the syntactic structures used in the material being read. Although written English is usually not an exact reproduction of oral English, there is enough similarity between standard oral and standard written dialects to predict structures from one to the other successfully. When the language patterns of the material closely match the language knowledge of readers, they have stronger bases for understanding the material. Therefore, they are better able and more likely to use syntactic clues. Because the degree of match affects the level of difficulty of certain materials for certain readers, some readers will be able to use syntactic clues more effectively in some materials than in others.

Dialect variations affect the use of syntactic clues. Since syntax is one dimension in which dialects differ, identifying word forms in standard written English through syntactic clues may be difficult, if not impossible, for pupils who speak nonstandard dialects. One simply cannot predict or anticipate what one does not know. Inability to anticipate words can interfere with word identification. For example, pupils who normally say "He work" in place of "He is working" may have difficulty identifying the word form ⟨is⟩ in the latter structure. On the other hand, pupils who habitually read *was* for *were* in sentences involving plural nouns may do so not because they cannot identify *were,* but because they read the way they speak. Hence they may read "There was three girls" for "There were three girls."

Within standard American English there is also syntactic variation. Suppose the question "Why don't you try Brand X?" appears in a selection and is followed by the sentence "I already did." If pupils read this sentence as "I already have," this may only be a reflection of their particular dialect. Both of these responses occur in standard American English.

Mature language users are usually fluent in several oral and written dialects and have a vast resource of syntactic knowledge at their disposal as they read. Beginning readers are usually fluent in only one dialect of oral language. If the syntax of the written material does not match the syntax of the one dialect they are familiar with, they are at a disadvantage in using syntactic clues. It is important for teachers to differentiate between dialect variations and word identification errors because the instructional implications are different.

Pupils for whom English is a second language may also experience difficulty in using syntactic clues. The placement of syntactic structures in sentences often differs from one language to another. In French, for example, adjectives usually follow the nouns they modify and always agree with them in number and gender. In English, adjectives normally precede the nouns they modify and their forms are constant. In the English phrase *the white house,* the adjective *white* precedes the noun *house.* In the French equivalent, *la maison blanche,* the adjective *blanche* follows the noun *maison.* Pupils who are accustomed to a particular pattern of word order in their native language may have difficulty following English word order. This can restrict their ability to use syntactic clues in reading English. Until such pupils become more familiar with the syntactic patterns of standard English, they probably need to rely on other techniques for word identification, particularly in the initial stages of reading development. This also holds true for native speakers of nonstandard dialects of English.

Advantages of Syntactic Clues

The use of syntactic clues, together with semantic clues, enables readers to identify words and word groups more rapidly and efficiently than they can by using any other techniques. The more familiar the syntax of the material is to readers, the more rapidly they can identify words. The more rapid word identification is, the more rapid readers' overall rates of reading can be. Thus the efficient use of syntactic clues for word identification usually results in rapid, fluent, and meaningful reading.

Another advantage of this technique is that entire groups of words representing complete syntactic units may be identified without requiring the reader to examine individual words or their components. More words can be identified in a single eye fixation if they are in meaningful sequences within recognized syntactic structures than if the words are unrelated to each other in any meaningful way. This, too, contributes to rapid, fluent, and meaningful reading. It is especially obvious when pupils read orally because readers infer appropriate intonation from the syntactic clues as they read.

Syntactic structure is a source of information that readers can use to predict and infer the words in a sentence. The better their predictions, the less visual-orthographic information they need. Identifying words in whole syntactic structures is possible with a minimum of visual-orthographic information and does not depend on familiarity with letter names or letter-sound correspondences. In the sentence "She is a very tall girl," the word *tall* is obviously a modifier of *girl* (because of its position between *very* and *girl*). Words like *tell, till, talk,* or *ball* would be ruled out as possibilities with minimal, if any, visual or phonic clues. In isolation, however, more visual-orthographic information would be needed to differentiate *tall* from these other words and to identify *tall* correctly.

One of the most important advantages of syntactic clues is that they are generalizable to the identification of all kinds of word forms in all kinds of contexts. Also, words that do not follow consistent letter-sound correspondences can be identified as readily as those that do. Syntactic clues are particularly useful for identifying structure words that are very often difficult to identify through other techniques. Furthermore, since syntactic clues are anticipatory in nature, they may be used to identify words that are encountered in written form by readers for the first time as well as words that are already familiar to them. Because of these advantages the use of syntactic clues leads to independence in word identification, particularly when they are used in combination with semantic clues and selected word-structure clues.

Limitations of Syntactic Clues

Syntactic clues are subject to the same kinds of limitations that semantic and picture clues are when used in isolation. Although a syntactic structure can be successfully predicted from context, the specific item of structure usually cannot. The final choice of the specific item can only be made in the light of additional information, usually semantic or orthographic-phonological. For example, in the sentence "The man went to the _____ of the house," the syntax indicates that a noun belongs in the blank space. However, the specific noun cannot be predicted or identified without additional clues. Syntactically, the context of the sentence indicates that the missing noun has some relationship to the house, but only semantic or orthographic-phonological information can reveal if it is the *top, front, side,* or *back* of the house. Syntactic clues can be used successfully only when enough of the other words in the context are identified easily enough for readers to follow writers' syntactic structures without difficulty. As a result, readers can use these clues only when the material they are reading is at their instructional and independent reading levels.

Another limitation of syntactic clues is that they are not readily available to beginning readers. Beginning readers must first learn to use other word identification techniques such as the use of picture, configuration, and phonic clues. By doing so they become able to identify a sufficient number of words to enable them to use syntactic clues. As their reading vocabularies increase, their proficiency in the use of syntactic clues can increase. But as long as their reading vocabularies are limited, their use of syntactic clues remains limited also.

The more difficulty readers have with reading, the less use they can make of syntactic clues and the more they have to rely on word-structure clues. This is equally true for beginning readers, retarded readers at any level of reading development, and for proficient readers reading difficult, unfamiliar material.

Finally, as is true of all word identification techniques, syntactic clues are not infallible when used alone. Word identification is always most effective and efficient when various techniques are used in combination with each other.

Exercises

The purpose of the following exercises is to illustrate how syntactic clues may be used for word identification purposes. For example, the homographs (italicized) in Exercise A can be differentiated and identified successfully only through syntactic clues. There is not enough lexical content to differentiate one homograph from the other through semantic clues. Since the homographs are spelled alike and therefore look alike, configuration, morphemic, and phonic clues cannot be used to differentiate between them. Picture and pronunciation spelling clues are not available. Hence, syntactic clues must be used to identify the italicized words.

Exercise A. Read each of the following phrases orally, identify the function or part of speech of the italicized word, and decide what kind of syntactic clue helped you distinguish the first italicized word from the second in each pair of phrases.

1a. the *wind*	1b. *wind* the
2a. his *conduct*	2b. will *conduct*
3a. *separate* books	3b. *separate* the books
4a. *invalid* document	4b. an *invalid*
5a. *close* the door	5b. *close* the door
6a. will *read* the book	6b. has *read* the book

Answer
Function/Part of Speech   *Syntactic Clues Used to*
                                   Differentiate Words
1a. Noun   1b. Verb   Word order and structure word

2a. Noun	2b. Verb	Structure words
3a. Adjective	3b. Verb	Word order and structure word
4a. Adjective	4b. Noun	Word order and structure word
5a. Verb	5b. Adverb	Word order and structure word
6a. Verb	6b. Verb	Structure words

Exercise B. The following sentences also demonstrate how sentence patterns, word order patterns, and structure words, in addition to semantic clues, help in the correct identification of words. Read each sentence orally, identify the function or part of speech of each italicized word, and decide what kinds of syntactic clues helped you to distinguish the first italicized word from the second in each sentence.

1. She *wound* a bandage around her *wound.*
     (a)   (b)

2. She will *entrance* you when she makes her *entrance.*
      (a)   (b)

3. His *excuse* was not sufficient reason to *excuse* him.
    (a)   (b)

4. *Duplicate* the keys and give the *duplicate* keys to your wife.
   (a)   (b)

5. The *learned* man *learned* to read Greek fluently.
      (a)   (b)

Answer

Function/Part of Speech	*Syntactic Clues Used to Differentiate Words*
1a. Verb	Subject/Verb/Object Sentence Pattern
1b. Noun	Structure Word Clue: Noun Marker *her* Possessive Pronoun/Noun Word Order Sequence
2a. Verb	Subject/Verb/Object Sentence Pattern Structure Word Clue: Verb Marker *will*
2b. Noun	Structure Word Clue: Noun Marker *her* Possessive Pronoun/Noun Word Order Sequence

3a. Noun	Structure Word Clue: Noun Marker *his* Possessive Pronoun/Noun Word Order Sequence
3b. Verb	Structure Word Clue: Verb Marker *to*
4a. Verb	Command Sentence Pattern That Starts with Verb Verb/Article/Noun Word Order Sequence
4b. Noun	Structure Word Clue: Noun Marker *the* Adjective/Noun Word Order Sequence
5a. Adjective	Article/Adjective/Noun Word Order Sequence
5b. Verb	Subject/Verb/Object Sentence Pattern

Exercise C. In the following exercise, use the suggested words to fill in the blank spaces and decide what kinds of syntactic clues enabled you to assign the words appropriately.

1a. _____ is he going home? 1b. _____ he is going home. (then, when)

2a. She borrowed _____ books from the library. 2b. She borrowed _____ book from the library. (a, some)

3a. Some _____ live in that house. 3b. Some _____ lives in that house. (child, children)

4. _____ time I have _____ gone to a cocktail party I have been _____ bored. (ever, every, very)

5. I don't know _____ _____ man is doing. (that, what)

6. I _____ you were _____ eating, _____ I see you are not. (though, thought, through)

7. The _____ customs officials looked _____ the luggage _____ly. (through, tough, thorough)

Answer	Syntactic Clues Available for Use
1a. when 1b. then	Punctuation and Word Order

2a. some	2b. a	Determiner/Noun Agreement
3a. children	3b. child	Subject/Verb Agreement
4. every, ever, very		Word Order and Sentence Pattern
5. what, that		Sentence Pattern
6. thought, through, though		Word Order
7. tough, through, thorough		Adjective/Noun Sequence, Word Order

Exercise D. If syntactic clues are used in conjunction with other clues, such as configuration, picture, or semantic clues, word identification becomes easier, faster, and more accurate. Referring to Figure 6.1, supply the missing words in the following exercise using all available clues.

1. The two _____ were flying south.
2. There were some _____ in the water.
3. Sam sat on deck and looked at the three ⌐⌐.
4. The fish were _mm_ away from the diver.
5. The fish swam ⌒ the boat.

Figure 6.1

Answer	Kinds of Clues Used to Identify Missing Word
1. birds	Syntactic, semantic, and picture clues
2. fish	Syntactic and picture clues
3. clouds	Syntactic, picture, and configuration clues
4. swimming	Semantic, syntactic, picture, and configuration clues
5. under	Semantic, syntactic, picture, and configuration clues

As is true with any whole-word identification technique, the effectiveness of syntactic clues depends on the number of unfamiliar word forms within a given amount of written text. The fewer unfamiliar word forms there are, the more successful readers can be in identifying them through any technique or any combination of techniques.

Suggested Activities for Pupil Practice

General Considerations for Teachers

It is important that activities focus on the specific skill(s) you want pupils to practice. Pupils should not be able to get the right answers except by applying the skill(s) you want them to practice. For example, in a sentence like "I object to your decision" the word *decision* supplies a semantic clue to the identification of ⟨object⟩ so that pupils need not rely on syntactic clues only in identifying that word form. However, if this semantic clue were deleted so that the sentence read, "I object," pupils would need to use the subject/verb word-order or sentence pattern as a syntactic clue to the identity of ⟨object⟩.

Guard against using items that have unintentional common elements since this might encourage pupils to make unwarranted generalizations. If homographs are used in all syntactic clue practice activities, pupils may conclude that syntactic clues are appropriate only for distinguishing between homographs.

Activities similar to those that are described for pupil practice may be used as diagnostic skills tests or as criterion-referenced tests to analyze pupils' proficiencies and deficiencies in the use of specific syntactic clues. Such diagnostic test activities may be administered before and/or after teaching the skills.

Activity 1

Purpose. To provide practice in using the article/adjective/noun word order sequence as a clue to the identification of words in sentences

Level. Upper primary.

Directions for Teachers. Use words whose meanings pupils already know and whose word forms they have learned to identify. Successful use of this kind of syntactic clue depends on pupils' being familiar with the syntactic pattern involved. If pupils are not native speakers of English, they may need to be taught the English article/adjective/noun sequence. For example, pupils whose native language is French or Spanish would have learned to use an article/noun/adjective word order sequence which could interfere with their use of the English article/adjective/noun word order sequence as a clue to word identification.

Select the nouns and adjectives to be identified. Prepare a set of phrases consisting of an article/adjective/noun word order sequence. (You may also use phrases taken from pupils' published reading materials for use in such exercises.) Either the noun or the adjective, but not both, should be blanked out in each phrase. The remaining words in each phrase should be familiar to pupils so that they present no word identification problems. The more familiar the content is to pupils, the more successfully they will be able to use the contextual clues.

The blanked-out word should be presented in a multiple-choice format with two or three other words of different parts of speech. The following are examples:

the angry _____	(lion, follow, little)
a _____ cookie	(bake, round, very)
an _____ breakfast	(elevator, over, early)
a loud _____	(dry, bell, grow)
the _____ nest	(empty, brook, fast)
an ugly _____	(funny, listen, house)

Write the set of phrases and word choices on the chalkboard or on a chart, transparency, or ditto sheet. Be sure that the blank spaces are the same length in all the phrases so that pupils cannot get any clues to the missing words from any differences. Word length is a type of configuration clue, not a syntactic clue.

Have pupils read the first phrase to themselves and select the appropriate missing word from the options provided. Call on a pupil to read the complete phrase aloud. If he or she has selected the appropriate word, ask why the other words did not sound right (were not appropriate in function; were not the right part of speech). Accept any explanation that conveys the idea.

If pupils select an inappropriate word, repeat the phrase as they have read it and ask them if it sounds right. Ask them to use each of the other word choices in the blank space and to choose the one that sounds best in the completed phrase. Elicit the reason why that particular word sounds best in that phrase. If they are familiar with the article/adjective/noun word order sequence, they should be able to select the appropriate word and give the reason for their choice.

Proceed in a similar manner with the remaining phrases. You may, if you wish, omit the word choices from this activity. In this case, any response that uses a word of the appropriate part of speech should be accepted. However, if you want to encourage pupils to combine semantic with syntactic clues, you should guide them to think of words that make sense as well as words that sound right. For example, the noun *cupcake* is syntactically acceptable in the first phrase, "the angry _____," but it is inappropriate semantically.

Sentences rather than phrases may be used in this activity. Again, they may be written by you or taken from pupils' instructional materials.

Pupils should be given opportunities to use other word order sequences and sentence patterns as syntactic clues. At a more advanced level, for example, sentences with similar semantic content but with variation in syntactic pattern may be used. In the sentence "The dog was _____ on the mat," either *asleep* or *sleeping* would be acceptable in the blank space. If, however, the sentence were changed to "The dog was fast _____ on the mat," only the word *asleep* would be acceptable.

At appropriate levels, pupils should also practice using syntactic clues that follow, rather than precede, target words in sentences. The following sentence illustrates this:

"Deer _____ on their speed and sharp sense of hearing to _____ themselves from their enemies."

Given the two verbs *defend* and *depend,* pupils should be able to select the appropriate one for each blank space, basing their choices on syntactic information. The structure word *on* following the first blank space is the syntactic clue to the word *depend.* The structure word *from* is the syntactic clue to the word *defend* in the second blank.

These kinds of activities may be done by pupils working independently at their desks. They can fill in the answers on ditto sheets or activity cards, or they may copy phrases and sentences from the chalkboard.

Activity 2

Purpose. To provide practice in using determiner/noun number agreement as a clue to word identification

Level. Primary.

Directions for Teachers. Use words whose meanings pupils already know and whose written word forms they have learned to identify. Successful use of this kind of syntactic clue depends on pupils understanding the difference between the terms *singular* and *plural.* Speakers of some non-standard dialects of English do not always differentiate singular and plural noun forms with inflectional endings, but rely on the determiner instead for this distinction. For example, the singular might be expressed as *this pencil,* the plural as *these pencil.* The following activity should not be used with such pupils until you have first taught them the difference in the forms of singular and plural nouns.

Select the determiners and nouns to be identified in the activity. Prepare a set of phrases or sentences that include determiners followed by nouns. (You also may use phrases or sentences taken directly from pupils' instructional materials.) Either the determiner or the noun, but not both, should be blanked out in each phrase or sentence. The remaining words should be familiar to pupils and present no word identification problems. The more familiar the content is to pupils, the more successfully they will be able to use the contextual clues.

The blanked out word should be presented in a forced-choice format, as in the following sentences:

> Lois picked _____ apples. (an, some)
> Sam used this _____ to paint his picture. (brush, brushes)
> _____ packages should be put in the trunk of the car. (that, those)
> Kathy fixed _____ broken chairs. (a, the)

Write the set of sentences and word choices on the chalkboard, or on a chart, transparency, or ditto sheet. Have pupils read the first sentence to themselves and select the appropriate missing word from the choices provided. Call on a pupil to read the complete sentence aloud. If he or she has selected the appropriate word to fill in the blank space, ask why the other word was not appropriate. Accept any explanation that conveys the idea.

If the pupils select the inappropriate word, repeat the sentence as they read it and ask them if it sounds right. Ask them to use the other word choice to hear how that sounds. Ask them to tell you which word sounds better when the whole sentence is read and have them explain why. (Hearing the sentence read aloud helps pupils determine which word choice "sounds right.") If they are still unable to select the appropriate word, you may have to point out the interdependence of the determiner and the noun in relation to singularity and plurality. Proceed in a similar manner with the remaining sentences.

Activities for practice in using this kind of syntactic clue may consist of phrases or sentences that are unrelated, as in the examples above, or of sentences in story format, as in the following example:

Lois picked _____ apples. She climbed up _____ ladder to
          (an, some)   (this, these)
reach _____ apples that were very high on _____ trees. She
   (that, those)   (a, the)
put many _____ into a _____. She put one _____ into
     (apple, apples) (basket, baskets)   (apple, apples)
each _____ of her blue jeans. Then she climbed down and
(pocket, pockets)
went home to bake a pie.

If pupils experience difficulty with any particular determiner/noun relationships, you should prepare activities that focus on those determiners. These activities may consist solely of determiner/noun phrases. For example, if pupils have difficulty choosing the appropriate noun form for the determiners *this* and *these,* activity items such as the following might be helpful:

this _____   (book, books)
these _____   (egg, eggs)
_____ desk   (this, these)
_____ kites   (this, these)

Activities involving determiner/noun relationships may be done by pupils working independently at their desks. They can fill in the blank spaces on ditto sheets or activity cards, or they may copy phrases and sentences from the chalkboard. This kind of activity can also be done by pupils working in pairs, reading to and checking each other.

Example of Combination Activity

Since syntactic clues are more effective when used in combination with other kinds of word identification clues, pupils should be given practice in so using them. Activity items such as the following, which combine syntactic with semantic clues, are illustrative:

1. Kathy likes to use pencil to draw _____, but Bill prefers to use paint to draw them.
2. Those tennis _____ don't have much bounce left in them.
3. The cheerleaders jumped up and down happily when their team _____ the game.

Answer

1. pictures   (The syntactic clues are the absence of a singular article before the blank space and the plural pronoun *them;* the semantic clues are the lexical meanings of the words *pencil, paint,* and *draw.*)

2. balls   (The syntactic clue is the determiner *those,* which signals a plural noun; the semantic clues are the lexical meanings of *tennis* and *bounce.*)

3. won   (The syntactic clues include the subject/verb/object clause pattern as a verb clue and the past tense of the preceding verb as a clue to the tense of the missing verb; the semantic clues are the lexical meanings of the words *cheerleaders, happily, team,* and *game.*)

PART THREE 3

Word Structure Techniques

Part III presents the word structure techniques of word identification. They can be divided into three categories: morphemic clues (discussed in Chapter 7), clues relating relating to phonics (Chapters 8, 9, and 10), and pronunciation spelling clues (Chapter 11). Chapters 7 and 11 follow the same pattern of organization as the chapters in Part II. They begin with brief introductions, followed by descriptions of the kinds of clues related to each technique. Discussed are how the clues are recognized and how they work, the conditions necessary for their proper use, and their advantages and limitations. Both chapters end with exercises for teachers and suggested activities for pupils.

Because of its extensive nature, three chapters are related to phonics. Chapter 8 briefly surveys the types of phonic clues and discusses how they work, what they depend on, and their advantages and limitations. Chapter 9 covers in detail syllabication (hyphenation) and accenting principles and includes teacher exercises and pupil activities for these topics. Chapter 10 presents grapheme-phoneme correspondences and also includes teacher exercises and pupil activities.

Part III is followed by Chapter 12, which summarizes the seven word identification techniques and reviews their applications to teaching word identification. Included is a teachers' mastery test based on the information presented in the text.

Two word identification techniques analyze words into subunits and use the subunits as clues to the identification of those words. The first technique, *morphemic analysis,* relates to the morphological structure of words. The second, called *phonic analysis* or *phonics,* relates to the phonological structure of words. Morphemic analysis uses meaning subunits as identification clues. Phonic analysis uses subunits of sound and pronunciation as identification clues. Morphemic analysis is discussed in this chapter. Phonic analysis is discussed in Chapters 8, 9, and 10. The rationale underlying these techniques is that a word is the sum of its parts, that if the individual parts can be recognized, the word can be identified by combining the parts.

Morphemic analysis is frequently referred to as *structural analysis, word-structure analysis*, or *word-part analysis.* Many authors and teachers who use these terms do not distinguish between meaning-related and pronunciation-related clues and usually intermingle under these headings the principles of syllabication and accenting with various kinds of semantic units. However, morphemic analysis relates *only* to the components of meaning. Principles of syllabication and accenting are really matters of pronunciation and thus relate primarily to phonics.

The term *morpheme* is somewhat difficult to define. Different linguists define it differently. In general, it refers to the minimal spoken or written unit of meaning. In reading, morphemic analysis refers to finding, isolating, and identifying such units.

Morphemes should not be confused with syllables. A morpheme is a unit in the grammatical and lexical systems of language; it always represents meaning. A syllable does not represent meaning; it is a unit of pronunciation. It is true that there are times when a given sequence of letters represents both a morpheme and a syllable as in the word *catnip* where ⟨cat⟩ constitutes a syllable and also represents the morpheme referring to a domesticated feline. However, the same sequence of letters represents only a syllable in words like *catalog* and *catalyst*. There are morphemes that are less than syllables (the ⟨-s⟩ in *girls*, the ⟨-ed⟩ in *slipped*), morphemes that are single syllables in themselves (*cat*, the ⟨un-⟩ in *until*), and morphemes that are composed of more than one syllable (*elephant*, ⟨anti-⟩ in *antidote*). Finding morphemes in words involves segmenting words into fragments and determining whether meaning can be assigned to them.

Kinds of Morphemic Clues

The effective use of morphemic clues for word identification depends on readers' familiarity with specific morpheme units. These include roots, prefixes, suffixes, and inflections. Each of these categories is discussed here.

Roots

The root of a word is that part which is neither prefix, suffix, nor inflection and which conveys the major portion of the word's meaning. The term *root* is used here because it is the term usually used in materials related to reading instruction. Linguists, on the other hand, commonly use the term *base*.

A root in English may be free or bound. Free roots are variously called *roots, root words* or *morphemes*, and *bases.* They are always whole recognizable English words—the smallest English words to which affixes (prefixes, suffixes, and inflectional endings) may be attached. Examples include *pay* in *repay*, *comfort* in *comfortable*, and *elephant* in *elephants.*

Bound roots are root units that cannot occur alone in English, but must be attached to other morphemes. They are variously called *word roots* or *bases*, or more frequently, *foreign word roots, parts,* or *particles.* Most of the bound roots in English have been borrowed from other languages, especially Latin, Greek, and Medieval or Old French. Some examples are ⟨-fer-⟩ in *transfer* (Latin), ⟨-chron-⟩ in *chronology* (Greek), and ⟨-cour-⟩ in *courage* (French). Since French developed from Latin, a number of borrowed words can be assigned to either language.

Because changes occurred in bound roots as they evolved from other languages, it can often be difficult to identify their meanings through their historical derivations. In fact, there is substantial evidence to indicate that evaluation of bound roots is not very helpful and that root identification should be limited to free roots. These are the kinds of root words that pupils can more readily recognize in affixed words.

However, identification of a few bound roots may be useful, particularly those most commonly found in pupils' reading materials. An example is the bound root ⟨-manu-⟩ (from the Latin word for *hand*) which appears in *manual, manuscript,* and *manufacture.* The study of bound roots for word identification purposes is probably best left for the secondary school level, when pupils are more sophisticated in their language skills.

Pupils should be taught to isolate letter combinations resembling affixes in unfamiliar word forms and to recognize what remains as whole English words, subject to spelling changes (dropped final ⟨e⟩, doubled final consonant, ⟨y⟩ changed to ⟨i⟩, ⟨f⟩ changed to ⟨v⟩, ⟨k⟩ added to ⟨c⟩). If whole English words do not remain, they should reconsider their first divisions. For example, if pupils encounter the unfamiliar word form ⟨receivable⟩, they may see spelling sequences that are familiar at the beginning and end of the word form: ⟨re-⟩ as in *repay* and ⟨-able⟩ as in *useable.* What remains is ⟨-ceiv-⟩ which does not look like a whole English word. Adding a final ⟨e⟩ does not make it a recognizable word. At this point, the pupils should look for other possibilities. If they isolate only the ⟨re-⟩, ⟨-ceivable⟩ is left and that is not an English word. If, however, they cut off ⟨-able⟩, what remains is ⟨receiv-⟩, which, with the addition of an ⟨e⟩ is an English word. They then can put together the meanings of the root *receive* and the suffix ⟨-able⟩ to arrive at the identification of the whole word.

Prefixes

Prefixes are bound morphemes since they are not independent units. They can occur only before roots and usually serve to modify the lexical meanings of those roots. Prefixes usually occur singly, but sometimes there are two of them in sequence at the beginning of a word. Each prefix also forms a separate syllable in the word. Most prefixes are not separated from the roots following them, but a few are sometimes separated from the roots by hyphens. This occurs when the lack of a hyphen would result in a sequence of letters that might be misleading, as in the word *co-worker* (vs. the unhyphenated form *coworker*).

The use of prefixes for word identification purposes can probably best be taught when the root parts of words are recognizable as individual English words. It is more difficult to use prefixes to identify words borrowed from other languages which were taken into English with prefixes already attached. In such words the root parts are not clearly distinguishable as morphemes. However, recognition of the prefix can be helpful in interpreting the words, although their identification may not be complete. Examples of such words are *translate* and *combine.* In these cases, the prefixes ⟨trans-⟩ (indicating *across)* and ⟨com-⟩ (indicating *with* or *together*) give readers a partial understanding of the words in which they appear.

The most effective way to completely identify words through their prefixes is to combine the meanings of the prefixes with the meanings of the roots. This is best accomplished when the roots are clearly recognizable whole English words. A good teaching strategy is to present pairs of words, one without the prefix and one with the prefix, in order to illustrate the meaning function of the prefix. Examples are *pay/repay, like/unlike,* and *worker/co-worker.*

Below is a list of prefixes that can easily be identified in English words. Some are used more frequently than others in the formation of new words. Only one spelling is given for each prefix, although some have alternate spellings, depending upon the spelling of the root to which they are affixed. The prefixes ⟨ad-⟩, ⟨com-⟩, and ⟨in-⟩ are examples of prefixes with variant spellings. In these and some other prefixes, the spelling of the prefix is modified to fit the initial consonant of the root. The process reflects a phenomenon of spoken language that is called "assimilation." There are also a few instances of prefixes that are spelled the same but that have different origins and retain different meanings. Although, strictly speaking, this difference in meaning would make them different morphemes, they are listed together here and the differences are illustrated by examples.

Table 7.1 Easily Identified Prefixes

Prefix	Example	Common Meaning
⟨a-⟩	atypical	not, without
⟨ab-⟩	abnormal	away, from
⟨ad-⟩	admit	to, toward, near
	accord	
⟨ante-⟩	anteroom	before, prior to
⟨auto-⟩	autobiography	self
⟨bi-⟩	biangular	two
⟨circum-⟩	circumnavigate	around
⟨com-⟩	commingle	together, jointly
	collaborate	
	coauthor	
⟨counter-⟩	counterattack	opposition
⟨de-⟩	defrost	opposition
⟨dis-⟩	disappear	opposition
	dishonest	not
⟨en-⟩	enslave	cause to
⟨ex-⟩	ex-president	former
⟨extra-⟩	extramarital	outside, beyond
⟨fore-⟩	forejudge	before
⟨hyper-⟩	hyperactive	overly, beyond
⟨in-⟩	indirect	not
	illegal	
	immeasurable	
	irrational	
⟨inter-⟩	interstate	between
⟨intra-⟩	intrastate	within
⟨mal-⟩	malfunctioning	poorly, badly
⟨micro-⟩	microwave	small
⟨mid-⟩	midyear	middle
⟨mis-⟩	miscount	wrongly, badly
⟨mono-⟩	monotone	one
⟨multi-⟩	multicolored	many
⟨neo-⟩	neoclassical	new
⟨non-⟩	nonliving	not
⟨per-⟩	permeate	thoroughly, through
⟨poly-⟩	polysyllabic	many
⟨post-⟩	postwar	after
⟨pre-⟩	prewar	before
⟨pro-⟩	pro-American	for, favoring
⟨pseudo-⟩	pseudoscience	false
⟨re-⟩	rewrite	again, repeat
⟨retro-⟩	retroactive	back

Prefix	Example	Common Meaning
⟨semi-⟩	semirigid	partly
⟨sub-⟩	subsoil	under, beneath
⟨super-⟩	superhuman	above, beyond
⟨syn-⟩	syndrome	together, with
	symbiosis	
⟨trans-⟩	transoceanic	across
⟨tri-⟩	triangular	three
⟨ultra-⟩	ultramodern	above, extremely
⟨un-⟩	unhappy	not
	untie	do opposite action
⟨uni-⟩	unicolor	one
⟨vice-⟩	vice-consulate	subordinate

Suffixes

Suffixes are morphemes usually consisting of one, but in some instances, two syllables, that are added to the ends of roots. They are also called *derivational suffixes* to differentiate them from inflectional endings or inflectional suffixes. Like prefixes, they are bound morpheme units since they cannot exist independently.

Suffixes affect the meanings of the roots to which they are affixed. Although other aspects of meaning are involved as well, a primary function of derivational suffixes is to indicate part of speech or syntactic function. English has four sets of such suffixes, one for each of the four major parts of speech: nouns, verbs, adjectives, and adverbs.

Many suffixes influence lexical meaning, whether or not they affect syntax. For example, the word *care* may be converted to *careless* or *careful*, which are both adjectives but whose suffixes give them very different lexical meanings. Note also the difference in meaning between *womanish* and *womanly*, both adjectives. In the above examples, differences in the suffixes produce differences in the lexical meanings of the two words, but not in their syntatic function. In other cases, suffixes can affect both. For example, the noun *race* may be converted to *racism*, also a noun but with quite a different meaning, and to *racist*, which may be a noun or an adjective, depending on the context in which it is used (*He is a racist* vs. *He is racist*).

There seem to be rules governing the order of suffixes, but they have not yet been fully analyzed. Suffixes seem to develop meaning progressively. For example, from the basic root *act* (a noun or a verb) is made the word *active* (an adjective). From *active* are made the words *activity* and *activism* (both nouns) and *activate* (a verb).

There is variation in the spelling of some suffixes. For example, one of the noun-making suffixes may appear as ⟨-tion⟩, ⟨-ation⟩, ⟨-ition⟩, or ⟨-sion⟩, but all end with ⟨ion⟩. The letters ⟨a⟩ and ⟨e⟩ are, in effect, alternates in some suffixes: ⟨-ant/-ent⟩, ⟨-ance/-ence⟩, and ⟨-ar/-er⟩. Similarly, the letters ⟨a⟩ and ⟨i⟩ alternate in ⟨-able/-ible⟩. These differences in spelling have historical bases but have nothing to do with the pronunciation or meaning of the suffixes.

It is important that readers remember that a suffix is only one clue to the possible identity of a word. The suffix ⟨-ly⟩ offers an example of how factors outside the suffix itself give clues to the possible meaning of a word. Most people think of ⟨-ly⟩ as an adverb-making suffix as in *quickly* and *quietly*. This is true when ⟨-ly⟩ is added to adjectives, but when it is added to nouns, it produces adjectives, such as *manly* and *worldly*. Also, there are some instances where ⟨-ly⟩ bears no adverbial relation to the root of the word as in *hardly* and *extremely*.

Most literate adults have some sense of derivational suffixes, but it is highly unlikely that one would understand their operation clearly without studying them closely. Reading teachers should have knowledge about the operation of suffixes so that they can answer pupils' questions; however, they should exercise restraint and avoid burdening pupils with more information on suffixes than they can utilize.

Below are lists of common suffixes. Their individual meanings should be interpreted according to the general explanation preceding each list.

Noun- and Adjective-Marking Suffixes. Noun-marking suffixes carry the implication that something with a particular quality or character is being referred to. Many of the nouns formed by the addition of suffixes are abstract nouns. They refer to qualities apart from although perhaps related to concrete objects. Adjective-marking suffixes convey, as part of their meaning, that something has a particular character or is like something else. The adjectives themselves convey this characteristic or similarity and ascribe it to the nouns that are being modified. In many instances the same spelling pattern serves as both a noun-marking and an adjective-marking suffix.

Table 7.2 Noun- and Adjective-Marking Suffixes

Suffix	Noun Example	Adjective Example
⟨-able⟩		break<u>able</u>
⟨-acy⟩	prim<u>acy</u>	
⟨-age⟩	orphan<u>age</u>	

Suffix	Noun Example	Adjective Example
⟨-al⟩	arrival	fictional
⟨-an⟩	republican	
⟨-ian⟩	Iranian	Iranian
⟨-n⟩	American	American
⟨-ance⟩	acceptance	
⟨-ancy⟩	ascendancy	
⟨-ant⟩	claimant	determinant
⟨-ar⟩	scholar	
⟨-ary⟩	commentary	budgetary
⟨-ate⟩	consulate	
⟨-ation⟩	affirmation	
⟨-cal⟩		historical
⟨-dom⟩	freedom	
⟨-ed⟩		cultured
⟨-ee⟩	appointee	
⟨-eer⟩	auctioneer	
⟨-en⟩		golden
⟨-ence⟩	preference	
⟨-ency⟩	consistency	
⟨-ent⟩	deterrent	abhorrent
⟨-er⟩	driver	
⟨-or⟩	sailor	
⟨-ery⟩	bravery	
⟨-ese⟩	journalese	
⟨-esque⟩		statuesque
⟨-ess⟩	authoress	
⟨-et⟩	floweret	
⟨-ette⟩	cigarette	
⟨-iferous⟩		odoriferous
⟨-fold⟩		tenfold
⟨-ful⟩		peaceful
⟨-ing⟩	meeting	
⟨-graph⟩	radiograph	
⟨-hood⟩	childhood	
⟨-ible⟩	convertible	
⟨-ic⟩		poetic
⟨-ice⟩	service	
⟨-ics⟩	athletics	
⟨-ile⟩		infantile
⟨-ine⟩	heroine	elephantine
⟨-ion⟩	regulation	
⟨-ish⟩		foolish
⟨-ism⟩	alcoholism	

Table 7.2 Noun- and Adjective-Marking Suffixes (cont.)

Suffix	Noun Example	Adjective Example
⟨-ist⟩	ra<u>cist</u>	
⟨-ity⟩	civi<u>lity</u>	
⟨-ive⟩		cre<u>ative</u>
⟨-kin⟩	lamb<u>kin</u>	
⟨-less⟩		wit<u>less</u>
⟨-let⟩	book<u>let</u>	
⟨-like⟩		child<u>like</u>
⟨-ling⟩	weak<u>ling</u>	
⟨-ly⟩		kind<u>ly</u>
⟨-ment⟩	develop<u>ment</u>	
⟨-ness⟩	kind<u>ness</u>	
⟨-ology⟩	etym<u>ology</u>	
⟨-ory⟩	deposi<u>tory</u>	compensa<u>tory</u>
⟨-ous⟩		joy<u>ous</u>
⟨-ry⟩	citizen<u>ry</u>	
⟨-ship⟩	friend<u>ship</u>	
⟨-some⟩		burden<u>some</u>
⟨-ster⟩	young<u>ster</u>	
⟨-ty⟩	certain<u>ty</u>	
⟨-ude⟩	defini<u>tude</u>	
⟨-ule⟩	mole<u>cule</u>	minis<u>cule</u>
⟨-ulent⟩		fraud<u>ulent</u>
⟨-ure⟩	fail<u>ure</u>	
⟨-y⟩	hones<u>ty</u>	mes<u>sy</u>

Verb-Marking Suffixes. Verb-forming suffixes carry the implication that something is being done or is happening.

Table 7.3 Verb-Marking Suffixes

Suffix	Example
⟨-ate⟩	activ<u>ate</u>
⟨-en⟩	short<u>en</u>
⟨-esce⟩	conval<u>esce</u>
⟨-fy⟩	beauti<u>fy</u>
⟨-ify⟩	solid<u>ify</u>
⟨-ize⟩	terror<u>ize</u>

Adverb-Marking Suffixes. Adverb-forming suffixes convey, as part of their meaning, an indication of the way or the conditions according to which something is being done or is happening.

Table 7.4 Adverb-Marking Suffixes

Suffix	Example
⟨-fold⟩	ten<u>fold</u>
⟨-ly⟩	slow<u>ly</u>
⟨-most⟩	top<u>most</u>
⟨-ward(s)⟩	west<u>ward(s)</u>
⟨-wise⟩	clock<u>wise</u>

Inflections

The term *inflection* refers to a change in a word form that indicates a new grammatical or syntactic relationship—a change, for example, that makes a noun plural or possessive, a verb into a past tense or a participle, or an adjective or adverb into a comparative or superlative degree. Regular inflections in current English are all endings, which are usually placed after roots and suffixes in words. If a word includes an inflectional ending, it is always the final unit of the word.

The term is also used for such internal spelling changes (called inflectional replacements) as *man* to *men, goose* to *geese*, and *ride* to *rode*. These irregular inflections are survivors from older stages of the English language. In a few instances, an inflection involves both an internal change and an ending, but for the most part a word can have only one inflection.

Inflected forms are not generally considered to be different words but specific forms of a root word. For example, *trees* is the plural form of *tree* and *touched* is the past tense of *touch*. The term *inflection* is not ordinarily used in connection with the forms of personal pronouns, but some linguists refer to *whose* and *whom* as inflected forms of *who*.

In a few instances it is difficult to tell whether a particular morpheme is an inflectional ending or a derivational suffix. For example, the ⟨-ing⟩ is ambiguous in the sentence "She is entertaining." Readers need to use semantic clues outside the immediate sentence to determine whether *entertaining* is an adjective or a verb:

> Everyone likes to be with Lois. She is entertaining (adjective).
> We are going to Lois's house. She is entertaining (verb).

This process is usually easy for proficient readers, but it can be very difficult for beginners. Therefore, such ambiguities should not be present in materials written for beginning readers.

The number of inflections in English is relatively small. The most common ones are listed below.

Noun Inflections—Plurality

If the singular form ends with one of the following consonant sounds: /s/, /z/, /ks/ spelled ⟨x⟩, /j/, /č/, or /š/, the plural ending is usually spelled ⟨-es⟩ and is pronounced as a separate syllable (churches, boxes, breezes).

If the singular form ends with any other consonant sound, the plural ending is usually spelled ⟨-s⟩ and does not add a separate syllable to the word (cars, roads, maps).

If the singular form ends with ⟨y⟩ preceded by a consonant, the ⟨y⟩ is changed to ⟨i⟩, and ⟨-es⟩ is added, but no additional syllable is formed (lady/ladies, fly/flies).

If the singular form ends with a silent ⟨e⟩, that ⟨e⟩ is kept (notes, toes, grapes).

If the singular form ends with a voiced consonant sound, the added ⟨-s⟩ represents the sound /z/ (tabs, toads, grooves).

If the singular form ends with a voiceless consonant sound, the added ⟨-s⟩ represents the sound /s/ (arcs, troops).

There are a number of irregular plurals (inflectional replacements) caused by internal spelling changes in the single form of the root (foot/feet, mouse/mice).

There are some irregular plurals that are identical to the singular form of the noun (deer/deer, moose/moose).

There are some plurals that are borrowed from other languages (alumnus/alumni, datum/data, locus/loci).

Noun Inflections—Possession

Singular possessive: to indicate ownership or possession by a single entity (be it person, place, or thing), ⟨-'s⟩ is added to the noun (Mary's friend, the book's cover).

Plural possessive: to indicate ownership or possession by more than one entity, usually ⟨-s'⟩ is added to the noun (the boys' books, the trees' trunks, two girls' hats). However, if the noun ends with the consonant sounds /s/, /z/, /ks/ spelled ⟨x⟩, /j/, /č/, or /š/, the plural possessive is spelled ⟨-es'⟩

and is pronounced as a separate syllable (the nurses' stations, the churches' spires).

Spellings and pronunciations involved when ⟨-s⟩ or ⟨-es⟩ is added to indicate possession are the same as for the ⟨-s⟩ and ⟨-es⟩ plural endings.

To indicate ownership or possession of most native and foreign irregular plurals, ⟨-'s⟩ is added to the plural noun (the mice's hole, the deer's food, the alumni's homecoming).

Verb Inflections

To indicate the third person, present-tense, singular form of most verbs, ⟨-s⟩ or ⟨-es⟩ is added, with pronunciation and spelling conditions the same as for plural nouns (she races, it jumps, he hurries).

To indicate past tense, the following conditions apply:

> The regular past tense spelling is ⟨-ed⟩ (jumped, spelled).
> If the simple verb form ends with silent ⟨e⟩, the ⟨e⟩ is dropped and ⟨-ed⟩ is added (urge/urged, carve/carved).
> If the simple form does not end with silent ⟨e⟩, the ⟨-ed⟩ spelling is added (join/joined, march/marched).
> The following pronunciation rules apply: If the simple verb ends with the sound /t/ or /d/, a syllable is added (parted, faded). If the simple form ends with a voiced sound (vowel or consonant), the ending is pronounced /d/ (raised, married). If the simple form ends with a voiceless sound, the pronunciation of the ending is /t/ (tapped, kissed).
> There are many irregular past tense forms of verbs that are inflectional replacements for the simple forms of those verbs (say/said, ride/rode, speak/spoke, is/was).

The regular form of the past participle follows the same principles as the past tense form [see items directly above].

The present participle is spelled ⟨-ing⟩. It usually indicates a present condition, a general fact, or a customary action. It also is used to convey the idea of "action going on at the present time" (They are talking. Barbara is attending college.). The ⟨-ing⟩ form of the verb is also used to indicate a past condition, a general fact, a customary action in the past, or "action going on in the past" (He was reading. They had been talking.).

All the modals (will/would, shall/should, can/could, may/might, must/ought) can be used with the present participle ⟨-ing⟩ to convey some sense of future (Shirley will be coming. Lisa would be reading.).

The ⟨-ing⟩ form may be used in a nominal function. If so, it is called a *gerund* or *verbal noun* (I get the meaning of what you say. Her singing is pleasant.). It is also found with adjective meaning (I have reached the turning point. This is a winding road.).

Adjective and Adverb Inflections

The comparative ⟨-er⟩ and superlative ⟨-est⟩ endings on adjectives and adverbs are considered inflections by most linguists.

The most common use of the ⟨-er⟩ comparative ending is in comparing qualities or attributes of two entities. It may be used when the comparison is only implied or when it is directly stated (John is the taller one. John is taller than Rose.).

The most common use of the ⟨-est⟩ superlative ending is to modify the word to which it is attached to indicate the greatest possible degree or extent of whatever quality or attribute is referred to. There is an implication that more than two instances are involved (The smartest always wins out. Pepe is the tallest boy in school.).

The ⟨-er⟩ and ⟨-est⟩ endings are not added to all adjectives and adverbs. In principle, they are added to one-syllable words, sometimes to two-syllable words, and never to words with more than two syllables. If the word is one that does not take the ⟨-er⟩ and ⟨-est⟩ endings, the comparative meaning is conveyed by a preceding *more* and the superlative meaning is conveyed by a preceding *most*(more expensive toys, most expensive toys). Also, adjectives in comparative or superlative forms with a preceding *more* or *most* are freely used in noun-like functions where the actual nouns are implied, but not named (These are the more expensive. These are the most expensive.).

There are some irregular forms of inflected adjectives and adverbs (better/best, worse/worst).

Morphemic Combinations

In English it is quite common to construct new words by combining two or more morphemes (*disambiguate, finalize*) or even by combining conventional morphemes with invented pseudomorphemes (*hamburger, truth-wise*). The word *hamburger* has nothing to do with ham but is an adaptation from the name of a well-known city in Germany—Hamburg. However, English-speaking people have divided the word into parts and used the second part to form such words as *cheeseburger, pizzaburger, fishburger,* etc. This has made ⟨burger⟩ into a morpheme. The morpheme ⟨-wise⟩ is another example of a pseudomorpheme used as a regular morpheme to extend the meanings of root words. Thus, there is the proliferation of such words as: *business-wise, money-wise, truth-wise, religion-wise,* and so on.

In English there are several kinds of morphemic combinations. They occur in fixed orders. From these fixed-order combinations, many English words can be formed. Words may contain one or more free morphemes or roots. Some words, those of foreign derivation, are composed of two or more bound morphemes. Additionally, words can contain one or more prefixes, one or more derivational suffixes, one inflectional ending, or a combination of these units. English words must contain roots. They may or may not contain other morphemic units. When other units are included in words, their fixed order of occurrence is: prefix(es), root(s), derivational suffix(es), inflectional ending. The following words are examples of various combinations of morphemic units.

rain: single free root

rainbow: compound word consisting of two free roots

rained: inflected form consisting of free root and inflectional ending

rainless: derived word consisting of free root and derivational suffix

unlike: derived word consisting of prefix and free root

receive: derived word consisting of prefix and bound root

receiving: inflected form of derived word consisting of prefix, bound root, and inflection

undoubtedly: derived word consisting of prefix, free root, and two derivational suffixes

A word can have only one inflectional ending. It may include multiples of the other units, but in practice seldom includes more than two of any single unit. The standard example of a very long English word, made up of many parts, is *antidisestablishmentarianisms*, which has two prefixes, a free root, at least four suffixes, and an inflectional ending. Another very long formation was used for humorous effect in the movie *Mary Poppins*. This was *supercalifragilistic-expialidocious,* by its form an adjective compound.

Contractions

Contractions are shortened forms of words in which sounds or letters are deleted. In writing, the deleted letter or letters are indicated by an apostrophe (*e'en* for *even, ne'er* for *never, 'n* for *and*). Contractions frequently appear in poetry, in written dialogue, or in writing that is informal in style.

A very common form of contraction consists of a compound word with the second root deemphasized and contracted (*he's* for *he is, can't* for *can not,* and *there'd* for *there would*).The contracted portions of such words are most frequently auxiliary and modal verbs and the negative particle *not.* The various kinds of compound contractions include the following combinations:

1. Noun or pronoun plus auxiliary or modal verb:
   The dog's barking./The dog is barking.
   Bill's already gone./ Bill has already gone.
   I'm going./I am going.
   I'll be glad./I will be glad.
2. Modal verb plus auxiliary verb:
   She may've already gone./She may have already gone.
   I could've saved him./I could have saved him.
3. Auxiliary or modal verb plus negative particle:
   We aren't going./We are not going.
   I can't sing./I can not sing.
   They mustn't leave./They must not leave.
   We won't cooperate./We will not cooperate.
4. Double contraction:
   Katie wouldn't've seen it./Katie would not have seen it.
   She'd've done it./She would have done it.
5. Other combinations:
   There's no one here./There is no one here.
   What's going on?/What is going on?
   Let's go./Let us go.
   'Tis the season to be jolly./It is the season to be jolly.

It is important to note that personal pronouns may be combined with forms of the auxiliary verbs *be* and *have,* but not with *do.* There are two contractions that are ambiguous in themselves and must be differentiated from each other by the context; usually the syntax is enough. If ⟨'s⟩ is the contraction, the ⟨'s⟩ may stand for *is* or *has.* If ⟨'d⟩ is the contraction, the ⟨'d⟩ may stand for *had* or *would.*

How Morphemic Clues Work

English morphemes can be divided into two broad classes, free and bound.

The dividing line between these two categories is not rigid, and the criteria for division should be regarded as general principles only.

A free morpheme is one that can occur as an independent word. It can also appear attached to other morphemes with no appreciable change in meaning. For example, *water* is a free morpheme meaning a liquid that falls from the sky as rain and fills oceans, rivers, lakes, and ponds. *Water* refers to the same liquid in words like *watercress, waterfall, waterfast,* and *rewatering.*

Bound morphemes appear only attached to another morpheme, which may itself be bound or free. Bound morphemes include prefixes, derivational suffixes, inflectional endings, and some roots. In this book, when bound morphemes are cited as separate units, they are enclosed in angle brackets and accompanied by hyphens to show their dependence on other morphemes. The hyphens appear where the joining of units is customary: at the ends of prefixes, at the beginnings of derivational suffixes and inflectional endings, and at both the beginnings and ends of bound roots.

If a word contains only one morpheme, that morpheme is, of course, free. Most such words are considered to be free roots and can take on other morphemes to modify or extend their meanings. However, some words never appear in combination with other morphemes, and it might be misleading to refer to them as roots. The term *root* implies some use as a base for the addition of prefixes, derivational suffixes, and inflectional endings. For instance, the word *the* is never attached by spelling to another word or morpheme. There are many others.

Another distinction to be made is between productive and nonproductive morphemes. A productive morpheme is simply one that is freely used to make new words. A nonproductive morpheme is one that is not so used. An example of a very productive morpheme is the prefix ⟨anti-⟩ meaning *against* as in *anti-Communist, antiliberal, antilabor, antiwar,* and so on. A nonproductive morpheme is the derivational suffix ⟨-th⟩ used to form such abstract nouns as *health, wealth,* and *strength.* Although it comes from a very common Old English suffix, it is no longer used in making new words.

When identifying morphemes for reading purposes, it is not always necessary to account for every sound or letter. Compare the following words:

legislate ·	(verb)
legislature	(noun)
legislative	(adjective)
legislatively	(adverb)

There is little point in arguing whether the second ⟨l⟩ goes with the root or not. Persons familiar with Latin will notice that the root of these words comes from the Latin word for *law*. Even those who do not know Latin may associate it with *legal*. People who know even one word in this set should be able to make an association and be a long way toward identifying the others.

If used in isolation, morphemic analysis is a slower, more tedious method of word identification than are whole word techniques. It is, however, a fairly reliable technique with which pupils can work independently. It helps readers build up their confidence and their competence in decoding writing. This is especially true when it is used with semantic and syntactic clues. If unfamiliar words forms are seen in the context of known words, it is often possible to infer what they are without identifying all of their parts.

Whole-word and word-structure clues together allow more effective and efficient word identification than can be achieved by either one alone. In beginning reading, pupils tend to rely heavily on word structure clues. The more proficient they become, the less they depend on word structure because they can identify whole words directly from semantic and syntactic context.

What Morphemic Clues Depend On

The efficient use of morphemic clues for word identification depends on a number of factors. First of all, morphemic analysis can be used only to identify words consisting of more than one morpheme. Single-morpheme words must be identified by other techniques.

To use morphemic clues, readers need to be aware that (1) words can consist of more than one morpheme, (2) morphemes are meaningful parts of words, (3) multimorphemic words can be divided into their individual morphemes, and (4) the meaning of the whole word is derived from the sum of its meaningful parts. They need to understand the concepts of *root*, *prefix*, *derivational suffix*, *inflectional ending*, and *contraction*. Moreover, they need to be able to recognize specific items in each of these categories. Morphemic analysis depends on the recognition of the specific meaning units within words. The more individual roots, prefixes, derivational suffixes, inflectional endings, and contractions that readers are familiar with, the more effectively they are able to use morphemic clues for word identification.

Since morphemic units are parts within whole words, readers must be able to distinguish readily parts within wholes. Pupils who have difficulty separating discrete parts embedded within total configurations of any kind (figure-ground discrimination) may not be able to use this technique effectively.

The effectiveness of this technique depends in part on pupils' reading vocabularies. Because all words contain roots, either free or bound, the more roots readers can recognize through configuration or phonic clues, for example, the more words they can identify in their derived and inflected forms.

Knowing certain foreign languages may be helpful in the use of morphemic clues. Many prefixes, suffixes, and roots derive from Latin, French, and Greek. This technique may be especially useful to older pupils for whom English is a second language.

Since morphemes are restricted to individual words, this technique does not depend on connected text, although its use can be facilitated by context. Readers do not need to search beyond the immediate word as they must with semantic and syntactic clues. Nor do morphemic clues depend as heavily on readers' intuitive knowledge. Morphemic clues can, in fact, be more easily taught to pupils than can contextual clues. The primary reason for this is that, being discrete units, morphemes can be located, isolated, identified, and recombined readily. Also, the principles pertaining to their use are more obvious and, therefore, more teachable.

Advantages of Morphemic Clues

The main advantage of morphemic clues is that their use enables readers to become independent in word identification. If readers use these clues correctly, they can be fairly certain that their identification of words is accurate. They do not need external verification. Morphemic clues are particularly useful in identifying word forms that readers have not previously encountered in print. If they can recognize a morpheme either as a discrete word or as part of a known word, they can use their knowledge to identify new words in which that morpheme appears. For example, if readers know that the prefix ⟨anti-⟩ means *against* and if they are familiar with the word *toxin*, they can independently identify *antitoxin* the first time they encounter it. If they know the words *dentist* and *dental*, and encounter words such as *dentifrice, dentition,* or *dentiform*, they should be able to infer that these words also refer to teeth in some way.

Morphemic analysis not only enables pupils to identify word forms in their reading, but also helps to increase their vocabularies. As pupils learn new morphemes, they can combine them into meaningful sequences to construct new words.

Morphemic clues are not as sensitive to the difficulty and interest levels of instructional materials as are, for example, contextual clues. Since they are restricted to word components, they can be relatively independent of context. At times, though, contextual clues are a necessary adjunct to morphemic clues in identifying words. For example, the syntactic clue provided by the pronouns *she* and *her* is essential for the successful identification of the word form ⟨dresses⟩ in the phrases *she dresses* and *her dresses.* The pronoun *she* indicates that *dresses* is a verb; the pronoun *her* indicates that it is a noun. Usually context is not as restricted as in this example so that more contextual information is available to readers. Note the following sentences:

> She dresses very nicely.
> Her dresses are very pretty.

There is more than one clue in each sentence relating to the function of ⟨dresses⟩. The adverb *nicely* in the first sentence is a clue to a verb. The verb *are* immediately following ⟨dresses⟩ in the second sentence is a clue to a noun. These additional clues supplement the information provided by the pronouns.

Limitations of Morphemic Clues

Some of the limitations of the word identification techniques already discussed also apply to morphemic clues. One has to do with dialect variations. In some nonstandard English dialects inflectional endings are used differently than in standard English. Consider the following pairs of sentences:

Nonstandard:	I have five cent.
Standard:	I have five cents.
Nonstandard:	Kate wear new shoes.
Standard:	Kate wears new shoes.
Nonstandard:	The boy hat felled off.
Standard:	The boy's hat fell off.

Another example pertains to foreign languages that use other kinds of linguistic structures to communicate the information that inflectional endings do in standard English. In Spanish, the words *más* and *el más* precede adjectives to indicate comparative and superlative degrees. In English, they are ordinarily indicated by the addition of ⟨-er⟩ and ⟨-est⟩ to the ends of adjective roots:

My father is the tallest in the family.
Mi papá es el más alto de la familia.

Because of such differences, pupils who speak nonstandard English and certain foreign languages may have difficulty in using standard English inflectional endings as clues to word identification.

Another limitation is that morphemic analysis can usually be used only to identify content words. It involves the analysis of words into their semantic units. Since most structure words consist of only a single morpheme, they cannot be divided into smaller subunits of meaning. The only exceptions are those structure words that are compounds such as *myself, however, heretofore,* and so on. Nouns, verbs, adjectives, and adverbs are more likely to consist of combinations of morphemes.

As is true of semantic and syntactic clues, morphemic clues are not used extensively by beginning readers. But the reasons for their limited use differ. Whereas beginning readers cannot use contextual clues effectively because of their own limitations, they are unable to use morphemic clues primarily because of the absence of such clues in their reading materials. Words used in beginning reading materials tend to be restricted to single morphemes. The only commonly included multimorphemic words tend to be inflected words, such as *plays, played, playing, toys, dresses, girl's.*

Morphemic clues also have some unique limitations posed by the inconsistencies of specific morphemic units. Although most prefixes are readily perceived, some present difficulties because they can be spelled in more than one way. For example, the prefix ⟨com-⟩ meaning *with* or *together* can be spelled: ⟨col-⟩ as in *collate*, ⟨cor-⟩ as in *corroborate*, and ⟨con-⟩ as in *congress*. Note the spelling of the prefix ⟨in-⟩ meaning *not* in *impossible, irrational, illegal*, and *ignoble*. Another problem is that many prefixes represent more than one meaning. The prefix ⟨in-⟩ may also mean *in* as in *include, within* as in *interior, into* as in *inject*, and *toward* as in *incoming*. Furthermore, many prefixes do not have obvious literal meanings restricted to themselves when combined with certain roots. Instead, they contribute a generalized sense or meaning to the entire word. An example is the prefix ⟨dis-⟩. In the words *disaster, disappear*, and *disappoint*, it contributes a negative quality to the words without being translatable into *not* as it is in *disagree* or *discontinue*. Teachers should be sure to work with general, as well as specific, meanings when they teach prefixes. This will enable pupils to identify words whether or not the prefixes can be converted into single word synonyms.

A problem that applies to derivational suffixes and inflectional endings as well as to prefixes relates to the visual similarity between these units and sequences of letters that are. parts of the spellings of roots. Some examples are the ⟨ly⟩ in *lily*, the ⟨re⟩ in *reason*, and the ⟨er⟩ in *her, river, over*, and *never*. In none of these instances do these sequences of letters represent units of meaning.

Words that include one or more free morphemes are usually easier to identify than words consisting of bound morphemes only. Many Latin, French, and Greek words have been absorbed into English in multimorphemic form, resulting in combinations of bound morphemes. Their division into morphemes may be difficult and, by reference to English meanings, quite unrealistic. For example, most structural linguists consider the words *conceive, receive*, and *deceive* to consist of two morphemes each, prefix and root. However, it is not possible to attach English meanings to both morphemes in each word. In reading instruction it is best to limit morphemic analysis to units whose meanings are relatively clear in English. Words consisting of only bound morphemes should be taught as whole words. An exception is older pupils who learn foreign roots, particularly Latin and Greek; they may be able to use their knowledge profitably for English word identification purposes.

Probably the major problem in using free roots for word identification is that adding some derivational suffixes and inflectional endings changes the spellings of the roots. Such spelling changes may render the roots unrecognizable to readers who are not familiar with such changes and so do not take them into account. It is important to make pupils aware of these spelling changes. Then, when they encounter derived and inflected words, they will be able to figure out what the root words are, and so be able to identify the whole words. Some common spelling changes follow:

When a suffix or ending that begins with a vowel letter is added to a root word that ends with ⟨e⟩, the ⟨e⟩ is dropped.

> skate+⟨-ing⟩=skating
> drive+⟨-er⟩=driver
> fame+⟨-ous⟩=famous

There are consistent exceptions to this principle. Roots that end with the letters ⟨ce⟩, ⟨ge⟩, and a few others may retain a final ⟨e⟩ to indicate that the final root phonemes remain unchanged after the addition of the suffix or ending. If the ⟨e⟩ were not retained in the root and the suffix or ending began with ⟨a⟩, ⟨o⟩, or ⟨u⟩, dropping the ⟨e⟩ would produce a spelling sequence that usually indicates a "hard" consonant sound. Hence, the ⟨e⟩ is retained in words like *noticeable* and *courageous*.

Native English words do not end with the letter ⟨v⟩ but with ⟨ve⟩. This final ⟨e⟩ has no consistent signal value. Note the two different pronunciations of ⟨live⟩: /lĭv/ and /līv/. This final ⟨e⟩ is usually dropped when a suffix or ending is added, but it may not be. The spellings ⟨livable⟩ and ⟨liveable⟩ are both acceptable, so are ⟨lovable⟩ and ⟨loveable⟩. On the other hand, only ⟨lively⟩, ⟨lovely⟩, ⟨living⟩, and ⟨loving⟩ are standard.

When a suffix or ending that begins with a vowel letter is added to a single-syllable word that ends with a single vowel letter followed by a single consonant letter, the final consonant is doubled. The doubling is done to retain the same stressed vowel and consonant pronunciations in the resulting two-syllable words (big/bigger, fad/faddish, mud/muddy, run/runner). Since the final ⟨x⟩ represents the /ks/ blend, it is not doubled.

This principle applies, but not consistently, to two-syllable words in which the final syllable has a similar spelling pattern *and is stressed*. Thus, *begin* becomes *beginning* and *beginner*, while *commit* becomes *committable* but *commitment*.

Words of two syllables in which ⟨fer⟩ is the second, and the stressed syllable, are inconsistent in the doubling of the final consonant. Furthermore, if the final consonant is doubled, the stress remains on the second syllable. But if the final consonant is not doubled the stress shifts to the first syllable. Thus, *refer* becomes *referred* and *referring*, but *reference* and *referable*. The same holds true for *confer, infer, prefer, defer,* and *transfer*.

A final ⟨y⟩ is changed to ⟨i⟩ before most suffixes and inflectional endings except those beginning with ⟨i⟩, and before the singular possessive ⟨'s⟩. Following this principle, *study* becomes *studied* and *studies* but *studying*; *baby* becomes *babies* and *babied* but *babying, babyish,* and *baby's*. There is one exception: if the ⟨y⟩ is preceded by a vowel letter, the ⟨y⟩ is retained. Thus *monkey* becomes *monkeys* and *play* becomes *player*. There are some exceptions to this, such as *lay/laid, slay/slain,* and *day/daily*.

In a few words a final ⟨f⟩ is changed to ⟨v⟩ when an ending beginning with a vowel is added. *Wolf* becomes *wolves, knife* becomes *knives,* and *mischief* becomes *mischievous*.

When a suffix or ending beginning with ⟨e⟩, ⟨i⟩, or ⟨y⟩ is added to a root ending with the letter ⟨c⟩, the letter ⟨k⟩ is added to the root. This provides a spelling pattern that preserves the /k/ sound at the end of the root word (*picnicking, panicked,* and *trafficking*).

Teachers must be aware of the difference between letter sequences that look like free roots and genuine free roots. Some books on reading instruction and many teachers advise pupils to look for "little words in big words." This can be misleading. Two little words can be found in a compound word consisting of two free roots (*class/room, rain/coat*). Little words can also be found in big words consisting of one or more free roots to which one or more affixes are added. For example, *govern* may be found in *misgovernment* and the *battle* and *field* in *battlefields*. On the other hand, no smaller words can be found in words consisting of single free roots. The word *father* cannot be identified by locating within it the two "little words" *fat* and *her*. They are not meaning units in *father*, nor are they even pronunciation units. In the same way, the word form ⟨goat⟩ cannot be identified by combining *go* and *at*.

The only little words that pupils should look for in big words are free roots. There is only one smaller word in the word *washed*, and that is *wash*. The letter sequences ⟨was⟩, ⟨as⟩, ⟨ash⟩, ⟨she⟩, ⟨he⟩, and ⟨shed⟩ are not little words in *washed* since they do not represent meaning units. Teaching pupils to look for little words that are not free roots within big words is counterproductive. It interferes with effective word identification.

Since morphemic analysis entails the identification of meaningful subunits within words, it is slower than whole word identification techniques. This disadvantage is compensated for by the relative independence it allows readers. The visual forms of morphemes are reasonably stable in English, so once a morpheme is known it can usually be recognized wherever it appears. If one morpheme of a word is known, the entire word is more easily identified.

As is true of all other word identification techniques, when this technique is used together with other techniques, its effectiveness is increased. In actual sentences meaning is conveyed not by morphemic units alone, but by morphemic units in combination with other kinds of units, particularly semantic and syntactic units. Pupils should be encouraged to use all the contextual clues that they can perceive and process. The need for semantic and syntactic information in addition to morphemic information is illustrated by the following set of sentences:

> Laura is *dressing* her daughter.
> Laura is *dressing* a chicken.
> I like salad *dressing*.

The word form ⟨dressing⟩ must be considered in the context in which it appears in order to be identified correctly.

Exercises

Exercise A. The following exercises illustrate how morphemic clues may be used in word identification. The italicized words in the sentences are to be identified through morphemic clues.

1. That document *antedates* the Civil War.
2. It was a *delightfully* sunny day.
3. *Bill's* coming home at the end of the semester.
4. My daughter associates with an *ultrafashionable* crowd.
5. The *attendants'* uniforms were neat and clean.
6. Sam is *friendlier* than Bill is.

Answer
1. *antedates*
   a. prefix ⟨ante-⟩ meaning *prior to*
   b. free verb root *date*, meaning *to reckon chronologically*
   c. verb inflectional ending ⟨-s⟩ indicating *third person, singular, present*
   d. morphemic combinations: *antedate, dates*
2. *delightfully*
   a. free noun root *delight*, meaning *a high degree of gratification or satisfaction*
   b. adjective suffix ⟨-ful⟩ meaning *full of*
   c. adverb suffix ⟨-ly⟩ meaning *in a (specified) manner*
   d. morphemic combinations: *delightful*
3. *Bill's*
   a. free proper noun root *Bill*, indicating *a person's name*
   b. contracted root ⟨-'s⟩ representing auxiliary verb *is*
4. *ultrafashionable*
   a. prefix ⟨ultra-⟩ meaning *beyond what is ordinary or moderate*
   b. free noun root *fashion*, meaning *the prevailing style during a particular time*
   c. adjective suffix ⟨-able⟩ meaning *tending, given, or liable to*
   d. morphemic combinations: *ultrafashion, fashionable*
5. *attendants'*
   a. free verb root *attend*, meaning *to look after*
   b. noun suffix ⟨-ant⟩ meaning *one who performs (a specified) action*
   c. noun inflectional ending ⟨-s'⟩ indicating *plural possession*
   d. morphemic combinations: *attendant*

6. *friendlier*
   a. free noun root *friend*, meaning *one attached to another by affection or esteem*
   b. adjective suffix ⟨-ly⟩, with final ⟨y⟩ changed to ⟨i⟩, meaning *in the manner of*
   c. adjective inflectional ending ⟨-er⟩ indicating *comparative degree*
   d. morphemic combinations: *friendly*

Exercise B. Morphemic clues are most effective when used with other kinds of word identification clues, especially contextual clues. This is particularly true when unfamiliar words are involved. Semantic and syntactic information may help in identifying morphemic units within words. In the following sentences identify the contextual clues that provide information about morphemic units in the italicized words.

1. Helen was the *unhappiest* one of all when her team lost the game.
2. Jennie attends school regularly but Susie has frequent colds and attends *irregularly* during the winter.
3. My brother's poems are published *pseudonymously* because he doesn't want anyone to know that he writes poetry.

Answer
1. *unhappiest*   "Team lost" is a semantic clue to the negative prefix ⟨un-⟩. "One of all" is a semantic clue to the superlative inflectional ending ⟨-est⟩.
2. *irregularly*   "But" is a syntactic clue that *irregular* is the opposite of *regular*. "Has frequent colds" is a semantic clue that the prefix ⟨ir-⟩ denotes negativeness.
3. *pseudonymously*   "Because he does not want anyone to know" is a semantic clue to the meaning of *pseudonymous*. The verb/adverb sequence is a syntactic clue to the adverbial suffix ⟨-ly⟩.

Suggested Activities for Pupil Practice

General Considerations for Teachers

It is important to focus activities on the specific skill(s) you want pupils to practice. Pupils should not be able to get the right answers except by applying the skill(s) you want them to practice. Once the meanings of component morphemic units are learned, activities intended to provide practice in using morphemic clues should include words that cannot be identified through clues in the sentence context itself. In the sentence "Her mother told her to *remake* her bed," knowledge of the component morphemes ⟨re-⟩ and ⟨make⟩ is essential to the identification of the whole word *remake*. In contrast, remake can be identified through semantic clues in a sentence like "Mother did not like the way Shirley fixed her bed and told her to remake it." Therefore, the latter sentence should not be included in an activity whose sole purpose is to provide practice in the use of specific morphemic clues. At times when you want pupils to practice using combinations of clues, such sentences might be included.

Guard against using items in activities that have unintentional common elements, since this might encourage pupils to make unwarranted generalizations. If the only prefixes you present are those with negative connotations such as ⟨un-⟩, ⟨non-⟩, ⟨dis-⟩, and ⟨in-⟩, pupils may generalize that all prefixes contribute a negative overtone to words.

Activities similar to those that are described for pupil practice may be used as diagnostic skills tests or as criterion-referenced tests to analyze pupils' proficiencies and deficiencies in the use of specific morphemic clues. Such diagnostic test activities may be administered before and/or after teaching the skills.

Activity 1

Purpose. To provide practice in using the prefix ⟨un-⟩ meaning *not* as a clue to the identification of derived words with free roots prefixed with ⟨un-⟩

Level. Intermediate.

Directions for Teachers. Use free root words which are familiar to pupils and to which the prefix ⟨un-⟩ meaning *not* can be added to form meaningful English words. (When first teaching the use of specific prefixes, it is advisable to avoid words with other affixes such as derivational suffixes and inflectional endings, as well as words with more than one prefix, such as the word *unreturnable*.)

Select several free roots to which the prefix ⟨un-⟩ meaning *not* will be added. (Be careful to avoid words in which the prefix ⟨un-⟩ does not mean *not* as in *unlock*, and words in which the prefix ⟨un-⟩ may be attached to a bound root as in *until*. Also avoid words where the sequence of letters ⟨un⟩ does not constitute a prefix as in the words *uncle* and *under*.)

Prepare several pairs of equivalent sentences. One sentence in each pair should contain a derived word with the prefix ⟨un-⟩ meaning *not* which pupils use in their oral language. The other sentence in each pair should be identical in content and structure except for substituting the word *not* for the prefix ⟨un-⟩. Be sure to include enough semantic content in the sentences to reveal the meaning of the prefix and the prefixed words.

Note the sentence pairs below:

> Jim was not kind to his dog when he kicked him.
> Jim was unkind to his dog when he kicked him.

> Barbara said her teacher was unfair because she failed her.
> Barbara said her teacher was not fair because she failed her.

> When Jennie is hungry, she is unhappy.
> When Jennie is hungry, she is not happy.

Write the pairs of sentences on the chalkboard, or on a chart transparency or ditto sheet. Have pupils silently read the first pair of sentences. Call on them to tell you whether both sentences mean the same thing. If the pupils reply that they do mean the same thing, ask if exactly the same words appear in both sentences. Have them underline the words that are common to both sentences. This may be done by matching individual words with each other or by matching word groups. When all words are underlined except the prefixed word and its equivalent phrase, ask how the remaining words are alike and different. Then ask how the word *not* is represented in the word *unkind*. Elicit that the part of the word spelled ⟨un-⟩ means *not*, then ask how the addition of the syllable ⟨un-⟩ to the word *kind* changes the meaning of the word *kind*. (If this is the pupils' first experience with prefixes, you need to explain (1) that this word part is called a *prefix*, (2) that a prefix is a syllable or syllables attached to the beginning of words to change their meanings, and (3) that the syllable ⟨un-⟩ is a prefix.)

If the pupils initially respond that the two sentences do not mean the same thing, ask them to explain their differences in meaning. Discuss the meanings of both sentences with them. Since the prefixed word is taken from their oral vocabulary, they should be able to reconcile the meanings of the two sentences. Once it is established that the meanings of the two sentences are equivalent, you may proceed in the manner described above. (It is important to permit the pupils to discover that the sentences are equivalent in meaning; you should not tell them this. If you do, they may accept your word for it without understanding the similarity at all.) Proceed in a similar manner with the remaining pairs of sentences.

After pupils understand that the meaning of a root can be changed to a negative form by adding the prefix ⟨un-⟩ meaning *not,* prepare an activity consisting of isolated prefixed words. Have pupils analyze each word and divide it into its two component meaningful parts by placing a slash mark between the prefix and the free root (*un/just*). Words which might be used include: unequal, unable, unclean, unborn, uncertain, uneven.

You might provide additional practice in contextual settings by presenting sentences in which words with the prefix ⟨un-⟩ meaning *not* are replaced by pupils with phrases beginning with the word *not,* as in the examples below:

> At the end of the week my work was *unfinished.*
>
> The peaches cannot be picked yet because they are *unripe.*
>
> Adam was *unsure* of the route to the Grand Canyon and got lost.

The above kinds of activities can be done independently by pupils, individually or in teams.

The prefix ⟨un-⟩ with meanings other than *not,* such as *the opposite of, the reverse of, to remove,* and *to free from* may be taught in a similar manner. Other prefixes, suffixes, and inflectional endings may be presented and developed in the same way.

Activity 2

Purpose. To provide practice in using ⟨-n't⟩ attached to the end of an auxiliary verb root as a clue to the identification of compound words consisting of an auxiliary verb plus the contracted form of *not*

Level. Upper primary.

Directions for Teachers. The use of this clue is usually easy to teach since informal spoken English makes frequent use of contractions and most pupils are familiar with them. However, pupils whose native language is not English may be unfamiliar with the forms of English contractions. Even though they may use contractions in speaking English, they may not recognize them as such. With these pupils, it is especially important to develop the correspondences between contracted and uncontracted forms.

Select several contractions consisting of ⟨-n't⟩ preceded by auxiliary verbs. Prepare several pairs of equivalent sentences. One sentence in each pair should contain the contracted form of the word *not* attached to an auxiliary verb. The other sentence in each pair should be identical except for replacing the contraction with the verb followed by the word *not*. Be sure to include enough semantic content in the sentences to reveal the meanings of the contracted and uncontracted forms of the words. Note the sentence pairs below:

> Because Bill had a cold, he did not go swimming.
> Because Bill had a cold, he didn't go swimming.

> Kathy wanted to go to the party but she wasn't feeling well.
> Kathy wanted to go to the party but she was not feeling well.

> Since Lisa hadn't been to school for a week, she missed a lot of work.
> Since Lisa had not been to school for a week, she missed a lot of work.

Write the pairs of sentences on the chalkboard, or on a chart, transparency, or ditto sheet. Have pupils silently read the first pair of sentences. Ask them to tell you whether both sentences mean the same thing. If the pupils reply that they do mean the same thing, ask if exactly the same words appear in both sentences. Have them underline the words that are not common to both sentences. Ask if the underlined part in one sentence means the same as the underlined part in the other sentence. If they reply that both sentence parts have the same meaning, elicit from them the differences in their spellings. The pupils should note that the word *didn't* in the second sentence is the equivalent of the the two words *did not* in the first sentence. Furthermore, they should realize that *didn't* is a single word made by putting together the words *did* and *not,* omitting the ⟨o⟩ from *not,* and replacing it with an apostrophe. Then elicit from the pupils that contracted forms of words retain the same meanings as the uncontracted forms.

(If the pupils are not familiar with the term *contraction,* you may wish to (1) use that term, (2) associate it with the contracted form *didn't,* and (3) explain that contractions result when two words are merged into one word with one or more letters omitted and replaced with an apostrophe. At a more advanced level, you may wish to draw the pupils' attention to the lack of stress on the negative particle when the contracted form is used in speech.)

If the pupils initially respond that the two sentences do not mean the same thing, ask them to explain their differences in meaning. Discuss the meanings of both sentences with them. Since the contracted word is taken from their oral vocabulary, they should be able to reconcile the meanings of both sentences. You should not tell the pupils that the sentences are equivalent in meaning; let them discover that for themselves. Once this has been established, you may proceed in the manner described above. Proceed in a similar manner with the remaining pairs of sentences.

After the pupils understand that auxiliary verbs followed by the word *not* can be contracted into one word, prepare an activity consisting of isolated contracted words. Have pupils analyze each word and either write down or tell you the two words from which the contraction was formed (for example, *hasn't* is the contracted form of *has not; isn't* is the contracted form of *is not*).

Additional practice in using ⟨-n't⟩ attached to an auxiliary verb root as a clue to a compound word consisting of an auxiliary verb plus the contracted form of *not* may be provided by presenting contractions in the context of sentences that are either independent of each other or in story form. See the example here:

> Susie and Jennie were very playful when they were kittens. They *weren't* as playful when they grew up. They slept most of the time and *didn't* play with each other. They lived in an apartment and *couldn't* go outdoors. They *hadn't* been outside to play since they were kittens. It *wasn't* much fun for them to be indoors all the time. One summer their owners took them to the country. The cats *wouldn't* stop purring because they were so happy to play outdoors again.

The above kinds of exercises can be done independently by pupils, individually or in teams.

Other contractions may be presented and developed in the same way. It is advisable to restrict each lesson to the teaching of one category of contractions at a time: contractions which consist of (1) pronouns plus auxiliaries (*I'm, you've, she's,* etc.); (2) nouns plus auxiliaries (the *boy's* going home, the *tree'll* turn green again, etc.);and (3) proper nouns plus auxiliaries (*Kathy'd* get well if she took her medicine, *Sam'll* go home soon. etc.). In teaching the contraction for *is,* you must be careful to differentiate ⟨-'s⟩ as a contraction and ⟨-'s⟩ as a singular possessive form.

Example of Combination Activity

Since morphemic clues are more effective when combined with other word identification clues, pupils should be given practice in using them with other kinds of clues. The following activity, which combines morphemic clues with syntactic clues, illustrates what can be done.

1. When the clown did her tricks, the children laughed happi _____.
2. Some children are happi _____ to be in school than to be on vacation.
3. My cat is happy but my dog is _____ happy when I feed them fish for dinner.
4. Sam was play _____ the piano.

Answers

1. $\langle$-ly$\rangle$ The morphemic clue is the adverb-forming suffix following the root word *happy* in which the final $\langle$y$\rangle$ has been changed to an $\langle$i$\rangle$; the syntactic clues are the verb/adverb word order and the subject/verb/adverb sentence pattern.
2. $\langle$-er$\rangle$ The morphemic clue is the adjective inflectional ending following the root word *happy* in which the final $\langle$y$\rangle$ has been changed to $\langle$i$\rangle$; the syntactic clues are the structure word *than* which sets up a comparative relationship and the subject/be/subject adjective complement sentence pattern.
3. $\langle$un-$\rangle$ The morphemic clue is a prefix preceding the root word *happy*; the syntactic clue is the structure word *but* which sets up a contrasting relationship.
4. $\langle$-ing$\rangle$ The morphemic clue is an inflectional ending following the root word *play*; the syntactic clues are the structure word *was* which signals a verb, the auxiliary verb/main verb word order, and the subject/verb/object sentence pattern.

Chapter 8
Phonic Clues

fŏn'ək clues

The use of phonic clues, or phonic analysis, is the second of the two word identification techniques that involve the analysis of whole words into subunits. The other technique, morphemic analysis, was discussed in the preceding chapter.

The basis for phonic division of words is different from that for morphemic division. Phonic clues are related to units of sound and pronunciation. In phonic analysis word forms are separated into their constituent spelling units, and these spelling units are related to their pronunciation equivalencies. When the spelling units are correctly associated with their corresponding pronunciation units, inferences can be made about the identities of the words.

The difference between morphemic and phonic analysis can be illustrated by the following comparison in relation to the word *hopeful.*

Morphemic Analysis

1. Free root *hope* meaning *expectancy* with no change in spelling
2. Derivational adjective suffix ⟨-ful⟩ meaning *full of* or *characterized by*

Phonic Analysis

1. Three separated vowel letter units, one of which is final ⟨e⟩ preceded by a single consonant, suggest two syllables
2. Root/Suffix division
3. Primary accent on root syllable
4. Initial ⟨h⟩ represents /h/
5. Medial ⟨o⟩ followed by a single consonant and ⟨e⟩ in an accented syllable represents /ō/
6. Final ⟨p(e)⟩ represents /p/
7. Initial ⟨f⟩ represents /f/
8. Medial ⟨u⟩ in unaccented syllable represents /ə/
9. Final ⟨l⟩ represents /l/

In general, phonic analysis requires that a word form be broken down into its smallest units. Note that *hopeful* is divided into only two units in morphemic analysis while complete phonic analysis calls for the identification of nine related principles and units. Phonic analysis of words is dependent on their morphological structure and, in addition, requires (1) knowledge of principles for segmenting written words; (2) knowledge of principles of accenting; and (3) knowledge of correspondences between graphemes and phonemes.

Phonic analysis is frequently called *phonetics* or *phonetic analysis, phonemics* or *phonemic analysis,* and *letter-sound* or *spelling-to-sound correspondences.* However, these terms are not all synonymous. Phonetics is the study of speech sounds per se; it is not concerned with correspondences between writing and speech. Phonemics considers speech sounds and their functions in speech; it, neither, is concerned with correspondences between writing and speech.

In contrast, phonics presupposes and depends on alphabetic writing. It deals with correspondences between writing and speech and hence is relevant to reading. Phonic clues are related to the spelling and sound systems of language. *Graphemes* derive from the spelling system; *phonemes* derive from the sound system. *Phonics* is simply the term for the body of information relating to the correspondences between them.

English phonology is divided into segmental and suprasegmental systems. Elements of both systems appear in any natural sentence. Loosely defined, *segmental phonology* involves the articulation of vowel and consonant sequences in speech; *suprasegmental phonology* involves the vocal effects that accompany such articulation. These include pauses between syllables, words, phrases, and clauses and differences in pitch level and stress that differentiate words and meanings.

In the phonic analysis of the word *hopeful*, the first three items, referring to syllabication and accent, are in the suprasegmental system; the last six are in the segmental system.

Kinds of Phonic Clues:
An Overview

Phonic clues are frequently referred to as *phonic elements, parts, components, or constituents.* Regardless of what such units are called, they bridge or connect the details of spelling with the details of phonology and can be used for the identification of written word forms.

The correspondences related to segmental phonology are those between vowel graphemes and phonemes and between consonant graphemes and phonemes. Graphemes are the letter symbols used in English spelling; phonemes the speech sounds of the language. These segmental grapheme-phoneme correspondences are often called *phoneme-grapheme, spelling-sound, letter-sound, spelling-pronunciation, or g-p and p-g correspondences.* In this book they are termed *grapheme-phoneme correspondences* since graphemes are part of the visual display to which readers must relate phonemes. The term refers to both single graphemes and phonemes and to combinations of them such as consonant blends, syllables, or grapheme bases.

The correspondences related to suprasegmental phonology involve syllabication and accenting. For reading purposes, syllabication and accenting principles are based on correspondences between conventional spelling patterns and juncture and stress components.

In multisyllabic words, suprasegmental phonology affects the segmental phonological correspondences. Grapheme-phoneme correspondences are dependent upon the syllabic divisions and accenting patterns of words. For instance, the phoneme represented by the grapheme ⟨e⟩ in each of the syllables in the word form ⟨rebel⟩ differs, depending on whether the first or second syllable is accented (/rĕb' əl/ and /rə bĕl'/). Note also that the phoneme for the grapheme ⟨a⟩ in the accented first syllables of *bacon* and *basket* depends on the syllabic division of the two words (/bā'kən/ and /băs'kət/).

Many grapheme-phoneme correspondences are commonly taught to pupils before syllabication and accenting principles, since they can be presented in relation to single syllable words. In words of one syllable, grapheme-phoneme correspondences are fairly stable. This is because both syllabic units and accent patterns are fixed in these words when they appear individually or in lists. Furthermore, the grapheme-phoneme correspondences of single syllable words can be applied to *the accented syllables of multisyllabic words* appearing in more advanced reading materials. The identification of multisyllabic words, however, requires application of syllabication and accenting principles prior to application of grapheme-phoneme correspondences. For this reason, syllabication and accenting principles are discussed in Chapter 9 and grapheme-phoneme correspondences in Chapter 10.

How Phonic Clues Work

Many phonic principles and generalizations deal with units of sound and pronunciation *within morphemic units.* Therefore, the morphological structure of word forms must be known before phonic analysis can be successfully applied. If a word consists of a single-syllable free root, such as *tree* or *jump,* only grapheme-phoneme correspondences need to be considered. If a word consists of a multisyllabic free root such as *potato*, or a multimorphemic combination such as *unlikeable*, then syllabication and accenting principles, as well as grapheme-phoneme correspondences, need to be considered.

The correspondences applicable to words depend on their syllabication and accent patterns, which, in turn, depend on their morphemic structure. For example, the grapheme-phoneme correspondences for the letters ⟨t⟩ and ⟨h⟩ in *father* and *fathead* are different. In *father*, they are part of the same morpheme and represent the single phoneme /d̶/. In *fathead*, ⟨t⟩ is the last letter in the first morpheme and ⟨h⟩ the first letter in the second morpheme. Therefore, these letters represent two separate phonemes, /t/ and /h/.

If readers can identify prefixes, suffixes, and inflectional endings as units within word forms, they may need to apply phonic analysis only to the unfamiliar roots of words. This emphasizes the importance of applying morphemic analysis before phonic analysis. Morphemic and phonic analysis together usually results in more rapid word identification than phonic analysis alone.

Grapheme use is somewhat different in phonics than it is in visual configuration. Configuration clues may consist of any features of letters that may be associated, however meaninglessly, with whole words. The association between features and words is direct. In phonics, on the other hand, letters are first associated with speech sounds. Then the speech sounds are associated with words. The association between letters and words is not direct. Phonic clues are valuable, for they appeal to pupils' oral competence in the language, which is usually well developed by the time they enter school.

To use phonic clues successfully, readers must discriminate visually among graphemes and grapheme sequences. They must discriminate aurally among phonemes and phoneme sequences. They must be able to recall correspondences between graphemes and phonemes and to synthesize units of sound and pronunciation into whole words. For example, to identify the word form ⟨bad⟩ by phonic clues alone, the following steps would be involved:

1. Recognize the graphemes ⟨b⟩, ⟨a⟩, and ⟨d⟩.
2. Recall the appropriate phoneme to associate with each of the three graphemes in a word based on a ⟨CVC⟩ spelling pattern.
3. Synthesize the phonemes /b/, /ă/, and /d/ into the word *bad.*

The actual process is, of course, less difficult in performance than in description.

Many teachers describe phonic analysis as a "sounding out" of words, either overtly or covertly. However, the sounding out of words by different pupils does not necessarily result in uniform pronunciations. English spelling is uniform across all dialects, but spoken English has wide variation. Pupils may pronounce words differently, depending on their dialects. For example, some may say /grēs/ for *grease* and others may say /grēz/. Some pupils may say ănt/ for *aunt* while others say /ônt/. As a result, one set of phonic principles cannot be made to apply across all dialects. Variation in pronunciation should not interfere with successful word identification. As long as pupils can associate their pronunciations arrived at through phonic analysis, with words in their oral vocabularies, they should be able to identify words successfully.

After assembling clues relating to syllabic division, accent patterns, and grapheme-phoneme correspondences, readers are in a position to approximate the pronunciations of words. If their approximations are similar enough to words in their vocabularies, they will succeed at identifying the words at that point. If their approximations do not sound familiar, they may reanalyze the word forms, trying alternate grapheme-phoneme correspondences, syllabic divisions, and/or accent patterns. Another possibility is that they assume that the words are new to them and either accept the pronunciation they have worked out or consult a dictionary or teacher. They may also decide not to concern themselves with pronunciations and learn to identify the written words without specific pronunciations.

Teachers should not insist on grapheme-phoneme correspondences that result in unfamiliar pronunciations of words so that pupils will not be able to associate them with words in their oral vocabularies. Doing so is likely only to make word identification more difficult. Phonic analysis is a strategy for *inferring* meanings of written words; it is not a strategy for pronouncing words. All of the grapheme-phoneme correspondences in a word need not be recognized to successfully identify that word. Even beginning readers can identify whole words, when the words are in context, from the grapheme-phoneme correspondences of only their initial letters.

Phonic analysis, like other word identification techniques, works most effectively when used in combination with other kinds of clues. If phonic clues are used as the sole means of word identification, all phonic units in word forms must be identified and synthesized into whole words. This is a slow, tedious procedure, even when the largest possible phonic units are used in the analysis. Using a combination of clues that provide redundant information about words eliminates the necessity of identifying all phonic components in words. No fixed amount of phonic information is required for successful word identification when other techniques are used concurrently. The purpose of phonic analysis in reading is simply to identify words, not to inventory all their grapho-phonological components. So, although pupils should know how to use all phonic clues, they should be discouraged from over-relying on phonic analysis.

Beginning and proficient readers differ in their dependence on phonic clues for word identification. Beginning readers rely heavily on phonic information because of their limited ability to use semantic and syntactic clues. Proficient readers resort to phonic clues only when other kinds of clues are insufficient.

Beginning readers tend to use phonic clues for their original identification of words and then contextual clues to confirm their identifications. Proficient readers tend to use contextual clues for their original identifications of words and phonic clues for confirmation purposes. Moreover, the more proficient that readers become, the larger the phonic units they can usually process. Thus, beginning readers rely on individual letter grapheme-phoneme correspondences, while proficient readers tend to use whole syllables and grapheme bases as phonic units. In addition, they are more likely to combine clues and use them concurrently than to use each kind separately and successively.

What Phonic Clues Depend On

Essentially, phonic analysis involves the systematic association of written words with spoken words. Its basic assumption is that pupils are already familiar with the spoken words. It is, however, possible for readers proficient in phonic analysis to work out pronunciations of unfamiliar words. They can make inferences from sequences of letters and recode these sequences of letters into speech. They may be able to do this even if they do not understand the meaning of what they recode.

Although phonic analysis depends less on pupils' oral language backgrounds than other word identification techniques, the closer the language of the pupils is to the language of written materials, the more effectively they can apply phonic clues. It is easier to infer or to confirm the identity of words if the words are already in readers' language patterns.

The fact that phonic analysis is less dependent on pupils' oral language backgrounds may be an advantage for speakers of non-standard English. They may be able to identify words more easily through phonics than through clues, such as semantic and syntactic clues, which depend heavily on language background. Regardless of pupils' previous language experiences, letter-sound correspondences can be learned to enable them at least to work out word pronunciations.

Since phonic analysis involves the association of letters with sounds, both visual and auditory abilities are essential. Readers must be able to visually perceive and discriminate among the letters of the English alphabet and among sequences of these letters. Many of the letters share similar features so that pupils who are visually deficient may have difficulty distinguishing letter forms or sequences. For example, ⟨M⟩ is frequently confused with ⟨N⟩ and ⟨W⟩; ⟨e⟩ with ⟨c⟩; ⟨house⟩ with ⟨horse⟩; and ⟨expect⟩ with ⟨except⟩.

In addition, each of the twenty-six letters can appear in different forms, such as upper case and lower case, and in various versions of print and script. Readers must learn which shapes represent the same grapheme; for example: ⟨G⟩, ⟨g⟩, ⟨G⟩, ⟨g⟩, ⟨𝒢⟩, ⟨𝑔⟩. In many instances differences between forms of the same grapheme are greater than differences between different graphemes. This is illustrated by the following three letters: ⟨E⟩, ⟨e⟩, ⟨c⟩, where the small ⟨e⟩ resembles the small ⟨c⟩ more than it does the capital ⟨E⟩. The graphic variations may cause pupils difficulty, especially when pupils are new to reading. Teachers of beginning reading should consistently use clear manuscript print in all teacher-prepared materials, both on the chalkboard and on paper. Also, in teaching letter recognition and initial position grapheme-phoneme correspondences, teachers should present both capital and lower cases forms of letters.

Knowledge of letter names is not essential to visual discrimation of letter forms, but such knowledge does facilitate pupil-teacher communication about letters. It is easier to talk about letters if they can be referred to by letter names, just as it is easier to talk about people if they are referred to by names.

Readers must also be able to perceive and discriminate among the more than forty sounds of spoken English and the various sequences of these sounds. Many sounds of English share similar features, so that pupils who are aurally deficient may have difficulty distinguishing sounds or sequences of sounds. For example, /f/ is frequently confused with /v/; /ĭ/ with /ē/; /băt/ with /băd/; and /ăks/ with /ăsk/.

Auditory perception and discrimination may be affected by foreign language and dialect variations and by speech impediments. One way in which languages and dialects differ is in the sounds that they include. Although children seem to have equal facility for all phonological systems, they seem to be conditioned rather early by the articulatory requirements and customs of the language or dialect they are learning. They find it easy to discriminate among the sounds of their language or dialect, but difficult to perceive and discriminate among phonemes that are not included. For example, native speakers of Spanish have difficulty distinguishing between /ĭ/ and /ē/ so that words like *ship* and *sheep, pick* and *peek*, and *chick* and *cheek* may not be differentiated. Nonstandard dialect speakers who do not differentiate /ð/ and /d/ do not distinguish between *they* and *day* or *breathe* and *breed.* If both teachers and pupils have the same language backgrounds, pupils will probably find learning grapheme-phoneme correspondences easier, since they share a common phonological system.

When dealing with sound and letter correspondences in beginning reading, teachers should consider the articulatory and discriminatory maturity of the pupils. Teachers should note if children's articulations and auditory discriminations of sounds are in harmony or if children are having difficulty in one of these areas in regard to certain sounds. Teaching the production of sounds can be of aid in teaching their discriminations.

There tends to be variation among children in the development of their abilities to articulate and discriminate between speech sounds. By the age of three or four months, most children, in their babbling, randomly produce all the vowel sounds of their dialects. On the other hand, some children do not produce all the consonant sounds of their dialects even by the time they enter school. For some children, the articulation and/or auditory discrimination of speech sounds may not be fully developed at the time of school entrance. The production of /č/ and /j/, for example, is rather complex; the production of /ə/ and /d̶/ is rather difficult. In addition, the acoustic differences between /ə/, /d̶/ and /f/, /v/, respectively, are rather slight. It may be necessary for teachers to help some pupils make the /f/ /ə/ distinction by demonstrating the correct lip movements. Saying /t/ instead of /ə/, or /d/ instead of /d̶/, may be either a developmental problem or a dialectal one. In either case, it probably should be approached through articulatory instruction accompanied by demonstration.

Another factor on which the effective use of phonic analysis depends is pupils' abilities to fuse or blend individual phonemes into syllables and words. Associating individual graphemes with individual phonemes will not necessarily result in the identification of words. The sequences of phonemes must be blended into whole units that are recognized by pupils as words in their oral vocabularies. Pronouncing the phonemes /k/, /ă/, and /t/ as separate units, for example, may not yield the familiar word *cat.* Pupils with deficiencies in blending may experience particular difficulty in learning to read through emphasis on phonic analysis.

Effective use of phonic analysis also depends on understanding that, in English, a phoneme may be spelled by different letters or combinations of letters. Furthermore, a letter or combination of letters may represent more than one phoneme. For example, the phoneme /f/ may be represented by ⟨f⟩, ⟨ff⟩, ⟨gh⟩, and ⟨ph⟩ as in the words *fun, muff, tough,* and *phone.* The letter ⟨o⟩ may represent different phonemes including /ŏ/, /ō/, /ĭ/, /ü/, /ŭ/, /ô/, and /ə/ as in *hot, cold, women, move, love, order,* and *lemon.* The various spellings of a phoneme are known as *allographs.* Each allograph must be taught and learned as a separate grapheme-phoneme correspondence.

The distinction between sounds and letter symbols must be recognized. For example, the statement "English has five vowels" cannot possibly be true of the sound system of English, although it has some limited validity when changed to "English is written with an alphabet that provides five vowel letters." Despite popular usage to the contrary, letters do not "have" sounds. At best, letters represent sounds, or sounds are represented by letters. Since phonic analysis starts with written symbols, the direction of analysis is from grapheme to phoneme (for example, ⟨ee⟩ represents /ē/). In describing grapheme-phoneme correspondences in this text, we indicate the spellings first, followed by the sounds that those spellings represent.

Advantages of Phonic Clues

The proficient use of phonic clues enables readers to be fairly independent in word identification, particularly when phonic clues are used in combination with other word identification techniques. It is probably safe to assume that all proficient readers rely on some phonic information regardless of what are their primary techniques in identifying words. Words tentatively identified through other kinds of clues can be verified through phonic information. Consider the two following sentences:

The fire *engine* raced down the street toward the burning building.

The fire *truck* raced down the street toward the burning building.

Neither semantic nor syntactic clues can differentiate the words *engine* and *truck* in these two sentences. Even if a picture accompanied the sentences, the two words still could not be differentiated. These whole-word identification clues suggest general categories of words, not specific words. However, using phonic information, readers can easily distinguish *engine* from *truck* and identify them.

Another advantage of phonic clues is that success in learning their use does not depend on a specific cultural and linguistic background. Any information that pupils need to use this technique can, with few exceptions, be taught to them by teachers in school. In fact, not even prior knowledge of the alphabet is prerequisite since letter discriminations can be developed at the same time as phoneme discriminations in preparation for learning specific grapheme-phoneme correspondences. This does not mean that knowledge of letter names is not helpful in phonic instruction. Such knowledge makes it easier for teachers and pupils to communicate about grapheme-phoneme correspondences.

Pupils who speak nonstandard dialects of English are likely to be more successful in learning to read through this technique than through techniques heavily dependent on familiarity with standard English vocabulary and syntax. In fact, pupils of certain foreign language background, such as Spanish and Italian, who know how to use phonic clues in reading their native language, may have a decided advantage in learning English phonics. When pupils' native languages use graphemes and phonemes similar to those used in English, they can transfer their knowledge from one language to the other.

Phonic analysis may be particularly helpful to pupils who have poor visual memories and who often have difficulty identifying words through visual configuration or morphemic clues.

Phonic analysis may also be advantageous to pupils whose inferential abilities have not sufficiently developed to use semantic and syntactic clues effectively. The grapheme-phoneme correspondences, as well as the syllabication and accenting principles, can be learned and applied fairly mechanically without higher-level thinking skills. For the same reason, it is easy to learn how to teach phonic analysis. Not only can teachers be easily trained, but so can subprofessionals. Educational aides such as tutors and paraprofessionals are frequently trained to supplement teachers' work with children in phonics.

Phonic analysis is the most frequently taught word identification technique, not only because it is easily learned and taught but because more is known about this technique than about others. The area of phonics has been researched and written about more extensively than have any of the other word identification techniques.

In general, teachers are well prepared to teach phonic analysis because of their own training and the abundance of available supporting materials. Training courses in the teaching of reading include instruction in phonics; textbooks on reading and reading instruction include sections or whole chapters on phonics. Published reading programs and supplementary materials include phonics as a major component; in fact, in some materials phonics is the only word identification technique developed. The guidebooks and manuals that accompany reading programs and supplementary phonic materials provide full and detailed directions for teachers.

The mechanistic aspects of phonic analysis lend themselves to teaching through programmed materials and mechanical aids (programmed workbooks, audio cassettes, filmstrips, computers). Use of such instructional materials for teaching phonics permits pupils to learn and practice their skills independently. The independent pupil activities free teachers to work on other reading skills that require more teacher supervision.

For all the reasons described above, phonic analysis, in one form or another, is a significant aspect of reading instruction. However, teachers should be cautious not to overemphasize it, teach it to the exclusion of other word identification techniques, or encourage pupils to use it as the primary means of identifying words.

Limitations of Phonic Clues

There are many limitations to the use of phonic analysis for word identification. When used by itself it is slow and tedious, since it deals with the smallest units of language structure. It may lead pupils to focus on the pronunciation of individual words rather than on word meanings and the comprehension of sentences. This can result in meaningless recoding or word calling. In addition, concern for pronunciation often leads to vocalization in silent reading. Even very proficient readers may continue subvocalizing habits while reading silently because of an early and continued emphasis on phonic analysis.

Since the identification of phonemes is a major component of phonic analysis, the use of this technique depends heavily on the auditory abilities of pupils. Phonic analysis has limitations not only for deaf and profoundly hard of hearing pupils but also for pupils who have lesser deficiencies in auditory perception and discrimination. Phonic analysis also depends on remembering correspondences between graphemes and phonemes so that pupils with poor auditory memories are likely to have difficulty in learning and using phonics.

Speech factors may be related to difficulties in the learning of phonic analysis. These factors include immature speech, speech impediments, and dialect variations in pronunciation. Speech impediments are more likely to affect consonant pronunciations while dialect differences are more likely to affect vowel pronunciations and accenting patterns. When pupils pronounce phonemes and words differently from their teachers, confusion may occur.

Teachers should be aware of limiting speech factors when they teach phonics and should modify their procedures accordingly. In the case of a dialect variation, for example, if teachers say /ŏs′trĕč/ for the word form ⟨ostrich⟩, but pupils say /ôs′trĕč/, it would be inadvisable to use this word to teach the pupils that ⟨o⟩ may represent /ŏ/. Pupils with immature speech and speech impediments may need to work with speech therapists to develop accurate pronunciations of particular phonemes. This should be done before or at the same time that related grapheme-phoneme correspondences are introduced.

Because of the complex system of English orthography, it is difficult to predict reliably some grapheme-phoneme correspondences. The grapheme patterns ⟨th⟩ and ⟨ch⟩ are particularly difficult to predict since their correspondences seem to depend upon word function or derivation. Initial ⟨th⟩ usually represents / đ/ in structure words (*the, then, they, this, that*) and /ə/ in content words (*thumb, thistle, threw, thick, thin*).

The grapheme pattern ⟨ch⟩, on the other hand, represents either /k/, /š/, or /č/, depending on the origin of the word in which the spelling pattern occurs. In words derived from Greek, ⟨ch⟩ usually corresponds with the /k/ as in *chemical*; in words derived from French or Old English, ⟨ch⟩ usually corresponds to /č/, as in *chase*, and less frequently to /š/, as in *chicanery*.

Due to these kinds of irregularities, phonic analysis has often been criticized as an unreliable means of identifying words. Some critics oppose the teaching of phonics altogether. Their arguments are apparently based on the assumptions that a phonic principle must work all of the time to be useful and that readers taught phonic analysis will rely exclusively on phonic clues for word identification purposes. Both of these assumptions are erroneous.

A phonic generalization does not need to be one hundred percent consistent to be useful for word identification purposes. Absolute consistency would be necessary only if phonic clues were the only kind of word identification clues used. Proficient readers can select from among the possibilities the appropriate sound correspondence for a letter sequence when they have enough information about the word form from other clues, especially semantic and syntactic clues. Although some irregularity of grapheme-phoneme correspondence does exist in English, it does not present as great a problem as some critics believe, as long as pupils read materials that are familiar to them in content and linguistic structure.

Those who expect phonic analysis to reveal the pronunciations of words become disenchanted when this does not occur. Their assumption is false. Phonics is not a method of determining specific word pronunciations; it only helps infer from grapho-phonological information what word forms may represent. Consider the word form ⟨route⟩. It may be pronounced /rüt/ or /röt/ depending upon the region of the country.

No one set of phonic generalizations can be applicable to all dialects of English. English spelling is essentially the same wherever English is used, but English pronunciation is subject to regional and social differences. For this reason, there is a limit to the comprehensiveness of phonic generalizations. In other words, although many grapheme-phoneme correspondences may apply to all varieties of English, some may apply to one dialect but not to others. A phonic generalization is reliable and useful only to the extent to which it relates standard spelling to the particular pronunciation details of the speech of the pupils involved. This means that teachers may need to adapt statements of grapheme-phoneme correspondences found in published instructional materials to the speech patterns of their pupils, particularly in dealing with vowel sounds and with final consonant blends or clusters.

Phonic clues cannot be used to differentiate between homographs, since their spelling patterns are the same. Semantic or syntactic information is needed to identify them. For example, the word form ⟨contest⟩ may represent either the noun /kŏn′əst/ or the verb /kəntĕst′/. Without the semantic and syntactic information available from a sentence such as "I want to *contest* the judges' decision in the beauty *contest*," the two words cannot be differentiated.

syl-lab-i-ca-tion and ac'centing principles

Syllabication and accenting of words are the aspects of phonics related to the intonational or suprasegmental phoneme system of the language. The components of intonation are *pitch, stress* and *juncture.* They operate in combination with consonant and vowel phonemes as well as sequences of them. They also separate such sequences of consonant and vowel phonemes into pronunciation and syntactic units. Juncture, the transition from one sound to another in speech, can be related to the syllabication of individual words. Stress refers to accent patterns within words. Pitch affects primarily whole sentence units, rather than individual words. For this reason, principles of pitch are not applicable to the phonic analysis of words, as are principles of juncture and stress.

The successful identification of multisyllabic word forms through phonics depends upon the syllabication and accenting principles that underlie them. All vowel grapheme-phoneme correspondences are dependent upon syllabic positions and accent patterns. Some consonant correspondences are too. Syllabication principles will be discussed first. It should be noted that accenting and syllabication principles must be used together for accurate identification of written words, since there is interplay between them. In accented syllables, single vowel letters at ends of syllables usually represent long vowel sounds *(he, ta'ble, ty'rant)*. In unaccented syllables, they usually do not *(be lieve', re bel', ca price')*. Accent or stress pattern takes precedence over syllabic position for vowel correspondences in unaccented syllables.

Syllables in Speech and Writing

A syllable is a unit of pronunciation. It may include one or more sounds. It is, by definition, a phonological phenomenon and, strictly speaking, does not have a written parallel. Because of this, the syllabic divisions of word forms cannot be determined until *after the words have been identified and their pronunciations established.* The role that syllabication principles can play in identifying *unfamiliar* word forms is both limited and largely misunderstood by teachers and authors of reading instructional materials.

A vowel sound occurs in every syllable in speech. One or more consonant sounds may precede and/or follow the vowel sound. Syllables that end in vowel sounds are called "open"; those that end in consonant sounds are called "closed." *Rat, ramp,* and *rate* are closed syllables; *ray* is an open syllable.

A syllable may be a whole word by itself or it may be only part of a word. It may be a morphemic unit or not. Morphemic units may consist of single syllables or more than one syllable, or they may be only parts of syllables. Examples of single syllable morphemes are: the word *run,* the prefix ⟨in-⟩, and the suffix ⟨-ness⟩. Examples of morphemes that constitute only parts of syllables are: the ⟨-ed⟩ past tense ending on *jumped* and the ⟨-s⟩ plural ending on *pals.*

Counting syllables in spoken words is seldom difficult, but one cannot always establish exact syllable boundaries on a phonological basis. True, syllable boundaries are often marked by consonant sounds, but some syllables have vowel sounds at their boundaries. Some consonant sounds are ambisyllabic; they appear between vowel sounds but can be exclusively designated neither as final consonant sounds of the preceding syllables nor as initial consonant sounds of the following syllables. This fact is illustrated in the ordinary pronunciations of *loyal* and *carry*. Dialect can affect our intuitive understanding of syllabic division. A stream of water may be heard as *riv/er* by some people and as *ri/ver* by others.

Vowel sounds are nuclear in syllabic structure; consonant sounds are peripheral. The sound patterns that English syllables can follow are listed below. The ⟨C⟩'s and ⟨V⟩'s enclosed in the slash marks refer to consonant and vowel sounds in general, not to specific phonemes.

Table 9.1 English Sound Patterns

Pattern	Examples
/V/	I, a/bout, ea/gle
/CV/	boy, she, ba/con, a/go
/VC/	at, out, each, ac/tion, el/bow
/CVC/	cat, rough, phone, sing, sil/ver
/CCV/	plow, try, through, trow/el
/VCC/	act, elk, aunt, Rich/ard
/CCVC/	trap, grass, phrase, climb, a/pron
/CVCC/	bend, mix, picked, a/shamed
/CCVCC/	blend, plunge, trained, com/plaint
/CCCV/	spry, straw, screw, squee/gee
/VCCC/	asked, arched, ends, imps
/CCCVCCC/	strengths, scrunched
/CCCVC/	stripe, sprain, squal/id
/CCCVCC/	strapped, scrounge
/CVCCC/	first, curled, at/tempt
/CCVCCC/	glimpse
/VCCCC/	angst
/CVCCCC/	tempts
/CCVCCCC/	glimpsed

These patterns do not imply that consecutive consonant sounds can consist of any sequence of two, three, or four consonants. The actual sequences of consonant sounds that occur in English are quite limited.

Spelling patterns of syllables vary according to the grapheme representations of the consonant and vowel phonemes included in syllables. A syllabic pattern that includes a /CVC/sequence of phonemes may have a corresponding letter pattern that looks like ⟨CVVCC⟩, as in the words *coach* and *teach*. Some short sound patterns may have long corresponding letter patterns, as does the syllable *through*, which has a /CCV/ sequence of sounds but a ⟨CCCVVCC⟩ sequence of letters. For this reason, it is always important to indicate whether syllable patterns represent sounds or letters.

In writing, it is easy to tell where one word ends and the next begins, whether one recognizes the word or not. It is not as easy to identify syllable divisions. There is no device in the English writing system to indicate breaks between syllables, with the exception of the occasional use of the hyphen. The written words *coop* and co-op, for example, are differentiated by the hyphen in the latter. The hyphen marks a division between syllables.

Once proficient readers have identified written words, they can usually divide the written words into syllables by matching spelling units with pronunciation units. However, unless they are doing a phonological exercise, readers do not need to divide into syllables words they have already identified. Doing so would only interfere with their reading. It can be helpful, though, when an unfamiliar word form is encountered. Readers can visually divide sequences of letters into smaller units, identify the smaller units, assign stress patterns and grapheme-phoneme correspondences, and synthesize them into whole words.

Since editors and printers frequently need to break written words at ends of lines of print, they have developed rules for hyphenating written words. Readers can get useful information about the syllabication of words by applying these writing segmentation principles. Speech syllabication rules are derived from the way words are pronounced and are based primarily on phonological variables, crossing morpheme boundaries. Writing segmentation rules are based first on morphological variables and then on phonological ones. Written segments frequently parallel morpheme units regardless of pronunciation. For example, while a division occurs after the first vowel in pronouncing *ska/ting,* the writing division is *skat/ing.* The morphemic units stay intact, with the exception of the dropped final ⟨e⟩, in the writing division. While we may say *ner/vous,* we write *nerv/ous* to preserve the two morphemes. Because morpheme units are not violated in writing segmentation, writing segmentation principles are more useful for word identification purposes than pronunciation syllabication principles are. But it should be remembered that written word segments may or may not be equivalent to spoken syllables.

The following segmentation principles serve as clues to identifying word forms. They show how readers can locate word segments from which direct identification of words can be made or to which grapheme-phoneme correspondence rules can be applied.

The principles are separated into two major categories. The first is division of words *between morpheme units*; the second is divisions *within morpheme units.* Intermorpheme divisions should be made before intramorpheme divisions when attempting to identify multisyllabic words.

To help illustrate the following principles, letter patterns will be enclosed in angle brackets. The capital letter ⟨C⟩ represents any consonant letter; the capital ⟨V⟩ represents any vowel letter. A lower case letter enclosed in angle brackets represents itself. A slash mark is used to designate a division between sequences of letters.

Segmentation Principles

Estimating Number of Syllables in Word Forms. There are at least as many syllables in a word as there are separated *vowel letter units.* Separated vowel letter units are individual or combined vowel letters that are separated from each other by one or more consonant letters. Some examples are:

1. *cat* (one vowel letter unit and one syllable)
2. *coat* (one vowel letter unit and one syllable)
3. *bacon* (two separated vowel letter units and two syllables)
4. *maiden* (two separated vowel letter units and two syllables)
5. *beautiful* (three separated vowel letter units and three syllables)

This generalization does not apply to two groups of words. One of these groups includes words that end in ⟨e⟩ preceded by a single consonant letter or by two letters representing a digraph. Examples are:

1. *rope* (has two separated vowel letter units, one of which is final ⟨e⟩ preceded by a single consonant; it has one syllable)
2. *breathe* (has two separated vowel letter units, one of which is final ⟨e⟩ preceded by two letters representing a digraph; it has one syllable)
3. *creature* (has three separated vowel letter units, one of which is final ⟨e⟩ preceded by a single consonant; it has two syllables)

Words in which final ⟨e⟩ is preceded by more than one consonant letter representing separate consonant sounds, or by a vowel letter, follow the original generalization. Note the following examples:

1. *constable* (has three separated vowel letter units, one of which is final ⟨e⟩ preceded by two consonants representing separate sounds; it has three syllables)
2. *ultrafashionable* (has six separated vowel letter units, one of

which is final ⟨e⟩ preceded by two consonants representing separate phonemes; it has six syllables)

3. *teepee* (has two separated vowel letter units, one of which is final ⟨e⟩ preceded by a vowel; it has two syllables)

4. *calorie* (has three separated vowel letter units, one of which is final ⟨e⟩ preceded by a vowel; it has three syllables)

There are occasional exceptions to this generalization, as in the words *adobe* and *recipe*.

The second group of words that constitutes an exception to the above generalization includes some verbs with the ⟨-ed⟩ past tense ending. When the ⟨-ed⟩ inflectional ending is added to verb roots that end with /t/ or /d/, the ⟨e⟩ is a clue to a syllable. If the verb root does not end with /t/ or /d/, the ⟨e⟩ is not a clue to a syllable. Examples are:

1. *spotted* (has two separated vowel letter units, one of which is part of ⟨-ed⟩ following /t/ at the end of the verb root; it has two syllables)

2. *shaded* (has two separated vowel letter units, one of which is part of ⟨-ed⟩ following /d/ at the end of the verb root; it has two syllables)

3. *jumped* (has two separated vowel letter units, one of which is part of ⟨-ed⟩ not following /t/ or /d/ at the end of the verb root; it has one syllable)

4. *rejoined* (has three separated vowel letter units, one of which is part of ⟨-ed⟩ not following /t/ or /d/ at the end of the verb root; it has two syllables)

When the inflectional ending ⟨-ed⟩ is added to a verb root ending with /t/ or /d/, a syllable (/əd/) is added to the word (*skate* + *ed* becomes /skā'tə d/; *shade* + *ed* becomes /šā'dəd/). However, when ⟨-ed⟩ is added to a verb root ending with any voiceless consonant except /t/, only the phoneme /t/ is added to the word (*jump* + *ed* becomes /jŭmpt/; *dance* + *ed* becomes /dănst/). When ⟨-ed⟩ is added to a verb root ending with a vowel or any voiced consonant except /d/, only the phoneme /d/ is added to the word (*hug* + *(g)ed* becomes /hŭgd/; *cry* + *ed* becomes /krīd/). In other words, the voiceless allomorph ⟨-ed⟩ follows voiceless root endings and the voiced allomorph ⟨-ed⟩ follows voiced root endings.

When words ending in the morpheme ⟨-ed⟩ are used as modifiers (adjectives or adverbs), the ⟨-ed⟩ tends to represent a syllable regardless of preceding phonemes:

"He *learned* his lesson" vs. "The *learned* man spoke."
"He *crooked* his finger" vs. "His *crooked* finger ached" and "He
walked *crookedly*."

For the most part, adjacent vowel letters represent single vowel phonemes
within morphemes. But, since they occasionally represent separate vowel
phonemes, as in the words *react, create,* and *science,* the number of
syllables in words cannot always be estimated correctly. A pupil could cope
successfully with *react* by applying morphemic analysis before phonic
analysis, which should be done as general procedure anyway. But *create*
and *science* are single free morphemes and pupils must be able to
recognize them in print before they can know the ⟨ea⟩ in *create* and the
⟨ie⟩ in *science* represent two phonemes and, therefore, two syllables each.

It should also be pointed out that dialect variations may affect the
number of syllables in words. Words like *lion, ruin, mayor,* and *giant* may
be pronounced with one syllable or two.

Divisions Between Morphemes

Divisions should be made between morpheme units in words before
intramorpheme divisions are made. Intermorpheme divisions do not take
into account letter sequence. They include the following:

1. root/root division (*rain/coat, horse/shoe, blue/bird, hot/head*)
2. prefix/root division (*mis/spell, re/call, un/tie*)
3. root/inflectional ending division when inflectional ending consists
   of more than one phoneme (*sew/ing, tall/er, nic/er, bench/es,
   grant/ed*)
4. root/suffix division (*kind/ness, calm/ly, skat/er*)
5. prefix/prefix division (*un/dis(closed), re/de(frost), re/im(plant)*)
6. suffix/suffix division (*(lone)li/ness, (respect)ful/ly,
   (courage)ous/ly*)
7. suffix/inflectional ending division when inflectional ending
   consists of more than one phoneme (*(kind)ness/es, (kind)li/est*)

Divisions Within Morphemes

Individual morphemes may be divided into syllabic segments if they include
more than one vowel letter unit (disregarding the exceptions previously
noted). These intramorpheme divisions are based on spelling patterns that
are more closely related to pronunciation variables than the intermorpheme

divisions are. Each principle listed below describes a single division within a multisyllabic morpheme. Several may apply at one time to a multisyllabic word.

The spelling patterns go from one vowel letter unit to the next, since syllabic divisions must be made somewhere between the separated vowel letter units. The consonant or consonants that precede the first vowel letter unit and follow the second are irrelevant to that division and are not mentioned as part of the spelling pattern. *Pilot* is described as having a ⟨VCV⟩ spelling pattern; *horrid,* a ⟨VCCV⟩ pattern; *deceit,* a ⟨VCVV⟩ pattern; and *village,* a ⟨VCCVCe⟩ pattern. Morpheme units with more than two syllables include overlapping spelling patterns describing each division. For example, two spelling patterns relate to the word *elephant:*

> ⟨VCV⟩ representing ⟨ele⟩ and
> ⟨VCCV⟩ representing ⟨epha⟩.

The word *prevaricate* includes the following spelling patterns:

> ⟨VCV⟩ representing ⟨eva⟩,
> ⟨VCV⟩ representing ⟨ari⟩, and
> ⟨VCVCe⟩ representing ⟨icate⟩.

The suffix ⟨-ibility⟩ has the following spelling patterns:

> ⟨VCV⟩ representing ⟨ibi⟩,
> ⟨VCV⟩ representing ⟨ili⟩, and
> ⟨VCV⟩ representing ⟨ity⟩.

⟨VCV⟩ Spelling Pattern. In a spelling pattern with one consonant letter between two vowel letter units, the division is ⟨V/CV⟩ approximately sixty percent of the time and ⟨VC/V⟩ forty percent of the time (*sea/son, la/dy, pi/lot,* but *cab/in* and *sol/id*). When the consonant letter is ⟨v⟩ a ⟨VC/V⟩ division usually results (*dev/il, sev/en,* and *heav/en*).

⟨VCCV⟩ Spelling Pattern. When a spelling pattern includes two consonant letters between two vowel letter units, the division depends on what the two consonant letters represent. If the two consonant letters represent a digraph or initial blend, the division is ⟨V/CCV⟩ (*fa/ther, ma/chine, cy/clone, se/cret*). If the two consonant letters represent double consonants, a final blend, or independent consonants, the division is ⟨VC/CV⟩ (*cab/bage, par/ty, hus/band*).

⟨VCCCV⟩ Spelling Pattern. When a spelling pattern includes three consonant letters between two vowel letter units, the division depends on what the three consonant letters represent. Combinations of consonant letters that represent digraphs or initial blends are not split up. In most cases the division is ⟨VC/CCV⟩ because the last two consonants represent the digraph or initial blend (or/phan, pan/ther, um/brage). Occasionally, the division is ⟨VCC/CV⟩ as in neph/ron. The division may also be ⟨V/CCCV⟩, as in a/strin/gent, where the three consonant letters represent a three-letter initial blend.

⟨VCCCCV⟩ Spelling Pattern. When a spelling pattern includes four consonant letters between two vowel letter units, the chances are that two digraphs are juxtaposed in the word and the division is ⟨VCC/CCV⟩ (diph/thong).

⟨VCle⟩ Spelling Pattern. When a spelling pattern at the end of a morpheme is ⟨le⟩ preceded by one consonant letter, the division is ⟨V/Cle⟩ (a/ble, ri/fle, bu/gle, ca/pa/ble).

⟨VCCle⟩ Spelling Pattern. When a spelling pattern at the end of a morpheme is ⟨le⟩ preceded by two consonant letters, the division is ⟨VC/Cle⟩ (bub/ble, gar/gle, can/dle). If the two consonant letters before ⟨le⟩ are ⟨ck⟩, the division is ⟨Vck/le⟩ (pick/le, buck/le).

Accenting Principles

The accenting of words relates to stress in intonation. Most phonemic analyses recognize four levels or degrees of stress or force with which syllables are produced in spoken English sentences: primary, secondary, tertiary, and reduced or weak stress. In the typical English sentence, primary stress occurs on the root syllable of the last word, as in "She played happily."

Words in isolation usually have three levels of stress: primary, secondary, and reduced. When words are pronounced in isolation or in lists, primary stress falls on a root syllable of all words. Thus, if the words in the abovementioned sentence were spoken as if in a list, she and played would also receive primary stress. In isolation, single syllable root words are pronounced with primary stress. Multisyllabic root words, derived, and inflected words have not only primarily stressed syllables, but unstressed syllables and perhaps secondarily stressed syllables. The accent patterns of words depend on the number of syllables and the morphological structure of the words.

Words spoken in isolation are frequently stressed differently than they are when spoken in sentences. This is one reason why pupils may still have difficulty identifying a word form even when they have applied all phonic principles correctly. Structure words are particularly vulnerable in this respect. Structure words are usually unaccented in context and do not sound the same as when spoken in isolation. For example, *an* is pronounced /ăn/ in isolation but usually /ən/ in context. A phrase like *an apple* may be pronounced /ə nă′pəl/, reducing /ăn/ to /ə/. Structure words should not be presented in isolation to pupils in the initial stages of reading development. They should always be presented as parts of phrases and sentences.

Probably the best way to realize the difference between a stressed and an unstressed syllable is to compare related words. For example, the pronunciation of the following italicized words in each pair differ primarily in the placement of the main stress, that is, in which vowel is produced with the greatest prominence or articulatory force.

> the *con′vict* — will *con vict′*
> the *pro′test* — will *pro test′*
> the *an′nex* — will *an nex′*

The following pairs of related words may also help distinguish between stressed and unstressed syllables. Compare the sounds represented by the underlined vowel letters in each pair. In each instance the underlined letter in the first word represents an unstressed vowel; in the second word it represents a stressed vowel.

hist<u>o</u>ry	—	hist<u>o</u>rical
c<u>o</u>ndemn	—	c<u>o</u>ndemnation
tel<u>e</u>graph	—	tel<u>e</u>graphy

Since vowel grapheme-phoneme correspondences are sensitive to stress patterns, phonic analysis cannot be successfully used with multisyllabic words without the identification of stress patterns. For instance, final ⟨a⟩ represents /ā/ in the accented first syllable of *ma′ple* but represents /ə/ in the unaccented first syllable of *ma chine′*; ⟨ai⟩ usually represents /ā/ in accented syllables, but /ə/ in the unaccented syllables of words like *curtain* and *mountain.* To avoid confusion and complication, the basic grapheme-phoneme correspondences should be first taught in relation to *single syllable root words.* This will ensure that the phonic principles of grapheme-phoneme correspondences actually do apply to the words used for demonstration and practice. Once pupils have learned the grapheme-phoneme correspondences, they should be encouraged to apply them to multisyllabic words in combination with other word identification clues. At this point, they should be taught how changes in stress can change vowel grapheme-phoneme correspondences.

Pupils automatically and intuitively accent words as they speak. They are usually unaware of doing so, but can be taught to predict accent patterns through visual clues in the spelling patterns of words. The following generalizations can be helpful in doing this.

Monomorphemic Words

1. Primary accent usually falls on any root syllable in which the vowel sound is spelled with more than one letter (*con ceal'*, *ex plore'*, *a bout'*, *Au'gust*, *bai'liff*, *oy'ster*).

2. Primary accent usually falls on the first syllable of two-syllable root words when the vowel sound in each syllable is spelled with only one letter (*stu'pid*, *or'phan*, *par'snip*, *a'corn*).

3. Primary accent usually falls on the syllable before double consonants (*let'ter*, *be gin'ner*, *mut'ton*).

4. Primary accent usually falls on the first syllable of two-syllable root words (that serve both as nouns and verbs) when they are used as nouns, and on the second syllable when they are used as verbs (*a per'mit/will per mit'*, *the an'nex/will an nex'*, *one pro'test/did pro test'*).

5. Root words ending in ⟨Cle⟩ are usually not accented on the final syllable (*ta'ble*, *can'dle*, *peo'ple*).

Multimorphemic Words

1. Primary accent usually falls on a syllable of the root when a word consists of a free or bound root and affix(es) (*en camp'ment*, *sur round'ing*, *a dapt'a ble*, *de fen'si ble*, *re mind'*, *ex hort'*).

2. Primary accent usually falls on a syllable of the first root word and secondary accent on a syllable of the second root word when a word is compound (*home'sick'*, *wa'ter fall'*).

3. Primary accent falls on the first root word in a compound contraction (*they'll*, *could've*).

4. Primary accent usually falls on the syllable before the suffixes ⟨-ion⟩, ⟨-ity⟩, ⟨-ic⟩, ⟨-ian⟩, ⟨-ial⟩, and ⟨-ious⟩ (*af fect'ion*, *af fect a'tion*, *pe di a tri'cian*, *con form'i ty*).

5. Primary accent usually falls on the second syllable before the suffix ⟨-ate⟩ (*dif fer en'ti ate*, *con'tem plate*).

Words having four or more syllables are likely to have both primary stress and secondary stress as in the words *mul'ti pli ca'tion, in oc'u la'tion,* and *de fen'si bil'i ty.* Morphemically complex words have complicated stress patterns, and it is questionable whether pupils need to know their underlying principles to identify written words successfully. The longer words are, the more likely they are to consist of multiple morphemes. Such words are identified more efficiently through morphemic clues than through phonic clues. For example, in *fatal* the first vowel is long, but in *fatality* the first vowel is partially or entirely neutralized. There is nothing in the spelling to suggest this, except for an obscure rule about syllable or morpheme addition. However, the similarity in spelling makes the identification of *fatality* relatively easy, for its morphemic relationship to the root word *fatal* is evident. Pupils usually have no difficulty in identifying words of this kind, and, although their oral renditions of the words may be faulty, they achieve the primary goal of reading. This is again to say that the underlying purpose of phonic analysis is word identification and not necessarily complete phonological accuracy.

Exercises

The purpose of the following exercises is to illustrate how segmentation and accenting principles may be used for word identification. Some of the items involve real words and some pseudowords. Presumably the only time that readers need to divide word forms into segments and infer stress patterns is when they do not recognize the word forms and cannot identify them through whole word and/or morphemic clues. Some pseudowords have been included to put you in the position of readers encountering unfamiliar words. Cover the answer column while working the exercises.

Exercise A. For each word below, indicate the number of pronunciation segments and identify the separated vowel letter units.

Real Word	Number of Segments	Vowel Letter Units	Answer
pauper	_____	_____	2 (au, e)
penicillin	_____	_____	4 (e, i, i, i)
truce	_____	_____	1 (u)
tentacle	_____	_____	3 (e, a, e)
metropolitan	_____	_____	5 (e, o, o, i, a)

Pseudoword	Number of Segments	Vowel Letter Units	Answer
kreagul	_____	_____	2 (ea, u)
fackle	_____	_____	2 (a, e)
crinded	_____	_____	2 (i, e)
glibe	_____	_____	1 (i)
alfensoipter	_____	_____	4 (a, e, oi, e)

Exercise B. Draw vertical lines to indicate the intermorpheme divisions of the following multimorphemic words. Underline the primary accented segment in each word.

Real Word	Answer
hatrack	hat/rack
disuse	dis/use
guided	guid/ed
carelessly	care/less/ly
unpleasantness	un/pleas/ant/ness

Pseudoword	
disfootous	dis/foot/ous
recurdedly	re/curd/ed/ly
bridewall	bride/wall
resquashment	re/squash/ment
stringballing	string/ball/ing

Exercise C. Draw vertical lines to indicate the intramorpheme divisions of the following words and underline the primary accented syllable in each word. Write the spelling pattern upon which the division is based.

Real Word	Spelling Pattern	Answer
total	_____	to/tal, ⟨ V/CV⟩: a single consonant letter between two vowel letter units more frequently begins the second segment
anvil	_____	an/vil, ⟨VC/CV⟩: the two consonant letters do not represent a digraph or initial blend

Real Word	Spelling Patterns	Answer
author	_____	au̲/thor, ⟨V/CCV⟩: the two consonant letters represent a digraph
cobra	_____	co̲/bra, ⟨V/CCV⟩: the two consonant letters represent an initial blend
repeat	_____	re/pe̲at̲, ⟨V/CV⟩: a single consonant between two vowel letter units more frequently begins the second segment
crackle	_____	cra̲ck/le, ⟨Vck/le⟩: the final ⟨le⟩ is preceded by ⟨ck⟩

Pseudoword

wrieple	_____	wri̲e/ple, ⟨V/Cle⟩: the final ⟨le⟩ is preceded by one consonant
corvate	_____	cor/va̲te ⟨VC/CV⟩: the two consonant letters do not represent a digraph or initial blend
eushult	_____	e̲u̲/shult, ⟨V/CCV⟩: the two consonant letters represent a digraph
barphex	_____	ba̲r/phex, ⟨VC/CCV⟩: the second and third consonant letters represent a digraph but the sequence of three consonant letters does not represent an initial blend
sasooch	_____	sa/so̲och̲, ⟨V/CV⟩: a single consonant letter between two vowel letter units more frequently begins the second segment

Exercise D. Draw vertical lines to indicate the segmentation divisions of the following words and underline the primary accented syllable in each word. Write the accenting principle on which the stress pattern is based.

Real Word	Underlying Principle	Answer
distrust	_____	dis/trust: the second syllable is the root syllable
vocation	_____	vo/ca/tion: primary accent usually falls on the syllable before ⟨-tion⟩
tennis	_____	ten/nis: the syllable before double consonants is usually accented or the first syllable of two-syllable root words is usually accented when there is one vowel letter in each syllable
account	_____	ac/count primary accent usually falls on any root syllable in which the vowel sound is spelled with more than one letter
music	_____	mu/sic: accent usually falls on the first syllable of two-syllable root words when each syllable has only one vowel letter

Pseudoword		
vashale	_____	va/shale primary accent usually falls on any root syllable in which the vowel sound is spelled with more than one letter
tapel	_____	ta/pel: accent usually falls on the first syllable of two-syllable root words when each syllable has only one vowel letter
respellance	_____	re/spell/ance: the middle syllable is the root syllable
cuzzon	_____	cuz/zon: the syllable before double consonant letters is usually accented or primary accent usually falls on the first syllable of two-syllable root words when each syllable has only one vowel letter
elgrean	_____	el/grean primary accent usually falls on any root syllable in which the vowel sound is spelled with more than one letter

Suggested Activities for Pupil Practice

General Considerations for Teachers

It is important to focus activities on the specific skill(s) you want pupils to practice. Pupils should not be able to get the right answers except by applying the skill(s) you want them to practice. For this reason, activities intended to provide practice in applying segmenting and accenting principles should include words that are unfamiliar to pupils in their written form. To eliminate pupils' using semantic or syntactic clues, practice activities should be restricted to words in isolation, except when your purpose is to have pupils practice using combinations of clues.

Guard against using items in activities that have unintentional common elements, since this might encourage the pupils to make unwarranted generalizations. If, in activities that focus on either segmentation or accenting, all words used consist of two syllables, pupils may assume that segmenting and accenting principles apply only to two-syllable words or to the first two syllables of longer words.

Activities similar to those that are described for pupil practice may be used as diagnostic skills tests or as criterion-referenced tests to analyze pupils' proficiencies and deficiencies in the use of specific phonic clues. Such diagnostic test activities may be administered before and/or after teaching the skills.

Activity 1

Purpose. To provide practice in using the $\langle VC/CV \rangle$ and $\langle V/CCV \rangle$ divisions in two-syllable root words with a $\langle VCCV \rangle$ spelling pattern as clues to the identification of such words.

Level. Upper intermediate.

Directions for Teachers. Use two-syllable root words with a $\langle VCCV \rangle$ spelling pattern. The combinations of adjacent consonant letters should represent a mixture of digraphs, initial blends, final blends, double consonants, and consonants that function independently of each other. Successful use of segmenting principles related to spelling patterns of words depends on distinguishing vowel letters from consonant letters and on the ability to identify syllables as pronunciation units in spoken words. Successful pronunciation of a word following the application of segmenting division principles depends on knowledge of grapheme-phoneme correspondences in open, closed, accented, and unaccented syllables. You must ascertain if pupils have this knowledge before presenting them with any segmenting exercises related to the spelling patterns of words. If they lack such knowledge, it should be developed first. It is important that you be aware of dialectal differences in the way that words are divided when they are pronounced by different pupils. When selecting words for this activity, select those that, in the pupils' natural speech, follow the patterns you plan to teach. Remember that there may be differences between divisions in pronunciation and divisions in writing across all dialects.

Prepare five sets of two-syllable root words with a ⟨VCCV⟩ spelling pattern. The two consonant letters in each set should represent, respectively, a digraph, an initial consonant blend, a final consonant blend, a double consonant, and two independent consonants. It is important that the words be those that pupils can identify in print in order for them to be able to make appropriate generalizations. They must also know how to distinguish consonant digraphs and initial consonant blends from other combinations of consonants. Note the following sets of words:

Set 1	Set 2	Set 3	Set 4	Set 5
trophy	apron	after	button	subject
father	between	winter	carrot	admit
machine	reply	wonder	rabbit	advent

Write the sets of words on the chalkboard, or on a chart, transparency, or ditto sheet. Double or triple space between the words of each set to leave space for later markings. Call on the pupils to read aloud the first word in the first set and to tell you how many parts they hear in that word. Have them underline each part in the written word and draw a slash mark between the parts (_tro/phy_). Direct the pupils to label letters from the first vowel letter to the second vowel letter with a capital ⟨V⟩ or ⟨C⟩ to indicate whether it is a vowel letter or a consonant letter ($\frac{tro/phy}{V/CCV}$).

Proceed in the same manner to complete the first set of words. Continue through the remaining sets, calling on a different pupil to do each word.

When all of the words in all of the sets have been completed, ask pupils if the spelling patterns from the first vowel letter through the second vowel letter are the same in all the words. Then ask if the division is at the same point in the spelling pattern for all the words. Have them identify where the division occurs in each set of words; that is, if it occurs before, between, or after the consonant letters.

Ask pupils why the words are divided between consonant letters in some sets and before the consonant letters in other sets. (They should be able to tell you that the words are divided before the consonants when the two consonant letters represent a digraph or an initial consonant blend, and between the consonants when they represent a double consonant, final consonant blend, or independent consonants. Accept any explanation that conveys this information.) If pupils are unable to discover the underlying patterns themselves, elicit from them what the two consonant letters represent in each set of words. Have them label each set appropriately. Then ask them in which three sets the words are divided between the two consonant letters and in which two sets the words are divided before the two consonant letters.

When pupils have reached this stage, they are ready to practice applying the ⟨VC/CV⟩ and ⟨V/CCV⟩ divisions in two-syllable root words with a ⟨VCCV⟩ spelling pattern. Prepare a list of words in which the several kinds of consonant letter combinations occur in mixed order (*betray, antic, magnet, typhoon, bonnet,* etc.). The words selected at this point need not be familiar to pupils since the purpose of this activity is to provide practice in applying word division principles to the identification of unfamiliar words. Have pupils draw vertical lines between the parts in each word and explain the basis for their division. Then have them pronounce each word, applying appropriate grapheme-phoneme correspondences to both accented and unaccented syllables.

You should provide additional practice in applying these principles to words in context. Present unrelated sentences or sentences in story context that contain words with the ⟨VCCV⟩ spelling pattern represented by different consonant letter combinations. In normal reading, pupils use these principles with continuous text. Identifying words in context enables them to practice combining various clues, which leads to greater efficiency in word identification.

The activity described above is for a summary type of lesson in dividing words of two syllables with ⟨VCCV⟩ spelling patterns. Since this lesson includes a spelling pattern that represents five different consonant combinations, it would be easier to teach if pupils previously had lessons involving one or more of these consonant combinations. Coping with all five for the first time at once may be overwhelming for many pupils. This kind of lesson should be followed by activities in which pupils are presented with three and four syllable words to divide. Such practice will enable pupils to apply the same principle of division to longer words.

It should be noted that many words with a ⟨VCCV⟩ spelling pattern in which the two consonant letters represent a digraph are divided after the digraph in pronunciation. The reason is that a digraph represents a single phoneme and, as a result, the ⟨VCV⟩ spelling pattern division principle can be applied to the word. In order not to complicate this lesson, such words have not been included. (If any pupils ask about this apparent contradiction, point out the similarity between a single consonant letter representing a single consonant phoneme and a digraph where two consonant letters represent a single consonant phoneme. Explain that just as the ⟨VCV⟩ spelling pattern is sometimes divided after the consonant, so is the ⟨VCCV⟩ pattern when the two consonant letters represent a single phoneme.) Words with ⟨st⟩, ⟨sp⟩, and ⟨sk⟩ have also been avoided in this activity since these combinations of consonant letters sometimes represent initial blends and other times final blends.

Activity 2

Purpose. To provide practice in using multiple vowel letters within word segments as clues to primary accent in two-syllable root words

Level. Intermediate.

Directions for Teachers. Use two-syllable root words with one vowel letter in one syllable and two vowel letters in the other syllable. The two vowel letters may be adjacent to each other as in *repeat* or separated as in *revise*. (Since accenting principles are related to syllables, pupils must understand the concept of a syllable or word part and be able to recognize accented syllables in spoken words. Determine if pupils have such knowledge before presenting them with accenting exercises related to the spelling patterns of words. If it is lacking, it should be developed first.) It is extremely important for you to be aware of dialectal differences in the way that words are accented when pronounced by different pupils. For some words, more than one pattern of stress may be acceptable within a dialect (*ad ver'tise ment* as opposed to *ad ver tise'ment* as opposed to *ad'ver tise ment*). Therefore, when selecting words for introducing principles of accenting, choose those that, in the pupils' natural speech, follow the patterns you plan to teach.

Prepare a set of two-syllable root words in which the vowel sound in one syllable is spelled by one letter and the vowel sound in the other syllable is spelled by more than one letter. Be sure that the vowel sounds spelled by two letters are not always in the same syllable. For this introductory exercise, use only words that pupils already recognize in print and that they pronounce uniformly. Avoid words such as *create* and *science*, where the two adjacent vowel letters represent separate vowel phonemes and are parts of separate syllables. The words should be divided when presented. If pupils know how to divide words by applying spelling pattern principles, they should be expected to perform the task. If they are unable to do so, you should do it. Note the following examples:

au/tumn	ex/plode
rai/sin	re/peat
toi/let	a/way

Write the words in two columns on the chalkboard, or on a chart, transparency, or ditto sheet. One column should consist of words in which the vowel sound spelled by more than one letter is in the first syllable; the other should consist of words in which the two-letter vowel sound appears in the second syllable. Call on the pupils to read the first word in the first column aloud and to tell you which syllable is accented. (They should be able to do this if they have all the prerequisite knowledge previously mentioned.) Then have them underline the accented syllable in the written word and place an accent mark to indicate this. Direct the pupils to write a capital ⟨V⟩ under all the vowel letters in the word and to tell you how many vowel letters there are in the accented and unaccented syllables. (This activity assumes that pupils know what an accent mark is and how it is placed in relation to stressed syllables in written words. If they do not have this knowledge, you should teach it to them. Accent marks may appear at the beginnings or ends of syllables, or above the vowel letters in the accented syllables. Be consistent in the placement you use and teach so as not to confuse the pupils.)

Proceed in the same manner with each word. When all the words have been completed, ask pupils if they see any relationship between the number of vowel letters in a syllable and the syllable that is accented in the words. Accept any explanation that indicates awareness of the accenting principle involved: primary accent usually falls on any root syllable in which the vowel sound is spelled with more than one vowel letter. If pupils are unable to identify the relationship between accented syllables and numbers of vowel letters, go back over the words one at a time. Ask the following questions about each word:

How many vowel letters are there in the first syllable?

How many vowel letters are there in the second syllable?
Which syllable is accented?
How many vowel letters does the unaccented syllable have?
How many vowel letters does the accented syllable have?

Ask again if they see any relationship between the number of vowel letters in a syllable and the accented syllable in two-syllable root words. If they are still unable to recognize the relationship, they probably are not ready for work on accenting.

When pupils understand the relationship between accent and the number of vowel letters in syllables, they are ready to practice applying this principle to two-syllable root words with different numbers of vowel letters in each syllable. Prepare an appropriate list of words, arranging the list so that the accent is sometimes on the first syllable and sometimes on the second syllable. The words selected at this point need not be words with which pupils are familiar since the idea is for pupils to apply accenting principles as clues to the identification of unfamiliar words. Have pupils mark the accented syllable in any way you wish (underlining, circling, placing accent marks, etc.) and ask them to pronounce each word.

You should also provide practice in applying this accenting principle to two-syllable root words in context, that is, in text or unrelated sentences.

Example of Combination Activity

Since syllabication and accenting clues are more effective when used with other word identification techniques, pupils should practice combining them with other kinds of clues. The following sample exercise combines syllabication and accenting clues with syntactic clues.

1. The winner of a *contest* usually does not *contest* the decision.
2. Barbara will *object* to your placing that *object* in her room.

Answer

1a. /kŏn′·təst/   The syllabication clue is that there is a ⟨VC/CV⟩ syllabic division in a two-syllable root word with a ⟨VCCV⟩ spelling pattern in which the two consonants represent a final consonant blend; the accenting clue is that two-syllable root word forms used as nouns and verbs are accented on the first syllable when used as nouns; the syntactic clue is the structure word noun marker *a*.

1b. /kən tĕst′/ The syllabication clue is that there is a ⟨VC/CV⟩ syllabic division in a two-syllable root word with a ⟨VCCV⟩ spelling pattern in which the two consonants represent a final consonant blend; the accenting clue is that two-syllable root word forms used as nouns and verbs are accented on the second syllable when used as verbs; the syntactic clue is the structure word verb marker *does*.

2a. /əb jĕkt′/ The syllabication clue is that there is a ⟨VC/CV⟩ syllabic division in a two-syllable root word with a ⟨VCCV⟩ spelling pattern in which the two consonants do not represent either a digraph or an initial consonant blend; the accenting clue is that two-syllable root word forms used as nouns and verbs are accented on the second syllable when used as verbs; the syntactic clue is the structure word *will* which signals a verb.

2b. /ŏb′ jəkt/ The syllabication clue is that there is a ⟨VC/CV⟩ syllabic division in a two-syllable root word with a ⟨VCCV⟩ spelling pattern in which the two consonants do not represent either a digraph or an initial consonant blend; the accenting clue is the principle that two-syllable root word forms used as nouns and verbs are accented on the first syllable when used as nouns; the syntactic clue is the demonstrative pronoun *that* which signals a noun.

Chapter 10

Grapheme-Phoneme Correspondences

⟨grapheme⟩-/phoneme/ correspondences

The aspect of phonics that relates to segmental phonology is the correspondence between graphemes and phonemes.

In conventional English spelling, graphemes represent phonemes up to a certain point. A grapheme is a letter or letter combination that represents a single speech sound. The phoneme /ē/, for example, may be represented by the grapheme ⟨ee⟩ as in *need,* ⟨ea⟩ as in *weak,* ⟨ie⟩ as in *believe,* ⟨ei⟩ as in *receive,* ⟨ey⟩ as in *key,* or ⟨e⟩ as in *even.* The grapheme is the smallest differentiating unit in writing; the phoneme is the smallest differentiating unit in speech. Graphemes are the visual representations of speech sounds in conventional spelling.

Readers need to know the various grapheme-phoneme correspondences in English in order to use phonic clues for word identification. When correspondences can be made between combinations of graphemes and combinations of phonemes, rather than between single graphemes and single phonemes, word identification can usually proceed more easily and rapidly. This is true both when phonics is used alone as a means of word identification and when it is used with other kinds of clues. For example, the recognition of consonant blends as units of correspondence is more efficient than the recognition of the individual consonant letter-sound correspondences of which the blends consist. In words like *clown* and *cluck,* associating ⟨cl⟩ with /kl/ as a unit is easier than associating ⟨c⟩ with /k/ and then ⟨l⟩ with /l/. Similarly, recognition of grapheme bases as pronunciation units is more efficient than identification of either individual or blend grapheme-phoneme correspondences. Realizing that ⟨east⟩ represents /ēst/ is more efficient than ⟨ea⟩ represents /ē/, ⟨s⟩ represents /s/, and ⟨t⟩ represents /t/ in words like *feast* and *yeast.* The larger the units of recognition, the more rapid word identification is likely to be and the more rapid and meaningful reading is likely to be.

The Spelling and Sounds of English

Segmental phonology is based on the vowel and consonant phonemes. They constitute the speech sounds of the language. Linguists generally agree that spoken English has about forty-five different phonemes. The actual number and identity of the phonemes may vary among speakers of various dialects. Of the total number, at least twenty-four are consonants. The number of vowel sounds varies with dialect and with linguistic description. This limited number of phonemes is used in various combinations to produce all the words and sentences of the language.

Speech sounds are produced by controlling the way air is released from the lungs. The basic difference between vowel and consonant phonemes is in the manner of their articulation. Vowels are sounds characterized by the use of the vocal cords and the free passage of air through the vocal mechanism. Differences in shaping the lips and in the relationship between tongue and palate produce the essential differences among the vowel phonemes.

Consonants are sounds characterized by complete or partial stoppage or redirection of the air stream as it passes through the vocal mechanism. Differences in the use of the vocal cords and differences in the type of obstruction of the air stream by tongue, lips, and teeth produce the essential differences among the consonant sounds.

There are only twenty-six letters in the English alphabet to represent in writing the forty-five phonemes. This is one reason why a consistent one-to-one correspondence does not exist between letters and sounds in conventional spelling. Since there are fewer letters than phonemes, some letters are used to represent more than one phoneme. For example, ⟨a⟩ may represent /ă/ as in *tap*, /ā/ as in *table*, /ô/ as in *all*, /ä/ as in *car*, and so on. Similarly, ⟨c⟩ may represent /s/ as in *cent*, /k/ as in *coat*, and /š/ as in *ocean*. Some letters are combined to represent certain phonemes. For instance, ⟨h⟩ is combined with ⟨c⟩ to represent /č/ as in *church* and /k/ as in *choir;* with ⟨s⟩ to represent /š/ as in *shoe;* with ⟨t⟩ to represent /ө/ as in *thin* and /đ/ as in *then;* and with ⟨g⟩ and ⟨p⟩ to represent /f/ as in *laugh* and *graph.* Many phonemes are spelled in more than one way. The /ā/, among many other ways, may be spelled ⟨ai⟩, ⟨ey⟩, ⟨ei⟩, ⟨ay⟩, ⟨eigh⟩, and ⟨ea⟩ as in *maid, they, rein, say, neigh,* and *steak.* The letters that spell a phoneme may be adjacent (⟨ai⟩ in *maid* and ⟨ph⟩ in *phone*) or separated by one or more intervening letters (⟨a⟩ and ⟨e⟩ in *bathe*). It is also possible for one letter to represent more than one phoneme at a time. For example, ⟨x⟩ at the end of *box* represents the consonant blend /ks/.

Statements of grapheme-phoneme correspondences must mention the letters as well as the sounds represented by the letters. Mentioning only the letters but not the sounds represented by them does not result in a correspondence. The statement "the sound of ph" does not specify a correspondence. The statement "the letters ph together represent the /f/ sound" does. In stating correspondences, it is important to differentiate between graphemes and phonemes. The terms *vowel* and *consonant* do not have the same referents in writing and in speech. Any reference to vowels or consonants must be made in terms of *letters* or *sounds* in order to be meaningful and accurate. Graphemes are designated by angle brackets in this book, while slash marks designate phonemes.

The phoneme symbols used throughout this book are listed earlier. They resemble those found in most current dictionaries and are not intended to differentiate very precise phonetic values; they allow for a wide range of variation. The symbols were compiled and selected from several dictionaries, including those most widely used in schools, and certain adaptations were made. In contrast to many dictionary pronunciation keys, we use symbols that consist of only single letters. This was done to emphasize the one-to-one correspondence between phoneme symbols and phonemes. For example, in this text the symbol /ö/ represents the phoneme frequently represented by the two-letter pronunciation symbol /oi/, and /ĉ/ represents the phoneme frequently represented by the two-letter pronunciation symbol /ch/.

Specific Grapheme-Phoneme Correspondences

In each correspondence presented below, the corresponding graphemes and phonemes are specified. Sample words are presented showing the indicated correspondence in various positions. In English words all phonemes do not necessarily appear in all positions (initial, medial, and final). For example, the two phonemes /ŋ/ and /ž/ never occur at beginnings of English words and others, such as /y/, /h/, and /w/, never occur at ends of words. And while a phoneme may occur in a given position, it may not be represented by certain letters in those positions. For instance, while ⟨ci⟩ is one spelling for /š/, as in *special,* this particular correspondence does not occur at beginnings of words. The letters ⟨ci⟩ at the beginnings of words usually represent two phonemes—/s/ and /ĭ/, /ī/, or /ə/—as in the words *civil, cider,* and *cigar.*

Very often the phoneme that a specific letter or letter combination represents in conventional spelling depends on the position of the grapheme within a syllable or word. Vowel letters and vowel sounds can occur in any of the three positions; however, the phonemes that vowel letters represent may be affected by their syllabic position. In general, single vowel letters in initial or medial positions of accented syllables or single syllable words represent "short" vowel sounds, while those in final positions represent "long" vowel sounds (for example, initial ⟨e⟩ represents /ĕ/ in *ebb,* medial ⟨e⟩ represents /ĕ/ in *met,* and final ⟨e⟩ represents /ē/ in *me* and *se/cret*).

Consonants occur only in initial and final positions within syllables or single syllable words, as, for example, initial ⟨f⟩ represents /f/ and final ⟨st⟩ represent /st/ in *fast.* The syllabic structure of English does not permit consonant phonemes to appear in medial positions in syllables. Since *medial position* implies both preceding and following phonemes, medial consonants would be both preceded and followed by vowel phonemes, creating more than one syllable. Multisyllabic words do have internal consonants but always at the beginnings or ends of syllables. For example, the internal ⟨b⟩ in *cab/in* ends the first syllable and the ⟨c⟩ in *ba/con* begins the second syllable.

Like single consonant phonemes, consonant blend phonemes occur only in initial and final positions. The ⟨r⟩ in *string* is the third letter of the initial ⟨str⟩ blend. Similarly, the ⟨r⟩ in *burst* is the first letter in the final ⟨rst⟩ blend. The consonant letters in the central portion of *portray* are divided *por/tray,* so that the first ⟨r⟩ ends the first syllable and the second ⟨r⟩ is part of the ⟨tr⟩ blend at the beginning of the second syllable.

Grapheme-phoneme correspondences of consonants are not affected by syllabic position to the extent that vowel correspondences are. However, there are instances in which syllabic position is influential. For example, if the letter combination ⟨gh⟩ appears at beginnings of syllables, as in *ghost,* it represents /g/; if it appears at ends of syllables, it may represent /f/ as in *laugh.* At ends of syllables, it may also be part of the vowel spelling, as in *nigh* and *bough.*

Some grapheme-phoneme correspondences may be affected by their phonological and/or orthographic environments, that is, by the sounds and/or letters that precede and/or follow them. If the consonant letter ⟨c⟩, for example, is followed by ⟨e⟩, ⟨i⟩, or ⟨y⟩, it usually represents /s/ as in *cell, city,* and *cyst.* If it is followed by ⟨a⟩, ⟨o⟩, or ⟨u⟩, it represents /k/ as in *cat, cop,* and *cure.* If it is followed by ⟨h⟩, it becomes part of the ⟨ch⟩ digraph and represents /č/, /k/, or /š/, as in *church, chorus,* and *chaise,* respectively. If ⟨c⟩ is followed by any other consonant letter, it represents /k/ as in *clock, crack,* and *accent.*

Vowel correspondences may also be affected by graphemic/phonological environment. An example of this is the effect that ⟨r⟩ has on vowels immediately preceding it in the same syllable. Although ⟨a⟩ in initial and medial positions of accented syllables generally represents /ă/, it usually represents /ä/ when it is followed by ⟨r⟩, as in *art* and *card.* In words like *arouse,* the ⟨a⟩ does not occur in the accented syllable, nor do ⟨a⟩ and ⟨r⟩ occur in the same syllable, so it does not have that effect.

Another factor that may affect grapheme-phoneme correspondences is the accent patterns of words. Intervocalic ⟨x⟩, that is, ⟨x⟩ occurring between vowel phonemes, usually represents /ks/ when primary stress is on the vowel preceding it, as in *extra* and *exercise.* It usually represents /gz/ if the primary stress is elsewhere, as in *exhibit* and *exhort.*

Vowel correspondences are more sensitive to stress conditioning than are consonant correspondences. Any of the vowel graphemes may represent a neutralized sound (schwa) in an unstressed syllable, as illustrated by the vowel letters in the first syllables of *above, effect, civilian, occur,* and *upon,* and in the second syllables of the words *pedant, hunted, raisin, season, circus, caution,* and *famous.* The schwa sound is very like that of the vowel sound in *but* and *hut* but is pronounced with less force. There is a common phonetic variant that sounds a bit like /ɪ/, and in some American dialects the two sounds are in contrast so that *roses* and *Rosa's,* are distinguished. There is no consistent spelling pattern associated with this sound or sounds. The nearest is the letter ⟨e⟩ in the past tense, plural, and superlative degree endings, as in *haunted, roses,* and *nearest,* unless the superlative degree ending is stressed enough to have the vowel sound /ĕ/.

Some words take on different stress patterns when used as different parts of speech. This results in different phonemes being represented by the same graphemes in the words, depending upon which syllable is stressed. The verb ⟨separate⟩ is secondarily accented on the final syllable and has /ā/ as the vowel sound in that syllable. On the other hand, ⟨separate⟩ as an adjective is accented on the first syllable, has schwa as the vowel sound in the final syllable, and is often pronounced with two rather than three syllables. In the noun ⟨rebel⟩ the first vowel sound is /ĕ/ and the second is schwa. If the word is used as a verb, the vowel sounds are reversed.

Because of the variations in vowel grapheme-phoneme correspondences produced by stress variations in multisyllabic words, it is advisable for teachers to use single syllable words when first teaching grapheme-phoneme correspondences, especially vowel correspondences. Multisyllabic formats should be introduced gradually afterwards.

Vowel Grapheme-Phoneme Correspondences

All vowel correspondences in the lists below pertain to one-syllable words and to stressed syllables in multisyllabic words, unless otherwise indicated by use of the unstressed vowel symbols. They are arranged according to patterns commonly found in reading instructional materials, and only the most common correspondences are included.

The correspondences listed reflect primarily the speech patterns of the authors of this book. The speech patterns of readers of this book may vary from these correspondences and be equally correct or appropriate. It is worth repeating that, for reading purposes, grapheme-phoneme correspondences need to be adapted to the speech patterns of the pupils involved.

Table 10.1 Common Vowel Correspondences

	Grapheme	Phoneme	Examples
One Letter	⟨a⟩	/ă/	at, tack, apple
Short Vowel Sound	⟨e⟩	/ĕ/	egg, red, edit
	⟨i⟩	/ĭ/	it, tip, little
	⟨o⟩	/ŏ/	odd, rot, pocket
	⟨u⟩	/ŭ/	up, cut, muscle
	⟨y⟩	/ĭ/	hymn, mystery
One Letter	⟨a⟩	/ā/	apron, favor
Long Vowel Sound	⟨e⟩	/ē/	he, equal
	⟨i⟩	/ī/	hi, nitrate
	⟨o⟩	/ō/	go, open
	⟨u⟩	/ū/	unit, bugle
	⟨y⟩	/ī/	sky, hyphen
Two Adjacent Letters	⟨ai⟩	/ā/	aim, paint, retain
Long Vowel Sound	⟨ay⟩	/ā/	gay, mayonnaise
(dipthongs)	⟨ea⟩	/ē/	eat, peace, tea teacher
	⟨ee⟩	/ē/	eek, reel, see, needle
	⟨oa⟩	/ō/	oats, road, toaster
	⟨oi⟩	/ȯ/	oil, void, poi, recoil
	⟨ou⟩	/ȯ/	ouch, south, mountain
	⟨ow⟩	/ō/	own, growth, low
	⟨ow⟩	/ȯ/	owl, town, how bower
	⟨oy⟩	/ȯ/	oyster, joy, loyal
Vowel + Consonant +	⟨a...e⟩	/ā/	ale, bathe, partake
⟨e⟩ Vowel Sound	⟨are⟩	/â/	care
	⟨e...e⟩	/ē/	scene, recede
	⟨ere⟩	/î/	here
	⟨i...e⟩	/ī/	hide, confine
	⟨o...e⟩	/ō/	ode, hope, remote
	⟨u...e⟩	/ū/	use, mule, dispute
	⟨u...e⟩	/ü/	rule, include

	Grapheme	Phoneme	Examples
Vowel + ⟨r⟩ Vowel Sound	⟨a(r)⟩	/ä/	ark, hard, tar, bargain
	⟨ai (r)⟩	/â/	air, chair
	⟨e (r)⟩	/3/	berth, her, merger
	⟨i (r)⟩	/3/	irk, bird, stir
	⟨o (r)⟩	/ô/	orb, torn, for
	⟨oo (r)⟩	/û/	poor
	⟨u (r)⟩	/3/	urn, hurt, fur
	⟨y (r)⟩	/3/	myrrh
Single Vowel Letter Schwa Sound	⟨a⟩	/ə/	alone, local
	⟨e⟩	/ə/	element, moment
	⟨i⟩	/ə/	compatible, pencil
	⟨o⟩	/ə/	oblige, pilot
	⟨u⟩	/ə/	upon, circus
Two Vowel Letters Schwa Sound	⟨ai⟩	/ə/	fountain
	⟨ei⟩	/ə/	villein
	⟨eo⟩	/ə/	dungeon
	⟨ia⟩	/ə/	parliament
	⟨io⟩	/ə/	caution
	⟨ou⟩	/ə/	famous
Vowel + ⟨l⟩ Vowel Sound	⟨a (l)⟩	/ô/	all, talk, alter
	⟨o (l)⟩	/ŏ/	doll, solemn
	⟨o (l)⟩	/ō/	old, folk, holster
	⟨u (l)⟩	/ù/	full, pulley
Vowel + ⟨r⟩ Unstressed Vowel Sound	⟨a (r)⟩	/3/	sugar, burglar
	⟨e (r)⟩	/3/	over, leper, silver
	⟨o (r)⟩	/3/	major, tenor, sailor

Vowel Grapheme-Phoneme Correspondence Generalizations

Each of the vowel grapheme-phoneme correspondences listed above may be considered a phonic rule when all information relevant to syllabic position, stress pattern, and graphemic environment is included. It is evident that there is a large number of grapheme-phoneme correspondence rules and that each correspondence is somewhat restricted in applicability. As a result, efforts are continually made to group various combinations of correspondences and to abstract more general rules, principles, or generalizations in order to reduce the number of correspondences that pupils need to learn and to increase the applicability of each correspondence.

One such generalization is that a single vowel letter at the beginning or in the middle of a single syllable word or in an accented syllable of a multisyllabic word is a clue to a short vowel sound while a single vowel letter at the end is a clue to a long vowel sound (*ebb, bet, he; at, bat, ta/ble; ox, top, mo/tor*). This generalization is fairly reliable, particularly with regard to single-syllable root words.

Another generalization involves accented syllables that end in ⟨e⟩ preceded by a single consonant letter or by two consonant letters representing one phoneme. Instead of specifying each of the correspondences in which a single vowel phoneme is spelled by two separated vowel letters, one of which is the final ⟨e⟩ preceded by a single consonant, all these correspondences are frequently subsumed under the "Magic ⟨e⟩ Rule." This generalization stipulates that when an accented syllable has a single vowel letter followed by a single consonant letter preceding a final ⟨e⟩, the final ⟨e⟩ is "silent" and the vowel phoneme in that syllable is the long sound represented by the first vowel letter. This generalization, too, is fairly reliable despite the imprecision of its linguistic content, (*mate, Pete, bike, hole, mule, style*). Words that do not adhere to this principle are some of the ones ending in ⟨ve⟩ (*give, live, have, move, glove, shove, love, above,* and the noun *dove*) and an occasional word like *come, some,* and *adobe*. But, provided pupils do not attempt to apply it to unaccented syllables in words like *menace, package,* and *genuine,* this principle can be useful. It should be noted that accented syllables that end in ⟨e⟩ preceded by two consonant letters representing a single consonant phoneme usually follow this generalization (*bathe, writhe,* and *cloche*). A notable exception are words ending in ⟨dge⟩ and pronounced with a single final consonant sound, such as *badge, edge, ridge, fudge,* and *lodge*.

Another general rule relates to vowel grapheme-phoneme correspondences when vowel phonemes are represented by adjacent vowel letters. This generalization is often expressed as "When two vowels go walking, the first does the talking." It states that two adjacent vowel letters usually represent the long vowel sound ordinarily represented by the first vowel letter alone. Close examination of this rule, however, suggests that this is a gross misrepresentation of the facts. When only the vowel letters ⟨a⟩, ⟨e⟩, ⟨i⟩, ⟨o⟩, and ⟨u⟩ are considered, as in the boxed area in Figure 10.1, the rule applies with any degree of consistency to only the five circled combinations. When the three semi-vowels ⟨y⟩, ⟨w⟩, and ⟨h⟩ are added only two additional combinations conform. (It should be noted that some of the combinations of letters shown in the figure do not occur in English syllables.)

Figure 10.1

Even the grapheme-phoneme correspondences for each of the circled combinations of vowel letters have many exceptions, such as ⟨ea⟩ in *bread,* ⟨ee⟩ in *been,* ⟨ai⟩ in *said,* and ⟨oe⟩ in *shoe.* Pupils who are taught to apply this two-vowel generalization become disenchanted with the "rules of phonics" very soon. It is more helpful to pupils to teach specific pairs of vowel letters and their correspondences.

Since the utility of other commonly taught generalizations may also be limited, teachers of reading should be wary of employing them and should instead emphasize specific grapheme-phoneme correspondences. Even where a generalization is actually functional, as in the case of ⟨oa⟩ conforming to the "walking-talking" vowel rule discussed above, the word identification process is much faster if the pupil can immediately call to mind the phoneme represented by the grapheme rather than attempt to recall the applicable generalization and fit it to the spelling pattern in question. In other words, it is much faster to infer /ō/ from ⟨oa⟩ directly than to relate the ⟨oa⟩ to the "walking-talking" vowel rule and reason that under the circumstances set forth in that rule ⟨oa⟩ must represent /ō/.

Consonant Grapheme-Phoneme Correspondences

The consonant grapheme-phoneme correspondences of American English are not as variable as are the vowel correspondences; that is, there is greater consistency between letters and the sounds they represent. This is true of both single consonant letters and consonant letter combinations. The consonant correspondences presented below are arranged according to patterns commonly found in reading instructional materials.

Table 10.2 Consonant Grapheme-Phoneme Correspondences

	Grapheme	Phoneme	Examples
Single Letter/	⟨b⟩	/b/	bat, rob
Single Sound	⟨c⟩	/k/	cat, sac
	⟨c⟩	/s/	cent, face
	⟨d⟩	/d/	doll, red
	⟨f⟩	/f/	fat, if
	⟨g⟩	/g/	go, dog
	⟨g⟩	/j/	gem, page
	⟨h⟩	/h/	he
	⟨j⟩	/j/	jam
	⟨k⟩	/k/	keep, seek
	⟨l⟩	/l/	light, coal
	⟨m⟩	/m/	me, am
	⟨n⟩	/n/	no, in
	⟨p⟩	/p/	pill, cup
	⟨r⟩	/r/	run, dear
	⟨s⟩	/s/	say, bus
	⟨s⟩	/z/	his
	⟨s⟩	/š/	sure
	⟨t⟩	/t/	tell, it
	⟨t⟩	/č/	future
	⟨v⟩	/v/	verb, love
	⟨w⟩	/w/	wet
	⟨x⟩	/z/	xylophone
	⟨y⟩	/y/	yes
	⟨z⟩	/z/	zeal, quiz
	⟨z⟩	/ž/	azure
Double Letter/	⟨bb⟩	/b/	ebb, rabbit
Single Sound	⟨cc⟩	/k/	account

Grapheme	Phoneme	Examples
⟨dd⟩	/d/	a<u>dd</u>, la<u>dd</u>er
⟨ff⟩	/f/	mu<u>ff</u>, mu<u>ff</u>in
⟨gg⟩	/g/	e<u>gg</u>, nu<u>gg</u>et
⟨gg⟩	/j/	exa<u>gg</u>erate
⟨ll⟩	/l/	pu<u>ll</u>, ba<u>ll</u>oon
⟨mm⟩	/m/	Gri<u>mm</u>, co<u>mm</u>on
⟨nn⟩	/n/	i<u>nn</u>, ma<u>nn</u>er
⟨pp⟩	/p/	La<u>pp</u>, ha<u>pp</u>y
⟨rr⟩	/r/	bu<u>rr</u>, pa<u>rr</u>ot
⟨ss⟩	/s/	lo<u>ss</u>, me<u>ss</u>age
⟨ss⟩	/š/	i<u>ss</u>ue
⟨ss⟩	/z/	sci<u>ss</u>ors
⟨tt⟩	/t/	mu<u>tt</u>, bo<u>tt</u>om
⟨vv⟩	/v/	fli<u>vv</u>er
⟨zz⟩	/z/	fu<u>zz</u>, da<u>zz</u>le

Sequences of consecutive consonant phonemes occur in English words. In writing, they are usually represented by sequences of consecutive consonant letters. These units of consonants are generally called *clusters* in linguistic writings and *blends* in reading instructional materials.

There seem to be built-in restrictions on the number of consonant sounds that can occur in a blend. The maximum number for the beginning of a syllable is three, in which case the third is always /r/ or /l/, as in *strain, scream,* and *splurge.* The maximum number for the end of a syllable is four; in such cases, the last one is always an inflectional ending *(glimpsed, tempts).* However, it is recommended that grapheme-phoneme correspondences be considered within individual morpheme units, not across morpheme boundaries. For the purposes of phonics, three consecutive consonant phonemes may be regarded as the maximum length of consonant blends in final as well as initial position.

Consonant blends are usually grouped in two categories: those that commonly occur at beginnings of single syllable root words and those that commonly occur at their ends. The distinction between these two classifications is important, since they function differently in the internal portions of multisyllabic words. Combinations of letters that represent final blend sounds are divided in segmenting multisyllabic morphemes, but those that represent initial blends are not. Hence, the letters ⟨rd⟩ in *par/don* are divided, but the letters ⟨pr⟩ in *a/pron* are not. There are some sequences of consonant sounds that never occur within the same syllable in English, such as /bj/ in *ob/ject,* /zb/ in *hus/band,* and /vr/ in *chev/ron.* Syllabic divisions automatically occur between them in multisyllabic words.

Only three consonant blends occur with approximately equal frequency as initial and final blends. They are (1) ⟨sp⟩ representing /sp/ as in *spell* and *grasp;* (2) ⟨sc⟩ or ⟨sk⟩ representing /sk/ as in *scale* and *ask;* and (3) ⟨st⟩ representing /st/ as in *stage* and *rust.* All other blends may be identified predominantly with one position or the other. In a number of cases final blends are reversals of initial blends as are, for example, the initial and final blends in *broad*/*barb, flop*/*elf,* and *drain*/*hard.*

Most consonants that occur singly at beginnings or ends of single syllable root words can also combine with selected other consonants to form blends in those positions. Exceptions are initial /z/, /č/, /j/, and /y/, which never occur in initial consonant blends.

Table 10.3 Consonant Blends

	Grapheme	Phoneme	Examples
Two Letters/	⟨bl⟩	/bl/	black, oblique
Two Sounds	⟨br⟩	/br/	break, library
(initial)	⟨cl⟩	/kl/	clip, seclude
	⟨cr⟩	/kr/	crust, across
	⟨dr⟩	/dr/	draw, quadrant
	⟨dw⟩	/dw/	dwell
	⟨fl⟩	/fl/	flood
	⟨fr⟩	/fr/	free, afraid
	⟨gl⟩	/gl/	glass, aglow
	⟨gr⟩	/gr/	green, vagrant
	⟨pl⟩	/pl/	play, diploma
	⟨pr⟩	/pr/	proud, apron
	⟨qu⟩	/kw/	queen, sequence
	⟨sc⟩	/sk/	scare, ascorbic
	⟨sk⟩	/sk/	skate, askance
	⟨sl⟩	/sl/	slow, aslant
	⟨sm⟩	/sm/	small
	⟨sn⟩	/sn/	snow
	⟨sp⟩	/sp/	speech, asparkle
	⟨st⟩	/st/	stop, astonish
	⟨sv⟩	/sv/	svelte
	⟨sw⟩	/sw/	swim
	⟨tr⟩	/tr/	trip, quatrain
	⟨tw⟩	/tw/	twin, between
Two Letters/	⟨ct⟩	/kt/	sect
Two Sounds	⟨dz⟩	/dz/	adz
(final)	⟨ft⟩	/ft/	raft

Grapheme	Phoneme	Examples
⟨lb⟩	/lb/	bul<u>b</u>
⟨lc⟩	/lk/	tal<u>c</u>
⟨ld⟩	/ld/	hol<u>d</u>
⟨lf⟩	/lf/	sel<u>f</u>
⟨lk⟩	/lk/	bul<u>k</u>
⟨lm⟩	/lm/	hel<u>m</u>
⟨ln⟩	/ln/	ki<u>ln</u>
⟨lp⟩	/lp/	pul<u>p</u>
⟨lt⟩	/lt/	sa<u>lt</u>
⟨mp⟩	/mp/	ju<u>mp</u>
⟨nd⟩	/nd/	ha<u>nd</u>
⟨nk⟩	/ŋk/	pi<u>nk</u>
⟨nt⟩	/nt/	pa<u>nt</u>
⟨pt⟩	/pt/	ra<u>pt</u>
⟨rb⟩	/rb/	bar<u>b</u>
⟨rc⟩	/rk/	ar<u>c</u>
⟨rd⟩	/rd/	boar<u>d</u>
⟨rf⟩	/rf/	scar<u>f</u>
⟨rg⟩	/rg/	ber<u>g</u>
⟨rk⟩	/rk/	dar<u>k</u>
⟨rl⟩	/rl/	cur<u>l</u>
⟨rm⟩	/rm/	fa<u>rm</u>
⟨rn⟩	/rn/	wa<u>rn</u>
⟨rp⟩	/rp/	har<u>p</u>
⟨rt⟩	/rt/	pa<u>rt</u>
⟨sk⟩	/sk/	ta<u>sk</u>
⟨sp⟩	/sp/	wa<u>sp</u>
⟨st⟩	/st/	te<u>st</u>
⟨tz⟩	/ts/	bli<u>tz</u>
Three Letters/		
Three Sounds		
(initial)		
⟨scl⟩	/skl/	<u>scl</u>erosis
⟨scr⟩	/skr/	<u>scr</u>eam, e<u>scr</u>ow
⟨spr⟩	/spr/	<u>spr</u>ing, o<u>spr</u>ey
⟨str⟩	/str/	<u>str</u>ipe, fru<u>str</u>ate
Three Letters/		
Three Sounds		
(final)		
⟨lct⟩	/lkt/	mu<u>lct</u>
⟨ltz⟩	/lts/	wa<u>ltz</u>
⟨mpt⟩	/mpt/	pro<u>mpt</u>
⟨nct⟩	/ŋkt/	disti<u>nct</u>
⟨ntz⟩	/nts/	chi<u>ntz</u>
⟨rld⟩	/rld/	wo<u>rld</u>
⟨rpt⟩	/rpt/	exce<u>rpt</u>
⟨rst⟩	/rst/	fi<u>rst</u>
⟨rtz⟩	/rts/	qua<u>rtz</u>

Digraphs are combinations of consonant letters that represent single phonemes that neither letter in the combination ordinarily represents alone. The letters ⟨wh⟩ are not a digraph. When ⟨wh⟩ occur in words, they most often represent the /hw/ blend as in *wheat, wheel,* and *when.* They may also represent /h/, as in *who,* or, in many English dialects, where there is no contrast at all between /w/ and /hw/, simply /w/. In none of the above alternatives do ⟨wh⟩ represent a single sound that is different from those usually represented by ⟨w⟩ or ⟨h⟩ alone.

Table 10.4 Consonant Digraphs and Digraph Blends

	Grapheme	Phoneme	Examples
Two Letters/	⟨ch⟩	/č/	chi<u>ld</u>, ea<u>ch</u>
One Sound	⟨ph⟩	/f/	<u>ph</u>one, gra<u>ph</u>
(digraphs)	⟨sh⟩	/š/	<u>sh</u>ip, fi<u>sh</u>
	⟨th⟩	/ə/	<u>th</u>in, bo<u>th</u>
	⟨th⟩	/đ/	<u>th</u>en, ba<u>th</u>e
	final ⟨gh⟩	/f/	rou<u>gh</u>
	final ⟨ng⟩	/ŋ/	si<u>ng</u>
Three Letters/	⟨chl⟩	/kl/	<u>chl</u>orine
Two Sounds	⟨chr⟩	/kr/	<u>chr</u>ome
(initial digraph	⟨phl⟩	/fl/	<u>phl</u>egm
blends)	⟨phr⟩	/fr/	<u>phr</u>ase
	⟨shr⟩	/šr/	<u>shr</u>imp
	⟨sph⟩	/sf/	<u>sph</u>ere
	⟨thr⟩	/ər/	<u>thr</u>ead
	⟨thw⟩	/əw/	<u>thw</u>art
Three Letters/	⟨dth⟩	/də/	wi<u>dth</u>
Two Sounds	⟨fth⟩	/fə/	fi<u>fth</u>
(final digraph	⟨lch⟩	/lč/	be<u>lch</u>
blends)	⟨lph⟩	/lf/	sy<u>lph</u>
	⟨lsh⟩	/lš/	We<u>lsh</u>
	⟨lth⟩	/lə/	wea<u>lth</u>
	⟨mph⟩	/mf/	ly<u>mph</u>
	⟨nch⟩	/nč/	pu<u>nch</u>
	⟨nth⟩	/nə/	mo<u>nth</u>
	⟨rch⟩	/rč/	sta<u>rch</u>
	⟨rsh⟩	/rš/	ha<u>rsh</u>
	⟨rth⟩	/rə/	wo<u>rth</u>

	Grapheme	Phoneme	Example
Four Letters/	⟨lfth⟩	/lfə/	twelfth
Three Sounds	⟨ŋgth⟩	/ŋkə/	length
(final digraph	⟨rmth⟩	/rmə/	warmth
blends)			

Some single phonemes are spelled by a combination of consonant letters in which one letter may not represent any phoneme. These letters are frequently called "silent" letters. They usually occur in words in which at one time the letters did represent phonemes, which were dropped from the words as spoken English has developed and changed. Certain combinations of these letters occur at beginnings of words and others at ends of words.

Table 10.5 Silent Consonant Combinations

	Grapheme	Phoneme	Examples
Two Letters/	⟨gh⟩	/g/	ghost
One Sound	⟨gn⟩	/n/	gnat
(initial)	⟨kn⟩	/n/	knock
	⟨mn⟩	/n/	mnemonic
	⟨pn⟩	/n/	pneumonia
	⟨pt⟩	/t/	ptomaine
	⟨rh⟩	/r/	rhyme
	⟨sc⟩	/s/	scent
	⟨sw⟩	/s/	sword
	⟨wh⟩	/h/	who
	⟨wh⟩	/w/	whale
	⟨wr⟩	/r/	write
Two Letters/	⟨bt⟩	/t/	doubt
One Sound	⟨ck⟩	/k/	back
(final)	⟨gn⟩	/n/	sign
	⟨ld⟩	/d/	would
	⟨lf⟩	/f/	calf
	⟨lk⟩	/k/	walk
	⟨lm⟩	/m/	calm
	⟨mb⟩	/m/	comb
	⟨mn⟩	/m/	solemn
	⟨tch⟩	/č/	match

Grapheme Base Correspondences

Units consisting of various combinations of consonant and vowel phonemes are very useful in word identification. Not only are they longer units than individual grapheme-phoneme correspondences, but they are complete pronunciation units as opposed to individual sound units. Therefore, they are easier to pronounce in isolation than are single consonants or combinations of only consonant sounds. Since they include both a vowel sound and a consonant sound or sounds, they are syllables in themselves.

Such units are frequently called *word families, phonograms, spelling patterns, syllabic units,* and *rhyming words.* Since they form the bases of words, they are also referred to as *grapheme bases.* They may consist of vowel-consonant or consonant-vowel phoneme sequences. The consonant sounds involved may be either single consonants or consonant blends. Vowel-consonant sequences such as ⟨at⟩ or ⟨ick⟩ are called final grapheme bases since they occur at the ends of words *(cat, bat, fat; Dick, kick, lick).* Consonant-vowel sequences such as ⟨bea⟩ and ⟨coo⟩ are called initial grapheme bases since they occur at beginnings of words *(bead, beak, beam; cool, coon, coop).* Consonants may be added to the beginnings of the final bases and to the ends of the initial bases to build a number of words that share the same grapheme base.

Pupils may be taught to respond to grapheme bases as units. They may also be taught to respond to whole words consisting of grapheme bases, prefaced or followed by consonants or consonant blends, such as *mad, pad, sad, shad, brad, glad,* and *grad.*   It is important that teachers be alert for possible vowel phoneme changes due to graphemic environment factors when building "families of words." For example, because the grapheme-phoneme correspondence of ⟨a⟩ is affected if preceded by ⟨w⟩, the word *wad* should not be included in the above "⟨ad⟩ word family."

One of the greatest shortcomings of grapheme bases is that words sharing a common spelling pattern are not necessarily pronounced alike in all dialects. The ⟨og⟩ grapheme base is a case in point. The following words share this letter sequence: *bog, cog, dog, fog, hog, jog, log, tog, clog, flog, frog, grog, slog,* and *smog.* In some dialects the vowel phoneme in all these words is /ŏ/, and in others it is /ô/. These cases present no problem. But in some dialects some of the words are pronounced with /ŏ/ while others are pronounced with /ô/, and the distribution of these vowel phonemes varies among the dialects. In these cases pupils may have problems making sense out of what is taught to them.

Another risk involved in using grapheme bases is that specific sequences of letters may serve different functions in different words. If pupils learn that the grapheme base ⟨me⟩ represents /mē/, they may have difficulty responding to the ⟨me⟩ in words like *met, time,* and *mechanic.* Such confusion can be avoided by not placing undue emphasis on phonics and by combining phonic clues with other kinds of word identification techniques.

Sometimes nonsense syllables are included in word families on the theory that they constitute syllables in multisyllabic words and so will be helpful in identifying such words. Although ⟨rad⟩ and ⟨gog⟩ do not spell English words, they might be added to the ⟨ad⟩ and ⟨og⟩ grapheme base families because they constitute syllables in many multisyllabic words such as *radical* and *goggle.* Recognizing them as familiar grapheme-phoneme correspondence units can help expedite word identification of multisyllabic words.

The grapheme base patterns may include only one vowel letter and one consonant letter or more than one letter of each kind (⟨ip⟩ represents /ĭp/, ⟨eal⟩ represents /ēl/, ⟨each⟩ represents /ēč/, ⟨edge⟩ represents /ĕj/, and so on). Since grapheme bases usually represent single syllables, only one vowel phoneme should be represented by the vowel letters. Occasionally, multisyllabic bases may be used. For example, the final grapheme base correspondence ⟨able⟩ represents /ā′bəl/ may be used to identify words like *table, gable, fable, sable, cable, and stable.*

Initial grapheme bases are more limited in number than final grapheme bases and are contained in fewer numbers of words. They involve vowel phonemes that are spelled with more than one letter. When vowel phonemes are represented by more than one letter in a stressed syllable, syllabic position is no longer a determining factor in the grapheme-phoneme correspondence. For example, ⟨ea⟩ represents /ē/ at the beginning, middle, or end of a syllable (eat, meat, sea). When the open syllable ⟨bee⟩ is used as an initial grapheme base, the vowel phoneme remains /ē/ as consonants are added to the end of it (beef, beet, beech). If a single letter represents the vowel phoneme in an initial grapheme base, the vowel phoneme changes when consonants are added to the end of it, changing the open syllable to a closed one. The vowel sound in ⟨be⟩ is /ē/, but it becomes /ĕ/ in *bet, beg,* and *bench.*

Implications for Teaching Grapheme-Phoneme Correspondences

Word forms may be analyzed into different combinations of grapheme-phoneme correspondence units for word indentification purposes. The grapheme-phoneme correspondences in the word *steed,* for example, may be itemized in any of the following combinations, all equally correct.

1. a. First letter ⟨s⟩ represents /s/
   b. Second letter ⟨t⟩ represents /t/
   c. Third and fourth letters ⟨ee⟩ represent /ē/ in accented syllable
   d. Last letter ⟨d⟩ represents /d/
2. a. Initial ⟨st⟩ represents /st/ blend
   b. Medial ⟨ee⟩ represents /ē/ in accented syllable
   c. Final ⟨d⟩ represents /d/
3. a. Initial grapheme base ⟨stee⟩ represents /stē/
   b. Final ⟨d⟩ represents /d/
4. a. Initial ⟨st⟩ represents /st/ blend
   b. Final grapheme base ⟨eed⟩ represents /ēd/

The first combination is based on individual phoneme units, which are the smallest correspondence units. There are four such individual grapheme-phoneme correspondences in the word *steed.* When graphemes and phonemes are combined into larger units, as in the second, third, and fourth combinations, the number of correspondences decreases and word identification speeds up. Pupils should be taught to analyze words using different kinds of grapheme-phoneme correspondences to acquire both flexibility and efficiency in the use of phonic clues. Pupils reading do not necessarily use the same type of phonic analysis each time they encounter and identify given words. They may use one combination of clues one time and other combinations other times, depending on how much information they already have about the words from other sources.

Exercises

The purpose of the following exercises is to provide practice in identifying phonic clues in word forms. The first exercise involves only grapheme-phoneme correspondences. The second exercise deals with the application of syllabication and accenting principles as well as grapheme-phoneme correspondences.

Exercise A. The purpose of this exercise is to provide practice in analyzing single-syllable root word forms into their grapheme-phoneme correspondences. Itemize all the grapheme-phoneme correspondences that are present in each word. Wherever appropriate, use consonant blends instead of individual consonant grapheme-phoneme correspondences. Indicate any grapheme bases which may be present in the words. Remember to use angle brackets and slash marks to differentiate graphemes from phonemes. Some items involve real words and some involve pseudowords. A sample item is done for you.

> *Example*
> *chase*
> a. initial ⟨ch⟩ represents /č/
> b. medial ⟨a(Ce)⟩ represents /ā/ in accented syllable
> c. final ⟨s(e)⟩ represents /s/
> d. final grapheme base ⟨ase⟩ represents /ās/
>
> *Real Words*
> 1. *scent*
> 2. *clown*
> 3. *phone*
> 4. *fright*
> 5. *choice*
>
> *Pseudowords*
> 6. *troick*
> 7. *knule*
> 8. *dwerd*
> 9. *scrump*
> 10. *theemb*
>
> *Answer*
1. *scent*
   - a. initial ⟨sc(e)⟩ represents /s/
   - b. medial ⟨e⟩ in accented syllable represents /ĕ/
   - c. final ⟨nt⟩ represents /nt/ blend
   - d. final grapheme base ⟨ent⟩ represents /ĕnt/
2. *clown*
   - a. initial ⟨cl⟩ represents /kl/ blend
   - b. medial ⟨ow⟩ in accented syllable represents /ö/
   - c. final ⟨n⟩ represents /n/
   - d. final grapheme base ⟨own⟩ represents /ön/

3. *phone*
   a. initial ⟨ph⟩ digraph represents /f/
   b. medial ⟨o(Ce)⟩ in accented syllable represents /ō/
   c. final ⟨n(e)⟩ represents /n/
   d. final grapheme base ⟨one⟩ represents /ōn/
4. *fright*
   a. initial ⟨fr⟩ represents /fr/ blend
   b. medial ⟨igh⟩ in accented syllable represents /ī/
   c. final ⟨t⟩ represents /t/
   d. final grapheme base ⟨ight⟩ represents /īt/
5. *choice*
   a. initial ⟨ch⟩ digraph represents /č/
   b. medial ⟨oi⟩ in accented syllable represents /ò/
   c. final ⟨c(e)⟩ represents /s/
6. *troick*
   a. initial ⟨tr⟩ represents /tr/ blend
   b. medial ⟨oi⟩ in accented syllable represents /ò/
   c. final ⟨ck⟩ represents /k/
7. *knule*
   a. initial ⟨kn⟩ represents /n/
   b. medial ⟨u(Ce)⟩ in accented syllable represents /ü/
   c. final ⟨l(e)⟩ represents /l/
8. *dwerd*
   a. initial ⟨dw⟩ represents /dw/ blend
   b. medial ⟨er⟩ in accented syllable represents /3/
   c. final ⟨d⟩ represents /d/
9. *scrump*
   a. initial ⟨scr⟩ represents /skr/ blend
   b. medial ⟨u⟩ in accented syllable represents /ŭ/
   c. final ⟨mp⟩ represents /mp/ blend
   d. final grapheme base ⟨ump⟩ represents /ŭmp/
10. *theemb*
    a. initial ⟨th⟩ digraph represents /ə/
    b. medial ⟨ee⟩ in accented syllable represents /ē/
    c. final ⟨mb⟩ represents /m/

Exercise B. The purpose of this exercise is to provide practice in analyzing multisyllabic root word forms into all of their phonic components, including syllabic divisions, accent patterns, and grapheme-phoneme correspondences. Indicate the syllabic divisions and accent patterns that apply to each word and the principles on which they are based. List all the grapheme-phoneme correspondences that are present in each word. Some items involve real words and some items involve pseudowords. A sample item is done for you.

> *Example*
> *audit*   /ô'dət/
> a. two separated vowel letter units suggest two syllables
> b. ⟨VCV⟩ spelling pattern suggests ⟨V/CV⟩ syllabic division because there is only one consonant letter between the vowel letter units
> c. vowel sound spelled by two vowel letters suggests primary accent is on first syllable
> d. open ⟨au⟩ in accented syllable represents /ô/
> e. initial ⟨d⟩ represents /d/
> f. medial ⟨i⟩ in unaccented syllable represents /ə/
> g. final ⟨t⟩ represents /t/
>
> *Real Words*
> 1. *cajole*
> 2. *dolphin*
> 3. *parsnip*
>
> *Pseudowords*
> 4. *staivron*
> 5. *shofle*
> 6. *splishete*
>
> *Answer*

1. *cajole*   /kə jōl'/
      a. three separated vowel letters, one of which is final ⟨e⟩ preceded by a single consonant, suggest two syllables
      b. ⟨VCV⟩ spelling pattern suggests ⟨V/CV⟩ syllabic division
      c. vowel sound spelled by more than one letter suggests primary accent on second syllable
      d. initial ⟨c(a)⟩ represents /k/
      e. final ⟨a⟩ in unaccented syllable represents /ə/
      f. initial ⟨j⟩ represents /j/
      g. medial ⟨o(C)e⟩ in accented syllable represents /ō/
      h. final ⟨l(e)⟩ represents /l/
      i. final grapheme base ⟨ole⟩ represents /ōl/
2. *dolphin*   /dôl'fən/
      a. two separated vowel letters suggest two syllables
      b. ⟨VCCCV⟩ spelling pattern, in which the second and third

consonants represent a digraph, suggests ⟨VC/CCV⟩ syllabic division

c. each syllable having only one vowel letter suggests primary accent on first syllable

d. initial ⟨d⟩ represents /d/

e. medial ⟨o(l)⟩ in accented syllable represents /ô/

f. final ⟨l⟩ represents /l/

g. initial ⟨ph⟩ digraph represents /f/

h. medial ⟨i⟩ in unaccented syllable represents /ə/

i. final ⟨n⟩ represents /n/

3. *parsnip*   /pär′snəp/

a. two separated vowel letters suggest two syllables

b. ⟨VCCCV⟩ spelling pattern, in which the second and third consonants represent an initial consonant blend, suggests ⟨VC/CCV⟩ syllabic division

c. each syllable having only one vowel letter suggests primary accent on the first syllable

d. initial ⟨p⟩ represents /p/

e. medial ⟨a(r)⟩ in accented syllable represents /ä/

f. final ⟨r⟩ represents /r/

g. initial ⟨sn⟩ represents /sn/ blend

h. medial ⟨i⟩ in unaccented syllable represents /ə/

i. final ⟨p⟩ represents /p/

j. final grapheme base ⟨ar⟩ represents /är/

4. *staivron*   /stāv′rən/

a. two separated vowel letter units suggest two syllables

b. ⟨VCCV⟩ spelling pattern, in which the two consonants do not represent either a digraph or an initial blend, suggests ⟨VC/CV⟩ syllabic division

c. vowel sound spelled by two letters suggests primary accent on first syllable

d. initial ⟨st⟩ represents /st/ blend

e. medial ⟨ai⟩ in accented syllable represents /ā/

f. final ⟨v⟩ represents /v/

g. initial ⟨r⟩ represents /r/

h. medial ⟨o⟩ in unaccented syllable represents /ə/

i. final ⟨n⟩ represents /n/

5. *shofle*   /šō′fəl/

a. two separated vowel letter units suggests two syllables

  b. ⟨VCle⟩ spelling pattern suggests ⟨V/Cle⟩ syllabic division

  c. the ⟨le⟩ ending on the second syllable suggests that primary stress is on the first syllable

  d. initial ⟨sh⟩ digraph represents /š/

  e. final ⟨o⟩ in accented syllable represents /ō/

  f. initial ⟨f⟩ represents /f/

  g. final ⟨le⟩ in unaccented syllable represents /əl/

6. *splishete* /splə šēt′/

  a. three separated vowel letters, one of which is final ⟨e⟩ preceded by a single consonant, suggest two syllables

  b. ⟨VCCV⟩ spelling pattern in which the two consonants represent a digraph suggests ⟨V/CCV⟩ syllabic division

  c. the second syllable having the vowel sound spelled by two vowel letters suggests primary accent on the second syllable

  d. initial ⟨spl⟩ represents /spl/ blend

  e. final ⟨i⟩ in unaccented syllable represents /ə/

  f. initial ⟨sh⟩ digraph represents /š/

  g. medial ⟨e(C)e⟩ in accented syllable represents /ē/

  h. final ⟨t(e)⟩ represents /t/

Suggested Activities for Pupil Practice

General Considerations for Teachers

It is important to focus activities on the specific skill(s) you want pupils to practice. Pupils should not be able to get the right answers except by applying the skill(s) you want them to practice.

 Activities intended to provide practice in using grapheme-phoneme correspondences should use words in isolation. In addition, when sentences are used, the target words in them should not be in the pupils' oral vocabularies. This way semantic clues will not lead to the identification of the target words. An example is the word *dab* in the sentence "Ellie put a dab of paint on the paper." The word *dab* is not likely to be in the vocabulary of many beginning readers, but since it is made up of consistent grapheme-phoneme correspondences, it can be identified phonically.

Guard against using items in activities that have unintentional common elements, since this might encourage pupils to make unwarranted generalizations. If, in an activity that focuses on the grapheme-phoneme correspondence between ⟨b⟩ and /b/, all the words begin with the letters ⟨ba⟩—such as *bat, bag, back,* and *ban*—the pupils may generalize that the ⟨a⟩ is an essential component of the grapheme-phoneme correspondence between ⟨b⟩ and /b/. It is important that the vowel following the ⟨b⟩ be varied.

Activities similar to those that are described for pupil practice may be used as diagnostic skills tests or as criterion-referenced tests to analyze pupils' proficiencies and deficiencies in the use of specific phonic clues. Such diagnostic test activities may be administered before and/or after teaching the skills.

Activity 1

Purpose. To provide practice in associating the initial grapheme ⟨p⟩ with the phoneme /p/ as a clue to the identification of written words

Level. Early primary.

Directions for Teachers. It is easier to teach pupils a grapheme-phoneme correspondence if they already know a few words that contain that correspondence and that they can recognize using other kinds of word identification clues. However, it is possible to teach it to them without this background. Since a grapheme-phoneme correspondence involves the association of a particular grapheme with a particular phoneme, pupils must be able to discriminate visually the grapheme from other graphemes and to discriminate aurally the phoneme from other phonemes. The first step in an activity on grapheme-phoneme correspondence should always be to determine if pupils can make these discriminations. If they cannot, these abilities must be developed before any effective work can be done in relation to the selected grapheme-phoneme correspondence.

Visual discrimination of a grapheme may be ascertained by letter-matching activities. One such activity might consist of showing pupils a letter shape and requiring them to find a similar letter or letters in a list or line, or on a page of random letters. If you plan to present the grapheme-phoneme correspondence with the grapheme appearing in both capital and lower case forms, your visual discrimination exercises should include both forms. You should make sure that pupils associate the lower case form with the capital form of the letter. The selected grapheme should be contrasted with other graphemes similar in appearance and, therefore, likely to be confused with it.

Auditory discrimination of a phoneme may be ascertained by sound-matching activities. One such activity might consist of having pupils listen to pairs of words, one word of each pair beginning with the selected phoneme and the other beginning with a different phoneme. It is important that the phoneme occur in words in the same syllabic position or positions (initial, medial, or final) in which the grapheme-phoneme correspondence will be developed. The selected phoneme should be contrasted with other phonemes that are similar in sound and, therefore, are likely to be confused with it.

Once the visual and auditory discriminations have been ensured, the grapheme-phoneme correspondence may be developed. The following activity to teach the correspondence of initial ⟨p⟩ with /p/ begins with exercises designed to check on pupils' ability to visually discriminate ⟨p⟩ and ⟨P⟩ and auditorally discriminate initial /p/. It then develops the correspondence itself.

For visual discrimination of the grapheme, prepare several lines of letter shapes. Each line should contain several instances of the letter ⟨p⟩ and other letters that share common configuration features with the letter ⟨p⟩, as in the given example:

```
p — q   p   b   q   d   p
P — B   D   P   F   P   R
p — F   P   B   R   P   P
P — p   b   q   p   d   p
```

Write the lines of letters on a chalkboard, chart, transparency, or ditto sheet, leaving adequate space between letters and lines. Elicit from pupils the name of the letter at the beginning of each line. If pupils do not know it, you should name it for them. In either case, use the letter name frequently throughout the lesson to ensure their familiarity with it. (Communication throughout the lesson is facilitated if pupils know the name of the grapheme. However, the letter name is not essential to establishing the grapheme-phoneme correspondence since the correspondence is between the visual *shape* and the phoneme.) Direct pupils to look at the first line of letters. Ask them to tell you the name of the letter at the beginning of the line. Tell them to find and draw circles around all the other ⟨p⟩'s in that line. Do the remaining lines of letters the same way.

If pupils are able to match the letters, continue with the lesson. If pupils are unable to match the letters, they are not ready to learn the grapheme-phoneme correspondence. Instead, you should work on developing their visual discrimination of ⟨p⟩.

For auditory discrimination of the phoneme, prepare several pairs of single-syllable words in which one of the words in each pair begins with the phoneme /p/ and the other word in the pair begins with another, similar sounding phoneme. (Since /p/ is a stop consonant, other stop consonants should be used for contrast.) In a few of the pairs the words should be identical and begin with the phoneme /p/. This is strictly an oral-aural activity; the spelling of the words is irrelevant. Minimal contrast pairs of words—words that are identical with the exception of one phoneme in comparable position in both words—are an effective means of ascertaining auditory discrimination of a given phoneme. Single-syllable words should be used to minimize the distracting elements that are present in longer words. The following pairs of words, including minimal pairs, are for discriminating /p/ in initial position:

pit	—	kit
park	—	park
bowl	—	pole
dig	—	pig
push	—	push
gun	—	pun
pack	—	tack
post	—	post

Pronounce one pair of words at a time and ask pupils to indicate whether both words in the pair begin with the same sound or with different sounds. Give directions to pupils *before* you pronounce the words so that they will know what to listen for as you say the words. If pupils are able to make the auditory discriminations successfully, continue with the lesson. If pupils are unable to make these discriminations successfully, they are not ready to learn the grapheme-phoneme correspondence involving /p/. Instead, you should work on the development of the auditory discrimination of /p/.

At this point, pupils are ready to develop an awareness and understanding of the correspondence between the grapheme ⟨p⟩ and the phoneme /p/ that it represents in the initial position of single-syllable words. This is best done by guiding pupils through an inductive reasoning process, leading them to develop their own generalization concerning the grapheme-phoneme correspondence. Present a list of words on a chalkboard, chart, transparency, or ditto sheet. Present enough words on which to base a generalization. The words should all begin with the letter ⟨p⟩ representing /p/ and preferably should be one-syllable words the pupils can recognize in print. The letter ⟨p⟩ should be followed by a vowel letter in all the words and not by a consonant letter to avoid digraphs, blends, and silent letters. The following are words that might be used: *pig, pet, pan, pat, put,* and *paint.* Have pupils read the list of words aloud. Then ask them if all the words begin with the same sound. If they reply affirmatively, ask them if all the words begin with the same letter. If they reply affirmatively again, ask them what letter spells the sound heard at the beginning of all the words. (The pupils can answer this last question only if they know the letter name.) Then ask if the same letter would spell the sound heard at the beginning of words like *past, pick,* and *punch.* (Note that these words were not included in any of the previous activities and also that responding to this question does not require knowledge of the letter name.) Try to avoid asking questions that will require pupils to answer by pronouncing /p/ in isolation since it is difficult to do without adding a vowel sound and distorting it. If pupils are able to answer correctly, continue with the lesson.

If pupils are unable to associate the grapheme ⟨p⟩ with the phoneme /p/, you should go back to the first activity in this lesson to review the visual discrimination of ⟨p⟩ and the auditory discrimination of /p/ in the initial position of words. Then repeat the grapheme-phoneme correspondence activity as described above but using a different set of words (*pal, pour, patch, pint, paste, pop*).

To provide pupils with practice in making the visual-auditory association of ⟨p⟩ with /p/, an activity using letter substitution can be useful. This kind of activity requires the replacement of a grapheme in a given position in a known word with a target grapheme. In this instance, the letter ⟨p⟩ would be used to replace the grapheme in the initial position of words already familiar to the pupils. A suggested procedure is to write on the chalkboard or on a transparency (so that pupils may erase and write in letters as needed) a familiar word such as *sat,* and ask pupils to read the word orally. Then ask one pupil to erase the first letter, replace it with the letter ⟨p⟩, and to read the new word orally. The same procedure may be followed with additional words, as in these examples:

mop	—	pop
rest	—	pest
tin	—	pin
men	—	pen
tie	—	pie

Another kind of activity useful for practicing the association of ⟨p⟩ with /p/ is one in which the ⟨p⟩ is used to fill in a blank space in words written on a chalkboard, chart, transparency, or ditto sheet. Note the following list:

_art
_ick
_al
_ine
_et

Call on one pupil at a time to write in the letter ⟨p⟩ and to read the whole word aloud until all the words have been completed. Then have one or more pupils read the whole list of completed words orally.

Since most reading involves words in meaningful context rather than unrelated words in lists the correspondence practiced above should be used in contextual settings. Context will permit the use of semantic and syntactic clues in conjunction with phonic clues for greater efficiency in word identification. For this purpose, construct sentences which include words involving the grapheme-phoneme correspondence developed previously. The target words should be familiar to the pupils in their oral form but unfamiliar in their written form. All of the other words in the sentences should be words that pupils can recognize in print without difficulty. Note the sentences below:

A cat is a nice pet.
Susie and Jennie went to the park.
Do not pick the flowers.
Bill is a good pal to me.
Pat will paint the house.

Write the sentences on a chalkboard, chart, transparency, or ditto sheet before the activity so that they will be ready for use. Have pupils note that in each sentence a word or two is underlined. Ask them to look at the underlined word or words and tell you with what letter all of these words begin. When they respond by saying that the underlined words all begin with the letter ⟨p⟩, tell them to keep in mind the sound that the letter ⟨p⟩ represents. Then call on one pupil at a time to read aloud a sentence, until all of the sentences have been read. Pupils should be able to identify each of the underlined words by using the ⟨p⟩ represents /p/ grapheme-phoneme correspondence, together with semantic and syntactic clues. If any pupils are unable to identify any of the other words in the sentences, you should tell them those words. Do not, however, tell them the target words and prevent them from practicing the skill you are teaching them.

Additional practice in using the grapheme-phoneme correspondence may be provided in the form of a brief paragraph or story. The paragraph or story should be written in advance on a chalkboard, chart, transparency, or ditto sheet to minimize the loss of pupil instructional time. The paragraph below is an example of what might be presented:

> Paul and Pat went to the park for a picnic.
> They took their pet dog, Patches, with them.
> They made popcorn in a pan and ate peanut
> butter sandwiches. Their pal, Pete, passed
> by on a pony. Paul gave Pete a peanut butter
> sandwich and Pat gave the pony some popcorn.
> Patches ate some popcorn, too, and licked his
> paws.

Have pupils read the paragraph silently. Call on one or more pupils to read it orally. Then you might ask several questions based on the content of the paragraph and call on individual pupils to answer the questions. Pupils should also read aloud the sentence(s) that substantiate their answers.

Paragraphs used for this kind of activity may be teacher-prepared or they may be taken from published materials at pupils' instructional reading levels.

Activity 2

Purpose. To provide practice in associating the grapheme ⟨oa⟩ in initial and medial positions in accented syllables with the phoneme /ō/ as a clue to the identification of written words

Level. Primary.

Directions for Teachers. Everything mentioned in the introduction of the "Directions for Teachers" for Activity 1 is applicable to this activity, as well as to all activities for teaching grapheme-phoneme correspondences.

For visual discrimination of the grapheme, prepare minimal contrast pairs of words. One word in each pair should contain the grapheme ⟨oa⟩ in either initial or medial position. The contrasting element in the other word of each pair should consist of the following three alternatives: ⟨o⟩ followed by a vowel letter other than ⟨a⟩, ⟨a⟩ preceded by a vowel letter other than ⟨o⟩, or by two vowel letters other than ⟨o⟩ and ⟨a⟩. (In instances where the letters of a target grapheme may appear in reverse order in words, such as ⟨ie⟩ and ⟨ei⟩, the reverse order should be included in the visual discrimination exercises.) Note the pairs of words below:

soap	out	read	coach	oars
soup	oat	road	couch	ears

Since this activity is only for the *visual* discrimination of the grapheme ⟨oa⟩, the words used need not be familiar to pupils either in their spoken or written forms.

Write the grapheme ⟨oa⟩ on the chalkboard. Elicit the names of the two letters from pupils and have them tell you which letter is first and which is second. It is very important for pupils to be aware of the sequence of graphemes consisting of more than one letter. If pupils are unable to name the letters, you should tell them the letter names. Be sure to use the letter names frequently throughout the lesson.

The pairs of words may also be written on a chalkboard, chart, transparency, or ditto sheet. Have pupils look at the grapheme ⟨oa⟩ which you have written on the board and have them circle the same grapheme in one word of each pair of words. Pupils who are unable to do this will need extra practice with the visual discrimination of ⟨oa⟩. An activity involving the visual discrimination of ⟨oa⟩ in isolation may be useful. A suggested format for such an activity is the one described in the preceding lesson for practice in the visual discrimination of ⟨p⟩. If pupils are successful in discriminating the grapheme ⟨oa⟩ in the above activity, continue with the lesson.

For auditory discrimination of the phoneme /ō/, prepare three lists of words. One list should include words in which /ō/ is contrasted with other vowel sounds in initial position. A second list should include words in which /ō/ is contrasted with other vowel sounds in medial position. The third list should include words in which /ō/ occurs either in initial or medial position, as well as words without /ō/. Note the three lists below:

List I	List II	List III
old	tone	oat
all	load	toast
own	moon	roof
ode	such	road
ape	coach	met
ouch	most	oak
oak	test	float
oaf	foam	oath

Since this is an auditory discrimination exercise and does not involve
looking at written words, the spelling of the target phoneme is irrelevant,
and words in which the phoneme /ō/ is spelled in various ways may be
used. However, care should be used in selecting phonemes with which /ō/
is to be contrasted. Phonemes that share articulatory features with /ō/ are
/ü/, /ô/, /ȯ/, /ū/, /ā/, and /ĕ/. Words including these phonemes should be
used for auditory discrimination purposes.

Begin with List I above. Tell pupils that you are going to say a list of
words, some of which will begin with the sound /ō/ as in the word *oatmeal*
and some of which will begin with different sounds. *(Oatmeal* is presented
as a meaningful key word to help pupils remember and recall the phoneme
/ō/ in initial position, since sounds by themselves are meaningless and
difficult to remember. However, in contrast to many consonant sounds,
vowel sounds can be uttered in isolation without distortion.) As you say
each word, have pupils indicate whether or not the word begins with /ō/ as
in *oatmeal.* Proceed in the same manner with List II, using the word *soap,*
for example, as the key word. If pupils experience difficulty with Lists I and
II, do not go on to List III. You should spend more time on developing their
auditory discrimination of the phoneme /ō/ in initial and medial positions of
words. If pupils are successful with Lists I and II, present List III.

Explain to pupils that you will read a list of words to them, some of which
will begin with /ō/ as in *oatmeal,* some of which will have /ō/ in the middle
as *soap* does, and some of which will not have an /ō/ sound at all. They
are to listen carefully to each word and indicate whether it includes an /ō/
sound, and if it does, whether the /ō/ is at the beginning or in the middle of
the word. (An easier form of List III would not include words without the /ō/
sound and would require pupils merely to locate the position of /ō/ in the
words.)

As pupils identify the words in List III in which /ō/ occurs and as they
indicate the syllabic position of /ō/, write those words in two columns on the
chalkboard. The following two lists would result:

oat	toast
oak	road
oath	float

Use these lists for developing the grapheme-phoneme correspondence,
using an inductive approach. Have pupils read the first list of words aloud.
Then ask them if all the words begin with the same vowel sound. If they
reply affirmatively, ask them if all the words begin with the same two
letters. If they reply affirmatively again, ask them which two letters spell the
sound heard at the beginning of these words and have a pupil underline

⟨oa⟩ in each word. Then have pupils read the second list of words aloud and ask them if all the words have the same vowel sound in the middle. If they reply affirmatively, ask them if all the words have the same two vowel letters in the middle, and have a pupil underline the ⟨oa⟩ in all these words. Then ask pupils if they can tell you what sound the letters ⟨oa⟩ represent in the middle of these words. If they can answer this question correctly, they are ready to generalize about the grapheme ⟨oa⟩ and the phoneme /ō/ in initial and medial syllabic positions. The generalization may be elicited from pupils through a sequence of questions such as:

> What sound do the letters ⟨oa⟩ represent at the beginnings of words?
> What sound do the letters ⟨oa⟩ represent in the middles of words?
> What is one way in which the /ō/ sound may be spelled at the beginnings and middles of words?

(After these questions are answered, you might tell pupils that the /ō/ sound is spelled in other ways in other words, and that if they do not already know these spellings, they will learn about them at a later time.)

If pupils have difficulty associating the grapheme ⟨oa⟩ with the phoneme /ō/, you should go back to the auditory and visual discrimination activities of this lesson and develop both of these aspects thoroughly. Then you may resume developing the visual-auditory association.

To provide pupils with practice in making the grapheme-phoneme correspondence, activities involving the substitution of ⟨oa⟩ for other vowel graphemes in words (for example, substituting ⟨oa⟩ for the ⟨ea⟩ in *beat)* may be used. Similarly, exercises involving the filling in of missing letters in words may be used (for example, *g - - t* for *goat).* Activities involving a simple teacher-prepared oaktag device can be useful. Use a piece of oaktag about four inches in width on which you write a list of words with the letters ⟨oa⟩ omitted in initial or medial position. Leave about a one-inch space between words. Write the letters ⟨oa⟩ on a small square of oaktag. Have pupils move the ⟨oa⟩ square down the column of incomplete words, placing it in either initial or medial position, according to where the letters ⟨oa⟩ have been omitted. As each word is completed with the addition of the ⟨oa⟩, have pupils read the word aloud. See the diagram here.

To provide pupils with practice in applying this grapheme-phoneme correspondence together with semantic and syntactic clues in meaningful context, you may use activities similar to those suggested for the application of the grapheme-phoneme correspondence in the previous lesson. An alternative kind of activity might consist of a paragraph or story

before   **after**

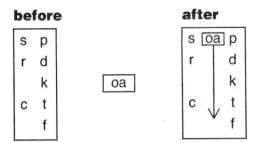

containing a number of words in which /ō/ is spelled with ⟨oa⟩, as in the following paragraph:

> It was Halloween night. Joan put on her grandmother's long white coat that looked like a cloak. She walked down the road to her friend's house and knocked on the door. Then she hid behind the big oak tree. Joan moaned and groaned like a ghost when the door opened. Her friend laughed at the hoax.

Have the pupils look through the paragraph and underline all the words that have ⟨oa⟩ in them. Call on one pupil at a time to read consecutive sentences orally. Then have one pupil read the entire paragraph aloud. Follow this with several questions based on the content of the paragraph. Call on individual pupils to answer the questions and to read aloud the sentence or sentences that substantiate their answers.

Paragraphs used for this kind of activity may be teacher-prepared or they may be taken from published materials at pupils' instructional reading levels.

Another approach that might be used for the contextual application of a grapheme-phoneme correspondence is to supply pupils with a list of words including the particular correspondence being taught. Have them write their own paragraphs and stories individually, in teams, or as a group, using as many of the words as they can. Pupils can read their own stories as well as those created by other pupils.

Example of Combination Activity

Since grapheme-phoneme correspondence clues are more effective when used in combination with other kinds of word identification clues, pupils should be given practice in combining them with other clues. The following activity, which combines grapheme-phoneme clues with semantic clues, illustrates the kind of thing that can be done:

1. Bill was riding in his w _____.
2. Pl _____ are my favorite fruit.
3. On Sunday, many people go to ch _____ ch to pray.
4. Kathy wr _____ Bill's birthday present in pretty paper.
5. The funny *cartoon* showed a clown in a cardboard *carton.*

Answer
1. wagon—The grapheme-phoneme correspondence clue is initial ⟨w⟩ which represents /w/; the semantic clue is the lexical meaning of the word *riding.*
2. plums—The grapheme-phoneme correspondence clue is initial ⟨pl⟩ which represents the initial /pl/ blend; the semantic clue is the lexical value of the word *fruit.*
3. church—The grapheme-phoneme correspondence clues are the initial and final ⟨ch⟩ which represent /č/; the semantic clues are the lexical meanings of the words *Sunday* and *pray.*
4. wrapped—The grapheme-phoneme correspondence clue is initial ⟨wr⟩ which represents /r/; the semantic clues are the lexical meanings of the words *present* and *paper.*
5a. /kär tün'/—The grapheme-phoneme clue that distinguishes *cartoon* from *carton* is the medial ⟨oo⟩ in the accented syllable which represents /ü/; the semantic clue is the lexical meaning of the word *funny.*
5b. /kär'tən/—The grapheme-phoneme clue that distinguishes *carton* from *cartoon* is the medial ⟨o⟩ in the unaccented syllable which represents /ə/; the semantic clue is the lexical meaning of the word *cardboard.*

Chapter 11

Pronunciation Spelling Clues

prə-nŭn'-sə-ā'-šən spĕl'-əŋ clues

The purpose of teaching pupils to use word identification skills is to give them independence in reading. However, there are times when even very experienced readers, after applying all the whole word and word structure techniques they know, are still unable to identify an unfamiliar word. When this happens, readers are likely to depart from the text to consult footnotes at bottoms of pages, glossaries at ends of books, or more often, unrelated dictionaries, to identify the words through pronunciation spelling clues. The pronunciation spelling technique provides a one-to-one correspondence between symbols and sounds. It is the only one of the seven techniques presented in this book that specifies pronunciations for word forms.

Pronunciation spelling is a word-based technique. It involves the identification of one word at a time and its clues do not depend on other words or on context. It is a nondirect technique that combines features of whole-word and word structure analysis.

The phonological units of individual words play a role in this technique but readers are not required to determine what these units are. That is, they are not required to analyze word forms into their phonological subunits in order to use pronunciation spelling clues. Pronunciation spelling is frequently referred to as *phonetic spelling, respelling,* or *transcription; phonemic* or *dictionary spelling;* and *pronunciation respelling.*

This technique is usually the last word identification technique taught to pupils. Rudiments of all the other techniques are generally introduced in the beginning stages of reading instruction. Pronunciation spelling is postponed until pupils are fairly competent in the use of all other techniques and until they are exposed to reading instructional materials that include words outside their oral vocabularies. However, some primary grade reading programs present as early as first grade a modified version of pronunciation spelling that adds diacritical marks to conventionally spelled words. Another, the I.T.A. Reading Program, is based on a transliteration of all words into pronunciation spelling, using an augmented alphabet.

Pronunciation spelling differs from phonics in a basic way. Grapheme-phoneme correspondences in phonics are between conventional spellings of words and their pronunciations. Correspondences in pronunciation spelling are between contrived spellings of words and their pronunciations. In pronunciation spelling, the pronunciations of words are specified by way of one-to-one symbol-sound correspondences. No graphic symbol is used to represent more than one phoneme and a phoneme is always represented by the same symbol. Thus, the sequences of symbols actually represent the pronunciations of words. In phonics, the pronunciations must be worked out by readers from the conventional spellings of words and from information about grapheme-phoneme correspondences stored in readers' memories.

The pronunciation spelling technique also differs from other word identification techniques in that pupils usually do not discover it independently. Pupils who are motivated to learn to read often figure out and spontaneously use their own adaptations of the other techniques. Only rarely do pupils use pronunciation spelling spontaneously, perhaps because these clues are not an inherent part of the reading material. Pupils usually need to be taught these clues systematically.

Kinds of Pronunciation Spelling Clues

Symbols to Indicate Phonemes

The pronunciation spellings of words reveal three components of word pronunciation: segmental phoneme sequences, syllabic divisions, and accent patterns. The clues to these components are discussed separately here.

The written symbols representing consonant and vowel phonemes are usually presented in pronunciation keys. These keys are usually located at the beginnings of glossaries or dictionaries. Pronunciation keys list a different symbol for each phoneme of the language and accompany each symbol with one or more words as examples of the given phoneme. For instance, the symbol /ā/ might be used to represent what is commonly called "the long ⟨a⟩ sound." The words *age, face,* and *pay* might accompany the symbol to illustrate "the long ⟨a⟩ sound" in initial, medial, and final positions of single syllable words. The /ā/ is called a *pronunciation symbol* and the words *age, face,* and *pay* are called *key words.* There is only one form of each symbol; there are no capital and lower case forms as in the conventional letters of the alphabet. In the pronunciation spelling of a word, the clues to the phonemes represented by the symbols are the key words listed in the accompanying pronunciation key. A pronunciation key is essential since without one there is no way of knowing which phonemes are represented by which symbols.

The key words are usually short, single-syllable, familiar words that are pronounced similarly across many dialects. Multisyllabic words are used only to demonstrate vowel phonemes that are unstressed and any consonant phonemes that occur only intervocalically in English, such as the internal consonant phoneme in the words *treasure* and *seizure.* Usually key words are selected to show a phoneme in all its normal syllabic positions in English words.

Most glossary and dictionary pronunciation keys use the conventional consonant letters as symbols for the phonemes they most commonly represent. Although efforts are made to maintain a relationship of one written symbol to one phoneme, many pronunciation keys make exceptions and use combinations of two letters to represent the initial consonant phonemes in *child, ship, thin, then.* The most frequently used symbols for these phonemes are /ch/, /sh/, /th/, and /th̸/, respectively. The intervocalic consonant phoneme in *measure* is represented frequently by /zh/ and the final consonant phoneme in *long* by /ng/. It should be noted that the pronunciation key prepared for this textbook has avoided the use of symbols with more than one letter. All phonemes are represented by single letter symbols to emphasize the one-to-one correspondence between them.

The disparity between the number of vowel letters in the alphabet and the number of vowel phonemes in English speech creates problems which are usually solved with diacritical marks. Diacritical marks are nonletter marks added to letters to indicate accent and to differentiate among phonemes, thereby extending the number of phonemes a letter may represent. The letter ⟨o⟩ is frequently used in pronunciation keys to represent the vowel phonemes in *rock, go,* and *all* by adding diacritical marks as follows: /ŏ/, /ō/, and /ô/. The most frequently used diacritical marks include: breve (ˇ), macron (ˉ), circumflex (ˆ), tilde (~), one dot (·), and two dots (¨).

As with consonants, many pronunciation keys maintain a one letter-one phoneme relationship for vowels. However, there are two common exceptions. The symbol /oi/ is frequently used to represent the initial vowel phoneme in *oil* and the symbol /ou/ to represent the initial vowel phoneme in *out.*

Symbols in pronunciation keys are usually arranged alphabetically according to the sequential arrangement of the English alphabet. Symbols representing vowel phonemes are interspersed with those representing consonant phonemes. A few pronunciation keys separate the vowel symbols from the consonant symbols, as has been done in the pronunciation key prepared for this book.

The correspondences between vowel symbols and vowel phonemes may be difficult for the average person to remember, necessitating continual reference to the pronunciation key. It is time-consuming and frustrating to keep turning to the front of the glossary or dictionary to consult the key. For this reason, symbols and key words representing *vowel* phonemes are often reproduced at the bottoms of the pages of glossaries and dictionaries for ready reference.

Using the symbols included in the pronunciation key prepared for this book, the pronunciation spellings of a sampling of single syllable words are given to show the relationship between conventional spellings and pronunciation spellings: *dough* vs. /dō/, *through* vs. /ərü/, *rough* vs. /rŭf/, *bough* vs. /bö/, and *cough* vs. /kôf/.

Typographic Devices to Show Syllabic Divisions

The pronunciation spellings of multisyllabic words must show where syllable divisions occur in the words. The syllabic divisions indicated in pronunciation spellings of words are always pronunciation divisions and not printers' usage or writing hyphenation divisions, which are more closely related to phonic segmentation divisions.

It is important for pupils to be aware of the differences between the syllabic divisions used by glossaries and dictionaries for indicating word pronunciations and the segmentation principles that pupils usually learn for writing purposes and as a part of phonics. The divisions in pronunciation spellings are based solely on phonological considerations. The divisions applied for writing and in phonic analysis are based on morphological and orthographic as well as phonological considerations. The pronunciation spelling division of the two-syllable word *milking* occurs between the letters ⟨l⟩ and ⟨k⟩ *(mil/king)*. In phonics and writers' hyphenation practices, morphemic units are not split up arbitrarily. Instead, divisions are made between morpheme units so that they remain recognizable *(milk/ing)*.

There are also some differences between the two sets of divisions within morpheme units that consist of more than one syllable. Dictionaries commonly indicate the pronunciation of the word *rabbit* as /răb'ət/. Writers' hyphenation and phonic analysis practices, however, commonly use the segmentation principle for the ⟨VCCV⟩ spelling pattern when the two consonant letters do not represent a digraph or initial consonant blend. Hence, the word is divided thus: *rab/bit.*

Pronunciation syllabic divisions in glossaries and dictionaries are usually indicated by blank spaces between segmental phoneme symbols. The syllabic division of the word *bacon* is most frequently indicated as /bā kən/. Sometimes centered dots, hyphens, or accent marks may be used to indicate syllabic divisions (/bā•kən/, /bā-kən/, /bā'kən/). In this book, blank spaces mark syllabic divisions in pronunciation spellings except at points where stress indicators are placed. The following pronunciation spellings illustrate the procedure used: /ə plôz'/ for *applause,* /əg zăkt'/ for *exact,* and /găl'əp/ for *gallop.*

Typographic Devices to Show Accent Patterns

The pronunciation spellings of multisyllabic words must show the stress patterns of the words. Usually, no more than three levels of stress are indicated for words entered in glossaries and dictionaries. Primary stress is usually indicated by a heavy diagonal mark (′) and secondary stress by a smaller and lighter diagonal mark (′). Tertiary or weak stress is left unmarked. The pronunciation spelling of the word *independent* shows the three levels of stress: /ĭn'də pĕn' dənt/. In single-syllable words stress is usually left unmarked.

Accent or stress marks in English have traditionally been placed at the ends of accented syllables (/plə tün'/ for *platoon*). However, some recently published materials have placed accent marks before accented syllables (/plə 'tün/ for *platoon*). Occasionally, other devices are used to indicate accented syllable in pronunciation spellings of words and sometimes even in conventional spellings of words. These devices include boldface type, italics, capital letters, and underlining. In this book, traditional markings are used to show stress patterns. Heavy diagonal marks at ends of accented syllables indicate primary accent. Lighter diagonal marks at ends of syllables indicate secondary accent. Unstressed syllables and single-syllable words are left unmarked. The following pronunciation spellings illustrate the procedure used: /bôt/ for *bought,* /də nī'/ for *deny,* /ŏf' əel mŏl' ə jəst/ for *ophthalmologist.*

How Pronunciation Spelling Clues Work

To use pronunciation spelling clues one must understand the one-to-one correspondence between written symbols and phonemes. One must also know the use of pronunciation keys. Readers can reproduce the specified pronunciations of words if they know how to use pronunciation spelling clues to recognize syllabic divisions and accent patterns and if they know what consonant and vowel sounds are represented by the symbols used.

Pronunciation spelling is related solely to the phonology of words, in contrast to conventional English spelling which may be related to the phonology, meaning, and etymology of words. All homophones are reduced to the same pronunciation spelling since they are all pronounced alike. Thus, the pronunciation spelling /rīt/ represents *right, rite, write,* and *wright.*

It is important to note that, despite the one-to-one correspondence between symbols and phonemes in pronunciation spelling, dialectal variations in the pronunciation of key words in the pronunciation key may result in variant pronunciations of the words whose pronunciation spellings are given. These variations are usually in vowel sounds, which frequently differ among dialects. Assume that the word *ostrich* is used as a key word for the phoneme /ŏ/. If readers pronounce *ostrich* as /ô'strəč/ in their own dialects, they will use /ô/ in their pronunciations of all words respelled with the /ŏ/ symbol. As a result, uniform pronunciations of words cannot be expected through the use of pronunciation spelling.

The use of pronunciation spelling clues can result in readers being able to pronounce word forms without actually identifying them. This happens most often when word forms represent words that are not already part of readers' speaking vocabularies. Such words are likely to be unfamiliar in meaning as well as in pronunciation. In these cases, readers cannot associate pronunciations of word forms with familiar oral counterparts in their vocabularies. However, by using pronunciation spelling clues and acquiring meanings from context, glossaries, or dictionaries, they can add the new words to their vocabularies. As is true of all the other word identification clues, pronunciation spelling clues can be used most effectively when reading materials are at appropriate levels of difficulty for pupils.

It should be noted in passing that most readers have at least a few words in their silent reading vocabularies that are not part of their oral vocabularies. They are likely to be words encountered only in written materials and whose meanings readers infer from context, but whose pronunciations readers do not take time to look up. Some readers make up private pronunciations for such words to use only when reading and avoid using these words in oral communication. These kinds of words do not necessarily present identification problems to readers. The naming or pronunciation of word forms is incidental to their successful identification.

What Pronunciation Clues Depend On

The efficient use of pronunciation spelling depends upon knowing the alphabetic sequence for locating words in glossaries and dictionaries. It also depends on knowing that derived and, especially, inflected forms of words may not be entered as separate words and must be identified through their morphemic units. If readers encounter the word *wanner* in their reading and try to look it up in a dictionary, they are not likely to find it. They will need to identify the root *wan* (with the final consonant doubled before the ⟨-er⟩ ending) and use the root as the entry word. The problem is even greater when pupils try to look up prefixed words like *reapply* since they are not likely to locate them in the ⟨r⟩ section of dictionaries.

To use pronunciation spelling clues one must be familiar with the pronunciation keys from which the symbols used in the pronunciation spelling come. One must be able to interpret syllabic divisions and accent marks for pronunciation purposes and to blend phonemes into syllables and syllables into whole words with appropriate stress.

The symbols used to represent the phonemes of English in pronunciation keys in glossaries and dictionaries have not been standardized. Each glossary and dictionary is free to use whatever symbols it chooses for this purpose. There is general agreement that the letters ⟨q⟩, ⟨x⟩, and ⟨c⟩ (unless ⟨c⟩ is part of the ⟨ch⟩ symbol) are never used as pronunciation symbols since none of these three letters is associated consistently with a single phoneme. Beyond this, there is little agreement and a great deal of disparity. Some pronunciation keys use the IPA (International Phonetic Alphabet) symbols in whole or in part; others do not. Some keys use the breve and macron diacritical marks to differentiate among vowel phonemes, while others use only one of these diacritical marks and not the other. Some pronunciation keys include a symbol to represent the schwa sound and others do not. Because of this lack of standardization, it is essential that readers refer to the pronunciation keys provided in the sources they happen to be using.

The difficulty level of the reading material is relevant to this technique to the extent that the more difficult the material, the greater the number of word forms likely to need identification through pronunciation spelling clues. Thus, the difficulty level of reading material affects the quantitative, not qualitative, use of these clues.

Advantages of Pronunciation Spelling Clues

The pronunciation spelling technique is reliable and broadly applicable, more so than any of the other word identification techniques. Once pupils know how to use this technique, they can transfer their skills from one glossary or dictionary to another. Even though the symbols in the pronunciation keys may differ, the underlying skills remain the same.

Another advantage of this technique is that it permits readers a great deal of freedom and independence as long as they have access to glossaries, dictionaries, or other sources. They do not have to guess at identifications of words or depend on someone else to tell them what the words are. They can independently verify tentative identifications of word forms made through other techniques by consulting dictionaries themselves. They do not need to wait for teacher confirmation.

Another benefit is that readers can acquire information about words beyond their pronunciations when they look them up in glossaries and dictionaries. For instance, glossaries generally provide word meanings as well as word pronunciations. Dictionaries provide additional information such as parts of speech, word origins, antonyms, synonyms, and inflected and derived forms of words. The more that readers know about a word, the more easily they will identify it when they encounter it again. Dictionaries, in brief, are reference tools which, when used with the various word identification techniques, give readers complete independence in word identification. Their use is limited only by readers' abilities to use them and by the quantity and quality of information they contain about words.

Limitations of Pronunciation Spelling Clues

Pronunciation spelling is probably the slowest and most tedious of the word identification techniques. Whole-word techniques are faster because readers infer words as they read, usually without stopping or, at most, pausing only briefly. Even morphemic analysis and phonic analysis, the word structure techniques, are more rapid. Pronunciation spelling is slower than the other techniques primarily because it involves departing from the text being read to consult an external source. Doing this takes time.

Departing from the text to locate the pronunciation of words in reference sources also interrupts the continuity of reading and makes it difficult for readers to follow its meaning. Rereading is usually necessary. Some readers do not interrupt their reading to look up unfamiliar words. Instead, they put check marks by such words and look them all up at the completion of their reading. This procedure may reduce their comprehension of the material read even though they make maximum use of semantic clues. Interrupting their reading may also reduce the pleasure that readers derive from their reading. In view of the time consumed in looking up words and in rereading material, the amount of material that can be read in a period of time is usually reduced when frequent use is made of pronunciation spelling clues. For all the reasons cited above, pronunciation spelling clues are usually used as a last resort when all other techniques fail to identify words successfully.

Another limitation of this technique is that a glossary or dictionary usually reflects the pronunciations of words within only one dialect of the language, a dialect selected (either consciously or unconsciously) by an author or editor. It presents no problems to pupils (and teachers) whose dialects match the ones represented in the dictionaries being used. But pupils whose pronunciations of words differ from those specified in particular dictionaries may become confused. Some dictionaries may be more appropriate for some pupils than others, depending on the dialects represented in the dictionaries and the dialects of the pupils. Some dictionaries do make efforts to provide common alternate word pronunciations, but others do not. Even if the prescribed pronunciations of words are different from those used by readers, they should be able to identify the words if the dictionary pronunciations approximate their own just enough to allow association. Therefore, the pronunciation spelling technique may be useful for word identification even when pronunciation spellings have a less than perfect correspondence with readers' speech patterns.

Still another limitation of this technique is that pronunciation spellings of words in glossaries and dictionaries reflect the pronunciations of words in isolation or in list form, not in connected discourse. Overall sentence intonation may alter individual word stress patterns and pronunciations. Such discrepancies may create problems of recognition for some readers. But, as mentioned above, if the prescribed pronunciation is a close enough approximation, word identification can be achieved. Once they have identified a word form, readers can then pronounce it as is natural in their dialects.

Exercise

The purpose of the following exercise is to provide practice in using pronunciation spelling clues for word identification. Write the conventional spelling for the words whose pronunciation spellings appear below. Refer to the pronunciation key in the front of this book for unfamiliar symbol-sound correspondences. Cover the answers until you are finished.

Pronunciation Spellings	Conventional Spellings	Answer
/sē′kwəns/	_____	sequence
/ăk′səl/	_____	axle
/kə někt′/	_____	connect
/pī′ə nēr′/	_____	pioneer
/nŏl′əj/	_____	knowledge
/eg zĭb′et/	_____	exhibit
/pär′ŝəl/	_____	partial
/prĕš′əs/	_____	precious
/kōld/	_____	cold
/rə nŏs′3 əs/	_____	rhinoceros

Suggested Activities for Pupil Practice

General Considerations for Teachers

It is important to focus activities on the specific skill(s) that you want pupils to practice. Pupils should not be able to get the right answers except by applying the skill(s) you want them to practice. Activities intended to provide practice in pronunciation spelling clues should include words whose pronunciation spellings are as dissimilar as possible from their conventional spellings, so that the words cannot be identified through phonic clues. The pronunciation spelling of *bat* is /băt/; pupils can identify it without applying pronunciation spelling clues at all. In contrast, the identification of *choice* from its pronunciation spelling /čòs/ requires the use of pronunciation spelling clues.

Guard against using items in activities that have unintentional common elements, since this might encourage pupils to make unwarranted generalizations. If all the words used in your pronunciation spelling activities contain consonant sounds represented by the same letter in both their pronunciation spelling and conventional spelling, pupils may assume that the same symbols represent phonemes in both conventional and pronunciation spellings. They may not realize that *f* may represent /f/ in words like *phone* and *rough* when pronunciation spelling of these words is used.

Activities similar to those that are described here for pupil practice may be used as diagnostic skills tests or as criterion-referenced tests to analyze pupils' proficiencies and deficiencies in the use of specific pronunciation spelling clues. Such diagnostic test activities may be administered before and/or after teaching the skills.

Activity 1

Purpose. To provide practice in using the macron (-) placed over vowel letters as a clue to long vowel sounds in the pronunciation spelling of single-syllable root words.

Level. Late primary.

Directions for Teachers. This activity presumes that pupils are able to discriminate long vowel sounds from other vowel sounds and can differentiate the five primary long vowel sounds (/ā/, /ē/, /ī/, /ō/, and /ū/). It presumes that pupils can distinguish vowel letters from consonant letters, can differentiate the five primary vowel letters (⟨a⟩, ⟨e⟩, ⟨i⟩, ⟨o⟩, and ⟨u⟩), and have knowledge of relevant long vowel grapheme-phoneme correspondences based on conventional spelling patterns. (Pupils should have acquired this knowledge in phonic lessons prior to this activity.) This activity also assumes that pupils have learned the consonant symbols used in the pronunciation spellings of the words as well as the sounds they represent (for example, the symbol /č/ represents the sound at the beginning of *child* and at the end of *which* and *watch*).

In presenting this activity to pupils, you should be careful to differentiate between the symbols used in pronunciation spelling and the letters that represent the same sounds in conventional spelling. A single pronunciation spelling may represent different conventional spelling patterns and different words. The pronunciation spelling symbol /ā/ represents the phoneme conventionally spelled by the letters ⟨ai⟩ in *wait*, ⟨ei⟩ in *rein*, ⟨eigh⟩ in *weight*, ⟨ay⟩ in *may*, and others. The words *break* and *brake* are represented by the same pronunciation spelling: /brāk/. It is important that teachers and pupils realize that pronunciation spelling is not related to the meanings of words but to their pronunciations.

Select single-syllable root words that have long vowel sounds in initial, medial, and final positions. Select words that include each of the long vowel sounds in each of the three syllabic positions. In presenting this activity for the first time, it is preferable to use words that pupils can identify in their conventional spellings and whose meanings they know. Once pupils associate the macron with the long vowel sounds, they should be expected to identify new words using this skill. The following words might be used to begin the activity:

age	cake	play
eat	feet	he
ice	ride	my
old	boat	go
use	cute	few

Write the words *age*, *feet*, *my*, *boat*, and *use* in a list on a chalkboard, chart, or transparency. Ask pupils to read the list of words orally. (Since they are familiar words, pupils should have no difficulty reading them.) In a second list, but in a different sequence write the pronunciation spellings of the words. The two lists might look like this:

age	ūz
feet	āj
my	bōt
boat	mī
use	fēt

Tell pupils that the second list is made up of the pronunciation spellings of the words in the first list, but that the order of the words has been changed. Call on one pupil to draw a line from the word *age* in the first list to what he or she thinks is its pronunciation spelling in the second list. (The words are different enough so that there should be no difficulty in doing this.) If the pupil is able to do so, ask how he or she made the choice. The pupil should be able to tell you that the two sounds in *age* are /ā/ and /j/, that the pronunciation spelling included the two letters ⟨a⟩ and ⟨j⟩, and that none of the others included either letter.

Now ask the pupil to tell you how many vowel letters are in the word *age* in the first list and how many are in its pronunciation spelling in the second list. When the appropriate answers are given, ask which vowel letter appears in both spellings of the word. He or she should be able to point out that the common vowel letter is ⟨a⟩. Ask why the pronunciation spelling of *age* includes the vowel letter ⟨a⟩ but not the vowel letter ⟨e⟩. The pupil should be able to respond that the only vowel sound heard in the word is /ā/ and that the ⟨e⟩ is silent and doesn't belong in the pronunciation spelling.

If the pupil cannot find the correct pronunciation spelling, or is unable to explain why he or she chose /āj/, ask what sounds are heard in the word *age*. Then ask if there is a pronunciation spelling in the second list that matches those sounds. Follow the same procedure for the other words in the list.

When the pronunciation spelling of each word has been associated with its conventional spelling, ask pupils if they hear short or long vowel sounds in the words listed. Ask pupils if the vowel letters in the words in the second list have any marks over them. Then ask them what they think those marks might indicate about the sounds of the vowels in the words. Pupils should respond that the mark above the vowel letter in each pronunciation spelling designates a long vowel sound. If pupils do not relate the macron to the vowel sound, you will need to explain its significance. In either case, tell them that this mark, which is a bar over the vowel letters in the pronunciation spellings of words, is called a "macron" and that it is used in many dictionaries to indicate long vowel sounds. Explain that the macron is placed over that vowel letter representing the long vowel sound in the pronunciation spelling of a word, regardless of how that sound may be spelled in the regular spelling of the word. When you feel they have understood this concept, erase the words in the first list. Then have pupils read aloud the words in the second list (pronunciation spelling list).

Prepare two sets of cards. On one set write the conventional spellings of the remaining words on your list. On the other set write the pronunciation spellings of these words. Distribute both sets of cards randomly among the pupils. Call on a pupil to come to the front of the room with his or her card and read it to the class. The pupil who has the matching card should then bring it up. Have the other pupils in the class verify whether the correct match has been made, that is, whether both cards represent the same word (one word card in conventional spelling, the other in pronunciation spelling).

On a ditto sheet, write the pronunciation spellings of several single-syllable root words that have long vowel sounds. The words need not be familiar to pupils. Call on one pupil at a time to read a word, or pupils can be paired and read the words to each other.

As a variation, you can have pupils write the conventional spellings of words whose pronunciation spellings you give them. Use either words whose conventional spellings they already know, or provide them with a list of conventionally spelled words to choose from. Include homophonous word pairs (such as *wait, weight; see, sea;* and *write, right*) to reinforce the understanding that pronunciation spelling is related to the pronunciations of words only and not to their conventional spellings or meanings.

Additional reinforcement in the use of the macron over a vowel letter as a clue to the long vowel sounds may be provided by having pupils write the pronunciation spellings of words whose conventional spellings you indicate. However, you should realize that this is not the way in which this skill is used in reading. Readers are never required to write their own pronunciation spellings. These are always provided for them in a glossary or dictionary or embedded in the text.

This activity presumed certain knowledge and skill on the part of the pupils, as explained in the introductory directions to teachers. It was not designed as a first lesson in pronunciation spelling. However, the specific skill developed here may be introduced as a first lesson in pronunciation spelling, or as an incidental part of lessons on specific vowel grapheme-phoneme correspondences in phonics. In such instances, the procedures for developing the understanding of the use of the macron would differ from those used in this activity.

This activity was limited to single-syllable root words to simplify presentation. However, this skill is applicable to multisyllabic and multimorphemic words and may be generalized to them. The procedures used in this activity may also be used to teach the use of other diacritical markings in pronunciation spelling (the breve, the tilde, the circumflex, the dots, and so on).

Activity 2

Purpose. To provide practice in using a short diagonal line (') at the end of a syllable in the pronunciation spelling of words as a clue to the accented syllable in two-syllable root words

Level. Early intermediate

Directions for Teachers. Prerequisite to this activity, pupils need to have learned all the symbols in the pronunciation key, including the schwa symbol, diacritical marks, and syllabic division indications, used in the pronunciation spellings of the words included in this activity. They need to understand the concept of stress or accent in words and to be able to identify accented syllables in two-syllable spoken words. If they lack any of this background, they will be unable to profit from this activity.

Select two-syllable root words in half of which the first syllable is accented and in half of which the second syllable is accented. These should be words that pupils can identify in their conventionally spelled written forms. The following list is an example:

complete
pilot
balloon
picnic
turtle
surprise

Write the first word on the board. Ask the pupils to read it orally and to tell you which syllable is accented. Next to the word write its pronunciation spelling, including syllabic division and accent mark. Continue in a similar manner with the remaining words on your list. When the pronunciation spellings of all the words have been written, have pupils pronounce the words from their pronunciation spellings and indicate whether the first or second syllable is accented in each word. Ask them if the pronunciation spellings of the words give any clue as to which syllable is accented. Pupils should respond that a short diagonal line appears at the end of the accented syllable in the pronunciation spelling of every word. If pupils do not note this independently, you will need to point it out to them, repronouncing each word as you point to the short diagonal line. In either case, tell them that the short diagonal line at the end of a syllable in a pronunciation spelling is called an accent or stress mark.

On a chalkboard or a ditto sheet write the pronunciation spellings of several two-syllable root words, some of which are accented on the first syllable and some of which are accented on the second syllable. Ask a pupil to look at the first word, tell you which syllable will be accented, and read the word orally. Follow the same procedure for the remaining words, calling on different pupils to read them. A list of words such as the following might be used:

pŏk'ət	(pocket)
ŭn'd3	(under)
rə kün'	(raccoon)
ĕks'trə	(extra)
bə găn'	(began)
cĭk'ən	(chicken)
drăg'ən	(dragon)

For additional reinforcement, you may have pupils write the pronunciation spellings of words whose conventional spellings you indicate. You should realize that this is not the way in which this skill is used in reading. Readers are never required to write their own pronunciation spellings of words. They are provided for them in a glossary or dictionary, or embedded in the context of what they are reading.

Most dictionaries indicate the accented syllable by the placement of the accent mark at the end of that syllable, as it was developed in this activity. Some dictionaries use the same kind of mark at the beginning of the accented syllable or over the vowel symbol in the accented syllable. Some pronunciation guides, instead of using an accent mark, use boldface type, italics, capital letters, or underlining to indicate which syllable is accented. In teaching pronunciation spelling clues to accent, you may select and teach the use of any of these means of indicating accent. You should begin by teaching the method used in the dictionary pupils use or will use in your class. Once they have become familiar with this method, make them aware of other ways in which accented syllables are indicated so that they will be able to use all dictionaries effectively.

This activity was limited to two-syllable root words only to simplify the presentation of the skill. This skill is applicable to words of more than two syllables and may be generalized to them. Similar procedures may be used for teaching pronunciation spelling clues to secondary accent.

Example of Combination Activity

Since pronunciation spelling clues are more effective when used in combination with other kinds of word identification clues, pupils should be given practice in combining them with other clues. The following activity combines pronunciation spelling clues with semantic clues.

Give an *oral* definition of the italicized word in each set of sentences below. Begin each definition with the italicized word.

1. We usually know only the *facade* (fə säd') of famous actresses like Greta Garbo. We seldom get behind their imposing fronts to find out what they are like as people.
2. That car is modeled after the nineteenth century horse-drawn *barouche* (bə rüš') It has a collapsible top and two double seats facing each other.
3. Of all the constellations in the Northern Hemisphere, *Cygnus* (sĭg'nəs), the Swan or Northern Cross, is the most fascinating to me. It contains the star Deneb.

The italicized words should be selected to be sure they are unfamiliar to pupils both in pronunciation and in meaning. Each sentence should be carefully written to include the semantic clues you want the pupils to practice. Since the activity is oral, pupils will need to apply pronunciation spelling knowledge; their unfamiliarity with the italicized words will ensure that they use semantic clues.

Chapter 12

Summary

sum+ma+ry=

Reading is the receptive component of written verbal communication and, as such, is a linguistic activity. It is a complex activity comprising several components. Reading instruction must cover these various components, particularly word identification and comprehension. The focus of this book is word identification.

There is a fundamental difference between word pronunciation and word identification. The pronunciation of words has to do with oral language only; the identification of words has to do with both oral and written language. Words in grammatical arrangements are the surface structure of language, from which listeners and readers comprehend what is spoken and written. Meaning is manifested through spoken and written words in grammatical arrangements. The comprehension of meaning is dependent on the identification of the words in their grammatical arrangements.

By the time children begin to learn to read, they have mastered the word identification process in oral language. They identify words subconsciously as they listen to speech. Intent upon meaning, they are unaware of the spoken words themselves, of which phonemes the words are composed, at which points in the flow of speech words begin and end, or what their intonational patterns are. In learning to read, children have to learn to do the same with written language. Pupils' proficiency in written language is usually related to their oral language development.

Pronunciation of words is not a necessary condition for the identification of written words; the fact that deaf and mute people can learn to read is dramatic evidence of this. However, the pronunciation of words is important for oral communication between teachers and pupils or among pupils themselves. It is also a means of teaching and checking on pupils' word identification skills. The teaching process, particularly in the primary grades, relies heavily on oral interaction between teachers and pupils. Written words must be referred to in some way. Hence, associating word forms with their oral equivalents becomes important in reading instruction.

A necessary condition of word identification is the association of word forms with the meanings they represent. Pedagogically, little is known about teaching pupils to associate word forms directly with meaning. Teachers usually circumvent the problem by teaching pupils to associate word forms with their spoken equivalents and by permitting pupils to associate the spoken words with meanings, which pupils are already able to do well. Gradually, pupils develop their own means of associating written words directly with meaning. Thus, in early reading instruction, word pronunciation is closely related to written word identification.

Summary of Word Identification Techniques

In this book, seven techniques are described as means of identifying written words. Clues from various sources enable readers to infer the identities of individual words or groups of words. No single technique is sufficient to function as a reader's sole means of word identification. Neither the orthography nor the lexicon of English lends itself to this. Proficient readers sample selectively the clues available through the various techniques; they continually compromise between speed and accuracy as they read. In this way they use the minimum number of clues to derive the maximum meaning from what they read.

Visual configuration clues are nongeneralizable, nonlinguistic whole-word clues by which associations are made between distinguishing visual features of word forms and the words represented by those word forms. These clues are dependent on visual information available in the graphic display of the material being read. They permit immediate, direct whole-word identification. When used alone, they are very limited and leave readers in a dependent position. Someone always has to tell them what the word forms represent before they can later identify them with visual configuration clues. Furthermore, if readers use these clues independently, someone always has to confirm their identifications of words. Mastery of other word identification techniques, of course, permits readers to verify their own word identifications.

Picture clues are also nongeneralizable, nonlinguistic whole-word clues. They involve associating word forms and related pictorial images. The source of information is the readers' knowledge of what is being represented in the picture. It is an indirect word identification technique. Whole words are identified as units, but the identifications are made indirectly through pictures. It is also a limiting technique when used alone, since the relation between pictures and specific words is not explicit and precise. Readers are dependent on others to confirm their word identifications unless they, themselves, can do so through other word identification techniques.

Semantic clues are context-based, generalizable, whole-word linguistic clues. They allow direct and immediate identification of whole words and even groups of related words. Readers do not need to analyze individual words or word parts. Using their knowledge of the semantic structure of the language, readers infer the identity of words on the basis of what "makes sense" in particular sentences. It is a more rapid technique of identification than the two previously described techniques. Like them, it is dependent on readers' knowledge of the world and the vocabularies stored in their memories. Like the picture clue technique, it is not a precise and exact word identification technique when used alone. Used in combination with other techniques, it results in fluent, meaningful reading.

Syntactic clues are also context-based, generalizable, whole-word linguistic clues. They also allow direct and immediate identification of whole words and groups of related words. Readers do not need to analyze individual words or word parts. Using their knowledge of the syntactic structure of the language, readers infer the identity of words on the basis of what "sounds right" in sentences. It is a rapid technique because it does not require the analysis of words into their constituent parts and because it involves large units of language structure. Like the semantic clue technique, it is not a precise and exact technique when used alone. It also results in fluent, meaningful reading when used in combination with other techniques.

Morphemic clues are generalizable, word-structure, linguistic clues. They are indirect or mediated clues, since word parts are identified which are then synthesized into whole words. The source of information is the morphological structure of the language. These clues involve the recognition of meaning units within words. This technique permits readers a greater degree of precision than do any of the whole-word techniques. Readers who preoccupy themselves with the analysis of individual words, however, can lose sensitivity to overall sentence meaning. For this reason, morphemic clues function most effectively in conjunction with context-based clues.

Phonic clues are also generalizable, word-structure, linguistic clues. They also are indirect or mediated clues, since word parts are identified which are then synthesized into whole words if this technique is used by itself. The source of information is readers' knowledge of the phonological structure of the language. These clues involve the identification of sound and pronunciation units within words and are sensitive to dialect variations. This technique also permits readers a greater degree of precision than do whole-word clues. Since this technique involves the analysis and synthesis of the smallest word parts, it is important to use it in conjunction with context-based techniques to ensure meaningful reading.

Pronunciation spelling is the only word identification technique that specifies the pronunciations of words as part of the word identification process. This technique is a generalizable, word-based, linguistic technique. It is the slowest of the word identification techniques since it usually involves departing from the text and consulting a reference source. At the same time, it permits readers the greatest amount of independence. It is a nondirect technique that combines whole-word and word-structure features. Like phonics, it is related to the sound and pronunciation units of words. But, unlike phonics, it is not dependent on phonological information stored in readers' memories. Instead, the clues exist in the contrived spellings that represent the pronunciations of words. In order to use pronunciation spelling clues, readers must know how to use the symbols presented in pronunciation keys to reproduce word pronunciations.

With the exception of picture and pronunciation spelling clues, these clues are always available to readers in the reading material at hand. The various types of clues provide redundant information, more than is ever required to identify a word or words. Readers should use only as much as they need to identify words. They do not need to use all the clues just because they are available. Which specific clues readers will use at a given time to identify words depends on how much information about the words they already have and how much more they need to identify them.

Beginning readers are restricted in the amount and kinds of clues they know about and can use. They may rely exclusively on one set of clues at a time. Proficient readers move continually from one kind of clue to another, selecting and using only those that they still need to identify words rapidly and accurately. For example, mature readers may move along at a rapid pace using configuration, semantic, and syntactic clues almost unconsciously. They may slow down only at unfamiliar words to "work them out." They may consciously apply morphemic analysis to the unfamiliar words and then quickly resume their pace, using a combination of whole-word clues again. If morphemic analysis helps only partially or not at all to identify the unfamiliar words, readers may resort to phonic clues. If a word still eludes them, or if they want to verify their tentative identification of a word form, they may refer to the spelling pronunciation of the word in a glossary or dictionary. They also have the option of just skipping particular words if their identification is not crucial to the overall understanding of what is being read.

Implications for Teaching Word Identification

It must be emphasized that, although the word identification techniques are presented separately in this book, this kind of separation is arbitrary and artificial. The focus on the characteristics of one technique at a time is solely to develop a thorough understanding of each one. Proficient reading is not possible when one technique is relied upon exclusively. Therefore, teachers should teach and encourage pupils to use a variety of clues flexibly. Different combinations of clues may be effective in identifying words in different reading situations. The effectiveness of any one technique is always enhanced when used in combination with others.

Beginning readers may use one type of clue at a time. They do so because they learn about one technique at a time. For example, they may be taught to use visual configuration clues first to develop a sight vocabulary. Then they may begin to learn to use phonic clues such as initial consonant grapheme-phoneme correspondences. Even when they have learned the rudiments of more than one technique, they may still tend to use consciously one technique at a time. If their attempt to identify a word through one technique does not succeed, they may try another. If the second technique does not bring success, they may try one at a time whatever other techniques they have in their repertoire. Teachers may intervene to remind pupils to use a different technique if they are aware that pupils are having difficulty with the technique being used. Once pupils have developed proficiency in using particular types of clues, they should be encouraged to use them in combination. Pupils should be permitted to use those techniques and combinations of techniques that they find to be most effective for them.

It is important for teachers to be familiar with all of the word identification techniques and to know when the use of certain techniques is more appropriate than others. For example, teachers should be aware that use of phonic analysis is not likely to be effective in the identification of many structure words. Similarly, visual configuration clues are not likely to be helpful in distinguishing among structure words with similar configurations (*on, in, an, or,* and so on). Semantic and syntactic clues are more productive in the identification of many structure words.

Teachers should also be aware of their own biases in regard to particular word identification techniques. Some teachers may prefer phonic clues and in their own reading may indeed find the use of these clues most effective. Others may be convinced that visual configuration clues are the most effective clues and may overemphasize the use of them by their pupils. Some teachers may dislike a particular technique to the point of omitting it completely from their reading instruction.

The basis for such teacher preferences may often be traced back to their own training. Teachers tend to teach as they were taught and as they were taught to teach. For example, teachers who themselves were taught to read using phonics will tend to emphasize this technique with their pupils. If a teacher training program emphasizes a particular technique, such as configuration clues, teachers trained in that program are likely to emphasize the use of that technique. Teachers who learned to read through one technique and whose teacher training emphasized that same technique are likely to be most restricted in their own teaching.

Published reading materials can contribute to and perpetuate biases concerning word identification techniques. They reflect the thinking and preferences of the authors, editors, and consultants involved in the development of the materials. Moreover, administrators and teachers, in selecting materials, tend to choose those that conform to their prejudices. Some textbooks on reading and reading instruction present only a limited number of word identification techniques. Some present only one.

For all the above reasons, many teachers do not teach all of the word identification techniques to their pupils. Yet, the development of proficient readers depends upon teaching all of the word identification techniques to pupils. The development of *proficient teachers of reading* depends on teachers knowing about all of the word identification techniques and knowing how to teach children to use all of them appropriately and effectively. The purpose of this book has been to provide this kind of information for teachers.

Review Test

The purpose of the following test is to assess your recognition of the seven word identification techniques described and discussed in this book. Name the kind of word identification clue or clues that a reader uses to identify the following words in the following ways. While it is recognized that proficient readers at all stages of development rely on combinations of clues for word identification, a specific clue (or clues) has been highlighted in each item for the purposes of this test.

1. He knows that the unfamiliar word form in the phrase "next door _____" must be /nā′bərz/ because people who live next door are called /nā′bərz/.

2. He identifies /pōst′môrt əm/ because ⟨post-⟩ is a prefix that means after and ⟨-mortem⟩ has something to do with death as in mortal and mortuary.

3. He thinks the word at the beginning of the sentence is /hwūt/ and not /ðăt/ because there is a question mark at the end of the sentence.

4. He knows that the word is /wīnd/ and not /wĭnd/ because the word the comes after it in the sentence.

5. He knows that the word must be /jŏn/ because the first letter in it looks like a big hook that his brother John uses for fishing.

6. He recognizes the word /kănt/ because it is the only written word he knows that has an apostrophe before the ⟨t⟩.

7. He identifies /mā′jər/ because the syllable break in two-syllable root words with a ⟨VCV⟩ spelling pattern is more often before than after the consonant letter.

8. He knows what the word is because the footnote indicates that ⟨righteous⟩ is pronounced /rī′čəs/.

9. He knows that the word is /rēd/ and not /rĕd/ because the word will precedes it in the sentence.

10. He works out the word /prē′həs tôr′ək/ because the word history is in the middle, fol-

lowing the prefix ⟨pre-⟩ meaning <u>before</u>, and the ⟨y⟩ at the end of <u>history</u> has been dropped and replaced with ⟨-ic⟩.

_____ 11. He thinks the word is /ə crôs/ because the picture shows a boy walking on a bridge over a river.

_____ 12. He thinks the unfamiliar word must be /kōŋk/ because the sentence says "The _____ is a large spiral mussel shell."

_____ 13. He identifies the word form ⟨sequence⟩ because the dictionary indicates that the pronunciation of that word is /sē′ kwəns/.

_____ 14. He identifies /nīt/ because he knows that ⟨igh⟩ represent /ī/.

_____ 15. He figures that the word must be /mā′ pəl/ because he recognizes the silhouette of the maple leaf on the accompanying map.

_____ 16. He identifies ⟨axle⟩ as /ăk′ səl/ because the wheel in the diagram is on a crossbar.

_____ 17. He identifies ⟨leg⟩ as /lĕg/ because the first letter of the word looks like a leg.

_____ 18. He identifies <u>short</u> because the sentence says "The girl was not tall, she was _____."

_____ 19. He identifies <u>orphan</u> because he knows that the sequence of letters ⟨p⟩ and ⟨h⟩ represents /f/.

_____ 20. He identifies the word form ⟨disagreeably⟩ because he recognizes the morpheme combination <u>disagree</u> at the beginning of the word and knows that the ⟨-ably⟩ at the end of the word consists of the suffixes ⟨-able⟩ and ⟨-ly⟩.

_____ 21. He infers that the word is /rīf′ əl/ and not /rī′ fəl/ because the second ⟨f⟩ goes with the ⟨le⟩ to form a syllable, and the first ⟨f⟩ ends the first syllable.

_____ 22. He assumes that ⟨wreck⟩ is pronounced /rĕk/ because initial ⟨wr⟩ represents /r/.

_____ 23. He figures out that the word is /jīm nā′ zē əm/ because the glossary lists <u>gynmasium</u> as one of its entries.

24. He identifies the word <u>viscera</u> because he knows that three-syllable root words with one vowel letter in each syllable tend to be accented on the first syllable.

25. He works out the word <u>alfresco</u> because he recognizes two bound morphemes in it and knows that primary accent tends to fall on the first syllable of a root morpheme if single vowel letters occur in each syllable.

26. He thinks that the word is <u>liberty</u> because the sentence says "While they were in New York, they visited the Statue of Liberty," and the only statue he knows in New York whose name begins with the correspondence ⟨l⟩ represents /l/ is the Statue of Liberty.

27. He decides that the unfamiliar word in the sentence must be /rāb′ ət/ because the picture shows a long-eared, fluffy-tailed animal eating a carrot and the two tall letters in the middle of the word remind him of the ears of a rabbit.

28. He identifies the word form ⟨rebel⟩ as /rə bēl′/ and not as /rē′ bəl/ because the auxiliary verb <u>will</u> precedes it, and he knows that two-syllable homographs used as nouns and verbs are accented on the second syllable when they are used as verbs.

29. He guesses that the word is <u>balloon</u> and not <u>ball</u> in the sentence "The boys went to the beach and played with balloons they blew up" because, although ball and balloon both make sense in the sentence, balloon is a longer word than ball.

30. He figures out that the word is /tȯz/ in the sentence "The toys are on the floor" because he knows the word <u>toy</u> and the verb <u>are</u> is plural.

Answer

1. Semantic clue
2. Morphemic clues
3. Syntactic clue
4. Syntactic clue
5. Configuration clue
6. Configuration clue
7. Phonic clue (syllabication principle)
8. Pronunciation spelling clue
9. Syntactic clue
10. Morphemic clues
11. Picture clue
12. Semantic clue
13. Pronunciation spelling clue
14. Phonic clue (grapheme-phoneme correspondence)
15. Picture clue
16. Picture clue
17. Configuration clue
18. Semantic clue
19. Phonic clue (grapheme-phoneme correspondence)
20. Morphemic clues
21. Phonic clue (syllabication principle)
22. Phonic clue (grapheme-phoneme correspondence)
23. Pronunciation spelling clue
24. Phonic clue (accenting principle)
25. Combination of morphemic clue and phonic clue
26. Combination of semantic clue and phonic clue
27. Combination of picture clue and configuration clue
28. Combination of syntactic clue and phonic clue
29. Combination of semantic clue and configuration clue
30. Combination of morphemic clue and syntactic clue

Norms

30 items correct	Excellent
25–29 items correct	Good
20–24 items correct	Fair
Below 20 items correct	You'd better go back and study some more.

Key to Suggestions for Further Reading

	Chapters in Word Identification Techniques											
	1	2	3	4	5	6	7	8	9	10	11	12
Selected Texts												
Bush and Giles	•	•	2,4,9	2	3,7	7	7	•	•	•	•	•
Carrillo	•	3,4	•	•	•	•	•	•	•	•	4	•
Dallman, et al.	2	5A	5A, 5B	5B	•	5A, 5B	5A, 5B	•	5B	•	•	•
Dawkins	•	•	•	•	•	X	•	•	•	•	•	•
Dawson	•	•	•	4	•	•	4	2,3, 4,5	•	5	2	5
Durkin	•	•	•	5	10	10	12	11	11	11	•	•
Ekwall (2)	•	•	•	•	•	•	•	X	X	•	•	•
Ekwall (1)	•	•	•	•	•	•	5	5	5	5	•	•
Fishbein and Emans	2,3, 4,6, 7	•	•	•	8,13, 14	14	•	13	•	•	•	•
Fry (2)	•	•	•	•	•	•	•	5,6,7	•	5,6,7	•	•
Fry (1)	•	4	•	•	•	•	•	2	2	3	•	•
Gibson and Levin	•	•	•	•	•	4	4	4	•	•	•	•
Goodman (1)	pp. 3-14	•	•	•	pp. 91-6	pp. 91-6	•	•	•	•	•	X
Goodman (2)	pp. 2-38	•	•	•	•	•	•	•	•	•	•	•

For each chapter in this textbook, we have noted corresponding chapters and portions of the selected texts for further reading. An X in a box indicates that the entire selected text relates to the content in the designated chapter of this textbook.

Chapters in
Word Identification Techniques

Selected Texts	1	2	3	4	5	6	7	8	9	10	11	12
Goodman and Burke	3	•	•	•	•	•	•	•	•	•	•	•
Gray	•	1,2	2	•	•	•	3,4, 5,6	3,4, 5,6	3,4, 5,6	3,4, 5,6	7	•
Guszak	•	•	•	•	•	•	4	•	•	4	•	11
Guthrie	8	•	•	•	•	•	•	•	•	•	•	6,7
Harris and Sipay (1)	•	•	•	•	•	•	•	9	9	9	9	•
Harris and Sipay (2)	•	3,4, 14	14	•	•	•	14	•	14	•	•	•
Heilman (2)	•	5	5,7	•	7	•	7	•	9	5,9	•	•
Heilman (1)	•	•	•	•	•	•	•	X	X	•	•	•
Herr	•	•	•	X	•	•	•	•	•	•	•	•
Hodges and Rudorf	•	4,5, 7	•	•	•	•	•	•	•	•	•	8
Horn	•	•	•	•	•	•	•	•	•	•	•	3
Jones	•	•	•	3	•	•	•	•	•	•	•	•
Karlin (1)	•	•	5	•	5	5	5	•	5	•	5	•
Karlin (2)	•	•	•	•	•	•	•	•	•	•	5	•
Levin and Williams	•	7	•	•	•	8,10	•	1	•	3	•	•

Chapters in
Word Identification Techniques

Selected Texts	1	2	3	4	5	6	7	8	9	10	11	12
Mazurkiewcz	•	•	•	•	•	•	•	X	•	X	•	•
Otto and Chester	•	3	•	•	•	•	3	•	3	3	•	•
Page	2	•	•	•	•	•	•	•	•	•	•	•
Robeck and Wilson	1,2,3	•	7	•	•	•	•	•	•	•	•	•
Robinson	•	•	•	•	4	4	•	•	•	•	•	•
Ruddell	2,3,4	•	•	•	10	10	10	10	10	10	•	10
Ruddell, et al.	2,3	6	•	6	6	6	•	6	6	•	•	•
Schell	•	•	•	•	•	•	•	•	X	X	•	•
Smith, F. (1)	1,3, 11	6,10	5,10	•	•	•	•	7,8	•	•	•	•
Smith, F. (2)	1,14	10	9,11	•	11,13	13	•	12	•	•	•	•
Smith, J.	•	•	6	2	6	6	•	•	•	6	•	1,3,5, 6,7
Smith, N.	•	•	•	8	•	•	•	•	•	•	•	8
Smith and Johnson	1,12	7	•	•	7	7	•	7	•	7	•	•
Smith, et al.	•	•	•	•	15,16	15,16	•	•	•	•	•	•

Chapters in
Word Identification Techniques

Selected Texts	1	2	3	4	5	6	7	8	9	10	11	12
Spache, E.	•	•	2,3	3	4	•	4	•	4	•	•	•
Spache, G.	•	8	•	•	•	•	•	8	8	•	•	•
Spache and Spache	•	•	•	13	•	•	12	•	12	12	13	9
Strang, et al.	•	•	•	•	•	•	•	•	•	•	6	•
Thorndike and Barnhart	•	•	•	•	•	•	•	•	•	•	X	•
Tinker and McCullough	1,3	8	8	8	•	•	8	8	8	8	•	•
Venezky	•	•	•	•	•	•	•	3,8	•	4,5, 6,7	•	•
Wallen	•	•	•	•	•	•	•	•	3,6,7	8,9	•	•
Wardhaugh	•	1,2,4	•	•	6	5	•	•	•	7	•	9,10
Wilson and Hall	•	•	•	•	•	•	•	•	•	•	7	•
Zintz	1	10	10	10	10	•	•	10	10	•	10	•

Suggestions for Further Reading

Bush, Wilma Jo, and Giles, Marian Taylor. *Aids to Psycholinguistic Teaching.* Columbus, Ohio: Charles E. Merrill, 1969.

Carrillo, Lawrence W. *Teaching Reading: A Handbook.* New York: St. Martin's, 1976.

Dallmann, Martha; Rouch, Roger L.; Chang, Lynette T. C.; and DeBoer, John J. *The Teaching of Reading.* New York: Holt, Rinehart and Winston, 1974.

Dawkins, John. *Syntax and Readability.* Newark, Del.: International Reading Association, 1975.

Dawson, Mildred A., ed. *Teaching Word Recognition Skills.* Newark, Del.: International Reading Association, 1971.

Durkin, Dolores. *Teaching Young Children to Read.* 2nd ed., revised. Boston: Allyn and Bacon, 1976.

Ekwall, Eldon E. *Diagnosis and Remediation of the Disabled Reader.* Boston: Allyn and Bacon, 1976.

_____. *Locating and Correcting Reading Difficulties.* 2nd ed., revised. Columbus, Ohio: Charles E. Merrill, 1977.

Fishbein, Justin, and Emans, Robert, *A Question of Competence: Language, Intelligence, and Learning to Read.* Chicago: Science Research Associates, 1972.

Fry, Edward. *Elementary Reading Instruction.* New York: McGraw-Hill, 1977.

_____. *Reading Instruction for Classroom and Clinic.* New York: McGraw-Hill, 1972.

Gibson, Eleanor J., and Levin, Harry. *The Psychology of Reading.* Cambridge, Mass.: The MIT Press, 1975.

Goodman, Kenneth S., ed. *Miscue Analysis: Applications to Reading Instruction.* Urbana, Ill.: ERIC Clearinghouse on Reading and Communication Skills, National Council of Teachers of English, 1973.

_____. Behind the Eye: What Happens in Reading. In *Reading Process and Program*, Kenneth S. Goodman and Olive S. Niles. Champaign, Ill.: National Council of Teachers of English, 1970.

Goodman, Yetta, and Burke, Carolyn. *Reading Miscue Inventory Manual.* New York: Macmillan, 1972.

Gray, William S. *On Their Own in Reading.* Revised ed. Chicago: Scott, Foresman, 1960.

Guszak, Frank. *Diagnostic Reading Instruction in the Elementary School.* New York: Harper and Row, 1972.

Guthrie, John T., ed. *Aspects of Reading Acquisition.* Baltimore: Johns Hopkins University Press, 1976.

Harris, Albert J., and Sipay, Edward R. *Effective Teaching of Reading.* 2nd ed., revised. New York: David McKay, 1971.

_____. *How to Increase Reading Ability: A Guide to Developmental and Remedial Methods,* 6th ed., revised. New York: David McKay, 1975.

Heilman, Arthur W. *Phonics in Proper Perspective.* 3rd ed., revised. Columbus, Ohio: Charles E. Merrill, 1977.

_____. *Principles and Practices of Teaching Reading.* Columbus, Ohio: Charles E. Merrill, 1967.

Herr, Selma. *Learning Activities for Reading.* 2nd ed., revised. Dubuque, Iowa: William C. Brown, 1970.

Hodges, Richard E., and Rudorf, E. Hugh, eds. *Language and Learning to Read: What Teachers Should Know About Language.* Boston: Houghton Mifflin, 1972.

Horn, Thomas D., ed. *Reading for the Disadvantaged: Problems of Linguistically Different Learners.* New York: Harcourt, Brace and World, 1970.

Jones, Daisy M. *Teaching Children to Read.* New York: Harper and Row, 1971.

Karlin, Robert. *Teaching Elementary Reading: Principles and Strategies.* 2nd ed., revised. New York: Harcourt Brace Jovanovich, 1975.

_____. *Teaching Reading in High School.* Indianapolis: Bobbs-Merrill, 1975.

Levin, Harry, and Williams, Joanna P., eds. *Basic Studies on Reading.* New York: Basic Books, 1970.

Mazurkiewcz, Albert J. *Teaching About Phonics.* New York: St. Martin's, 1976.

Otto, Wayne, and Chester, Robert D. *Objective-Based Reading.* Reading, Mass.: Addison-Wesley, 1976.

Page, William D., ed. *Help for the Reading Teacher: New Directions in Research.* Urbana, Ill.: National Conference on Research in English, 1975.

Robeck, Mildred C., and Wilson, John A. R. *Psychology of Reading: Foundations of Reading Instruction.* New York: John Wiley, 1974.

Robinson, H. Alan. *Teaching Reading and Study Strategies: The Content Areas.* Boston: Allyn and Bacon, 1975.

Ruddell, Robert. *Reading-Language Instruction: Innovative Practices.* Englewood Cliffs, N.J.: Prentice Hall, 1974.

Ruddell, Robert; Ahern, Evelyn J.; Hartson, Eleanore K.; and Taylor, Joellyn. *Resources in Reading-Language Instruction.* Englewood Cliffs, N.J.: Prentice-Hall, 1974.

Schell, Leo M. *Fundamentals of Decoding for Teachers.* Chicago: Rand McNally, 1975.

Smith, E. Brooks; Goodman, Kenneth S.; and Meredith, Robert. *Language and Thinking in the Elementary School.* New York: Holt, Rinehart and Winston, 1970.

Smith, Frank. *Psycholinguistics and Reading.* New York: Holt, Rinehart and Winston, 1973.

_____. *Understanding Reading–A Psycholinguistic Analysis of Reading and Learning to Read.* New York: Holt, Rinehart and Winston, 1971.

Smith, James A. *Creative Teaching of Reading in the Elementary School*. 2nd ed., revised. Boston: Allyn and Bacon, 1975.

Smith, Nila B. *Reading Instruction for Today's Children*. Englewood Cliffs, N.J.: Prentice Hall, 1963.

Smith, Richard J., and Johnson, Dale D. *Teaching Children to Read*. Reading, Mass.: Addison-Wesley, 1976.

Spache, Evelyn B. *Reading Activities for Child Involvement*. Boston: Allyn and Bacon, 1972.

Spache, George D. *Diagnosing and Correcting Reading Disabilities*. Boston: Allyn and Bacon, 1976.

Spache, George D. and Spache, Evelyn B. *Reading in the Elementary School*. 3rd ed., revised. Boston: Allyn and Bacon, 1973.

Strang, Ruth; McCullough, Constance M.; and Traxler, Arthur E. *The Improvement of Reading*. New York: McGraw-Hill, 1967.

Thorndike, E. L., and Barnhart, Clarence L. How to Use This Dictionary. In *Thorndike and Barnhart Dictionaries*. Chicago: Scott, Foresman, 1962.

Tinker, Miles A., and McCullough, Constance M. *Teaching Elementary Reading*. 4th ed., revised. Englewood Cliffs, N.J.: Prentice Hall, 1975.

Venezky, Richard L. *The Structure of English Orthography*. The Hague, Netherlands: Mouton, 1970.

Wallen, Carl J. *Competency in Teaching Reading*. Chicago: Science Research Associates, 1972.

Wardhaugh, Ronald. *Reading: A Linguistic Perspective*. New York: Harcourt, Brace and World, 1969.

Wilson, Robert M., and Hall, Maryanne. *Reading and the Elementary School Child*. New York: Van Nostrand Reinhold, 1972.

Zintz, Miles V. *The Reading Process: The Teacher and the Learner*. 2nd ed., revised. Dubuque, Iowa: Wm. C. Brown, 1975.

Glossary

Accent (stress): the popular term for stress or force given to one or more syllables in a word. In sentences, four levels of stress are recognized—primary, secondary, tertiary, and reduced. In isolation, words have three levels of stress—primary accent, secondary accent, and unaccented syllables.

Affix: a general term referring to a prefix, suffix, or inflectional ending.

Angle brackets: the symbols used to enclose letters, graphemes, and spelling patterns in this book (⟨e⟩, ⟨ph⟩, ⟨anti-⟩, ⟨-ous⟩, and ⟨sat⟩).

Antonyms: words that have opposite meanings (good/bad, tall/short).

Basal readers (basic reading series): a series of reading textbooks that forms the basis of classroom reading instruction. The series is graded and may range from reading readiness, preprimer, and primer levels to sixth and eighth grade levels.

Base word: a free or bound morpheme that functions as the root part of a word, such as *base* in *basement* and ⟨-manu-⟩ in *manuscript.*

Clause: a group of words containing a subject and predicate and performing as a unit some grammatical function. Traditionally, clauses are categorized as independent (main) or dependent (subordinate).

Communication: the process by which information is exchanged between people through a common system of symbols, signs, or behavior. Verbal communication involves speech and writing. Nonverbal communication involves pictures, gestures, and behavior.

Compound: a word consisting of two or more free morphemes. Compounds are written in one of three forms: as one word (raincoat), with a hyphen (teen-ager), or as two or more words (dime store).

Configuration clues: see visual configuration clues.

Connotation: the implications or suggested meaning of a word beyond its literal meaning.

Consonant: a speech sound produced by interrupting or modifying the outgoing air or breath by an organ of articulation such as the lips, teeth, tongue, hard palate or soft palate. Consonant sounds occur at the beginnings and ends of syllables. They are found in the middles of syllables only if they are part of a consonant blend or cluster.

Consonant blend or cluster: two or more immediately adjacent consonant sounds. Initial blends occur frequently at the beginnings of one-syllable root words (black, grass, stripe); final consonant blends occur frequently at the ends of single syllable root words (ha<u>nd</u>, pa<u>rt</u>, fi<u>rst</u>). Final blends are often reversals of initial blends (<u>d</u>rop/ha<u>rd</u>, <u>t</u>rain/hea<u>rt</u>). The only three consonant blends that occur frequently in both initial and final position are /st/, /sp/, and /sk/ spelled either as ⟨sk⟩ or ⟨sc⟩. Since *initial* and *final* refer to syllabic position, there are no medial consonant blends. The consonants /s/, /l/, and /r/ occur most frequently in blends and for this reason are called the *common blenders*. Consonant blends are treated as single units instead of separate consonants in teaching grapheme-phoneme correspondences.

Content words (form class words): one of the two major classifications of English words (the other being function or structure words). Content words make up the bulk of our vocabulary and carry most of the lexical or dictionary meaning in a sentence. There are four content classes in English, traditionally termed: *nouns, verbs, adjectives,* and *adverbs*. All words within a class occupy the same position in a construction and share a pattern of morphologic or syntactic features.

Context (contextual format): the words and syntactic structures that surround a word or other language unit and that affect its meaning. *Contextual clues* (frequently called meaning clues) refer to semantic and syntactic information that readers may use for identifying written words.

Contraction: a combination of two words written as one so that only part of the second is spelled. English has two major types of contractions: (1) the combination of a personal pronoun and an auxiliary (I've, she's) and (2) the combination of an auxiliary and the negative particle (wouldn't, hasn't).

Decode: to identify the meanings of words in the surface structure of language. In reading, decoding is the identification of the pronunciations and meanings of word forms.

Deep structure: the abstract structure postulated as underlying a sentence. It contains all the information necessary for the semantic interpretation of that sentence.

Denotation: the literal meaning of a word, stripped of its emotional overtones.

Derived word (derivative): a word composed of a root plus a prefix, derivational suffix, or both (believable, unbelievable).

Determiner: a structure word that signals the form class or syntactic function of the word or words which follow (for example, *will* signals that a verb follows in the phrase *will turn*; *my* signals that a noun follows in the phrase *my turn*).

Diacritical marks (diacritics): used in pronunciation spelling transcriptions to produce additional symbols to represent the phonemes of English. The most common are the following:

1. breve: a u-shaped line (˘) placed over a vowel letter to indicate a short sound (/ă/ as in *cat*).
2. circumflex: a reversed V (^) placed over vowel letters to distinguish among vowel letters when they are used as phonetic symbols (/ô/ as in *order*).
3. macron: a straight horizontal line (−) placed over a vowel letter to indicate a long sound (/ā/ as in *aim*).
4. one and two dots: dots (˙ and ¨) placed over vowel letters to distinguish among vowel phonemic symbols (/u̇/ as in *book*; /ö/ as in *out*).
5. reversed circumflex: a small v (ˇ) placed over some consonant letters to distinguish among consonant phonemic symbols (/š/ as in *shoe*).
6. tilde: a wavy line (˜) frequently placed over vowel letters to distinguish among vowel phonemic symbols, particularly those followed by r ⟨kär/ as in *car*).

Dialect: any form of a language spoken by a group of people within a larger linguistic community (including the form that is considered standard). There are social dialects as well as regional dialects. *Idiolect* is the term for the form of the language spoken by an individual.

Digraph: two consonant letters regularly used in conventional spelling to represent a single consonant sound. Both letters lose their identity of sound in the merger and emerge with a single sound different from that usually represented by both participating members individually. Some examples are /f/ spelled ⟨gh⟩, /Θ/ spelled ⟨th⟩, and /c/ spelled ⟨ch⟩.

Diphthong: a succession of two vowels sounds joined in a single syllable under a single stress. A diphthong is produced by a continuous glide of the tongue from one vowel position to the other (/ȯ/ as in *oil*).

Discourse: expression via connected speech or writing.

Encode: to represent meaning through speech and writing.

Grapheme: a letter character or significant written unit; the basic unit of written expression of the English language. Each grapheme may have one or more *allographs* that do not differ functionally (g, G, gg). Graphemes are usually indicated by angle brackets (⟨g⟩).

Grapheme base (phonogram): a succession of orthographic letters that occurs with the same pronunciation value in several words (⟨ight⟩ as in *light, night, fight*).

Graphemic environment: the letter or letters that surround a letter in a written word.

Grapheme-phoneme correspondences: relationships between phonemes and the spelling patterns that represent them in writing. They are also called *orthographic-phonological correspondences*.

Homograph: a word with the same spelling as another but with different pronunciation and meaning (*bow* as in *the bow of the boat* and *bow* as in *the bow in her hair*).

Homophone: a word with the same pronunciation as another but with different spelling and meaning (*steel* and *steal*).

Homonym: a word with the same spelling and pronunciation as another but with different meaning (*fair* meaning "market" and *fair* meaning "just").

Independent reading level: the level of reading materials that a pupil can read with approximately 99% word recognition and at least 90% comprehension.

Inflectional ending: an ending added to a root that indicates case, gender, mood, number, person, tense, voice, etc. but that affects neither the lexical meaning of the root nor part of speech. An *inflected word, inflected form,* or *variant* is a root word with an inflectional ending. The rules of standard English grammar require that certain kinds of words conform to each other in certain ways. The process of such adjustment is called *inflectional agreement* (for example, the subject and verb of a sentence must agree in number and person).

Instructional reading level: the level of reading materials that a pupil can read with approximately 95% word recognition and at least 90% comprehension.

Intonation: complex patterns of pitch, stress, and juncture that contribute to meaning in speech. In writing, intonation is represented by punctuation.

Juncture: the breaking off or interrupting of the flow of speech according to the structure of the sentence, or the way in which two units of linguistic structure are joined, as in the difference between *nitrate* and *night rate*. There are four juncture phonemes in English.

Language: a systematic means of communicating ideas or feelings by the use of conventionalized signs, sounds, gestures, or marks with understood meanings. *Linguistic or verbal clues* are cues from the orthographic, phonological, semantic, and syntactic systems of language that readers may use for the identification of written words. *Nonlinguistic clues* are nonverbal cues that may be used for word identification.

Lexicon: the stock of morphemes and words in a language. *Lexical reservoir* refers to an individual's stock of morphemes and words. *Lexical or semantic meaning* is the referential meaning that stays the same from one inflectional form to another (*play, plays, played, playing*). *Lexical clues* are semantic information that readers can use to identify written words.

Linguist: one who systematically studies a language or languages.

Markers: letters and words whose sole purpose in certain positions is as a signal. A letter marker in a written word serves only to indicate the pronunciation of another letter or digraph in the word (for instance, the final ⟨e⟩ in *mate*); a work marker is used solely to indicate the grammatical class of some other word (*to* is a marker in the phrase *to run*).

Morpheme: the smallest meaningful unit of language. Morphemes take the form of free or bound roots, prefixes, suffixes, and inflectional endings. *Allomorphs* are variant forms of morphemes, an example being the diverse plural endings on *cats, dogs, boxes*. A *free morpheme* is a unit of meaning that can occur alone (*chair, dance, also*). A *bound morpheme* is a unit of meaning that does not occur alone but only when attached to another morpheme. Examples are *eating* (eat + *ing*), *remove* (*re* + move), and *dogs* (dog + *s*), each of which contains two morphemes, one of which is bound. Most prefixes, suffixes, inflectional endings, and foreign roots in English words are bound morphemes. English words may consist of a single free morpheme (*coat*), a combination of free morphemes (*raincoat*), a combination of free and bound morphemes (*coats*), or a combinaiton of bound morphemes (*receive*). A word that consists of more than one morpheme may be referred to as a polymorphemic or multimorphemic word. The *morphological structure* of a word relates to its units of meaning. *Morphemic analysis* is the identifiction of the meaning units within words. *Morpheme clues* may be prefixes, suffixes, inflectional endings, free or bound roots, or combinations of these units.

Orthographic information: cues available from the spelling patterns of words that readers may use for word identification.

Orthographic units: the spelling patterns representing individual phonemes and sequences of phonemes.

Orthography: the system for written representation of linguistic utterances, including phonemes and punctuation; spelling.

Paragraph: a subdivision of a written composition comprised of one or more sentences dealing with one idea and marked in writing by the indentation of the first word.

Phoneme: the smallest unit of spoken language by which utterances can be differentiated. A difference in phonetic quality is phonemic when and only when this difference differentiates words or structures. *Allophones* of a phoneme are its variant forms, which are not functionally different from each other. An example of allophones would be the aspirated and unaspirated forms of a consonant. *Segmental phonemes* are the vowel and consonant sounds of the language.

Suprasegmental phonemes are the features of speech accompanying one or a sequence of segmental phonemes such as pitch, stress, and juncture. As yet there is no unanimous agreement over the total number of phonemes in American English, but most linguists identify about 45 of them. In writing, phonemes are usually indicated by slash marks (/m/, /ă/). *Phonology* is the general term for the study of speech sounds and embraces both phonetics and phonemics.

Phonic clues: the syllabication and accenting principles and the spelling-sound correspondences within words that may be used for word identification purposes. *Phonic analysis* is the process of identifying words through these clues. A *phonic rule* or principle is a statement of correspondence between the pronunciation and conventional spelling of a word or phoneme.

Phonics: the study of the relationship between spoken sounds and written symbols. The term is often used interchangeably but incorrectly with *phonetics, phonemics, phonic analysis, phonetic analysis,* and *phonemic analysis*. Phonetics is the study and systematic classification of speech sounds without regard to whether these sounds differentiate among morphemes or not. Phonemics is the study and classification of the speech sounds and distinctions of a language that differentiate morphemes in that language. Phonetics deals with sounds as *perceptibly* different, phonemics, with sounds as *functionally* different. Many people are conditioned to hear only distinctions that are functional *in their own dialects*.

Phonogram: a syllabic unit consisting of a vowel-consonant or a consonant-vowel phoneme sequence. Words sharing a common syllabic unit are frequently called a "word family." For example, the ⟨at⟩ phonogram is the basic unit of the word family that includes *bat, cat, fat, hat,* and so on. (See also grapheme base.)

Phrase: a group of words performing some function as a unit. A phrase lacks a subject and predicate, although it may have a clause as a subordinate element.

Picture clues: cues available from a pictorial representation that may be used for word identification. A picture may portray a single item or concept, or it may portray multiple items or concepts in a complex picture.

Pitch: the melodic aspect of speech; the musical contour for speech units. English intonation is usually divided into four levels: the normal level for an individual, one level below that, and two levels above. The highest level is used only for special emphasis of some kind.

Prefix: a bound morpheme that precedes a root and modifies its lexical meaning (⟨un-⟩ as in *unkind*).

Pronunciation spelling (phonemic or phonetic respelling): the use of phonetic symbols to indicate pronunciations of words (for example, the pronunciation spelling of *right* is /rīt/). The sounds represented by the symbols in pronunciation spelling are presented in a *pronunciation key* or *key to pronunciation*. *Pronunciation spelling clues*, frequently called *dictionary* clues, can be used for word identification.

Punctuation: the graphic representation of certain boundaries between syntactic units. The system of punctuation is parallel to the system of intonation, although there is not perfect correspondence between the two systems.

Recode: to convert one code to another, such as going from print to speech or from speech to print.

Redundancy: the practice in language of including repetitive information or more information than is absolutely needed. "She helps her mother" contains three clues that the subject is singular: the two personal pronouns and the ⟨-s⟩ on the verb. The redundancy of cues enables readers to identify words with a minimum amount of cues and without having to carefully take note of every word.

Root: the base or core to which prefixes, suffixes, and inflectional endings may be added. Linguists are more likely to use the term *base* in this sense. *Free roots* are morphemes that can occur alone. *Bound roots* are those that cannot occur alone in English but must be attached to other morphemes. For example, *speak* is a free root in *unspeakable* and ⟨-manu-⟩ is a bound root in *manufacture*.

Schwa: an unstressed vowel sound such as the first vowel sound in *about* or the second vowel sound in *circus*. It may be spelled by any vowel letter or combination of vowel letters. Although it never occurs in an accented syllable, it is not the only unstressed vowel in American English.

Segmental phoneme: a consonant and vowel sound of a language that functions as a recognizable, discrete unit in it. To have phonemic value, a difference in sound must function as a distinguishing element marking a difference in meaning or identity.

Semantic clues: the lexical or referential aspects of words in sentences and larger units of discourse that may be used for word identification purposes. They are frequently called *context clues, meaning clues,* and *connected text clues*. They include *intrinsic clues*, which are the normal attributes or context such as the topic or subject matter of the passage, and *extrinsic clues*, which are deliberately built into the context such as synonyms set off by commas, dashes, or parentheses.

Sentence (complete): a grammatically independent unit which contains one or more finite verb forms and, except for requests or commands, one or more subjects for these verbs. In writing, such units must be separated by a coordinate conjunction, a semi-colon, or an end mark of punctuation. When either of the first two methods is used, the result is usually called a compound sentence. In speech, such units are marked by rising or fading juncture, usually the latter. It should be noted that sentence fragments, marked by similar intonation, appear in connected speech and are very common in dialogue. Minimal sentences conform to one of a short list of patterns but may be expanded or combined in various ways so that the number of possible sentences is infinite.

Sight word: any written word recognized instantly without analysis; a word whose identification has been mastered to the point that response to it is immediate.

Slash marks: see virgules.

Spelling pattern: the graphemic representation of a phoneme or sequence of phonemes.

Stress: see accent.

Structural analysis: ambiguous term that some writers use to mean the identification of some pronunciation units and some meaning units in words.

Structure words (*function words, service words*): words whose primary meanings are grammatical and whose lexical meanings are minimal. There are only about 300 function words in the English language. They include determiners like *a, the, their;* auxiliaries like *is, can, do;* prepositions like *in, on, with;* subordinators like *which, since, after;* coordinators like *and, but, or;* interrogators like *who, which, what;* intensifiers like *very, more, rather;* expletives like *there, it;* and sentence starters like *well, oh, now.* They are the most frequently recurring words in the language.

Suffix: a bound morpheme that follows a root and modifies its meaning. Derivational suffixes usually change the part of speech to which the original word belongs. Where prefixes affect only lexical meaning, suffixes affect grammatical and/or lexical meanings of the words to which they are affixed. For example, the noun *fame* becomes an adjective when the derivational suffix ⟨-ous⟩ is added to form the word *famous*.

Surface structure: the grammatical arrangements of words in speech or writing.

Syllable (*syllabic unit*): in speech, the basic unit of pronunciation consisting of one vocal impulse and containing one vowel sound. It may also contain consonants or consonant blends in initial and/or final position. An *open syllable* consists of a single vowel sound or a vowel sound preceded by a consonant sound or sounds; a *closed syllable* is a vowel sound followed by a consonant sound or sounds. Syllables in written words may and frequently do differ from those in spoken words. In other words, the division of a spoken word into syllables does not always match the hyphenation division of written words when dividing words at ends of lines of print. Spoken syllables are based on phonological variables only; written syllables or segments are based on morphological as well as phonological variables. For this reason the hyphenation or writing syllabication principles are more useful for word identification purposes than are pronunciation syllabication rules. A *monosyllable* is a word with only one vowel sound (man, spring, kite); a word like *noble* is not a monosyllable because a second syllable is indicated either by a schwa or the /l/. A *polysyllable, multisyllable,* or *plurisyllabic word* is a word of more than one syllable. *Syllabication* is the process of dividing polysyllabic words into their separate component syllables or segments.

Syllabic: any sound that functions as a syllable-making sound, that is, any sound that is vocalic in function. By definition, all vowels are syllabic. The consonant nasals and liquids may be syllabics (such as, the /l/ in noble), but, except for /r/, they appear as syllabics only in unstressed syllables.

Synonym: a word with nearly the same meaning as another (cool/chilly).

Syntax: the structure and organization of meaningful sequences of morphemes (above the morphological level) in a language. *Syntactic units or structures* are grammatical units containing more than one word but having, as units, some identity of their own. They may be classified by composition (clause or phrase), by function as part of speech (nominal, adjectival, etc.), or by function as a sentence part (subject, modifier, etc.). Syntactic structures of one type may appear within a syntactic structure of another type. English sentences are thus hierarchial rather than strictly linear in structure. *Syntactic clues* are the grammatical or relational aspects of words in sentences and in larger units of discourse that may be used for word identification purposes.

Target words: those that are the focus of specific items and activities in practice exercises. The same definition applies to *target phonemes, target graphemes, target phrases and sentences.*

Virgules (*slash marks***):** the symbols used to enclose pronunciation notations (sounds and pronunciations) in this book (for example, /g/, /ē/, /sāt/, and /fōn/.

Visual configuration clues: distinctive visual features of written words which may be used for word identification purposes. They include whole-word features as well as details of words.

Voiced, voiceless: terms used to differentiate consonants by the presence or absence of vocalization as they are articulated. Voiced consonants are those in which the vocal cords vibrate; voiceless consonants are those in which the breath stream passes unimpeded through the larynx. All vowel sounds are voiced.

Vowel: a speech sound formed by the relatively free passage of the breath stream over the center of the tongue. The tone of vowel sounds is formed by the vibration of the vocal cords. When the cords are tautly strung, the vowels produced are high-pitched or tense vowels; when the cords are relaxed, the vowels produced are low-pitched or lax vowels. The resonance of vowel sounds is shaped by the modification of the oral and nasal chambers. Vowel sounds are free of audible friction. Vowels are classified as long and short; as high, mid, or low according to the raising and lowering of the tongue; or as front and back according to the putting forward or retracting of the tongue. Vowel sounds perform a different syllabic function than do consonant sounds. The phonemes /w/, /h/, and /y/ are called *semivowels*. They are sounds of short duration with no precise point of articulation, being formed as the tongue shifts toward or away from pure vowels. They are used in the position of vowels and consonants. Some phonemicists also consider /r/ to be a semivowel.

Whole word clues: those features, characteristics, and/or understandings that enable readers to infer meanings of whole written words without having to identify the component morphemic or phonic parts of the words. Specifically, they include visual configuration clues, picture clues, semantic clues, and syntactic clues.

Word: a "primitive" term in that it cannot be satisfactorily defined verbally but is intuitively perceived as a free unit in speech or in writing—the smallest unit to be recognized. Some words contain only one morpheme (*train*), some more than one (*entrain, entrainment*).Some compound words are written with space left between the elements (filling station) but are still considered to be single words. Certain expressions consisting of more than one word are best dealt with as single grammatical entities, or "words" (according to , put up with).

Word form: the orthographic representation of a word; an orthographic configuration.

Word identification: the process of associating pronunciation and meaning with word forms. Other terms used for this process include *word attack, word analysis, word perception, word recognition,* and *decoding.* .

Word structure clues: those correspondences between orthographic units and units of meaning and sound or pronunciation that enable readers to infer what written words are by identifying their meaning and/or pronunciation components. Word structure clues include morphemic clues and phonic clues.

Index

lesson materials, 40–52
    exercises, 40–43
    suggested activities, 43–52
limitations of, 39–40
types of clues, 33–35
    maps, diagrams, picture graphs, 35
    multiple-object pictures, 34–35
    single-object pictures, 33–34
Pitch, 84, 152
Post-appositive synonyms, 59
Prefixes, 109–11
Primary stress, 160–62
Productive morphemes, 121
Proficient reading, 6, 7, 11
Pronunciation keys, 212–13
Pronunciation spelling clues, 210–26
    advantages of, 217–18
    basis for, 216–17
    defined, 210–11
    how they work, 215–16
    lesson materials, 219–26
        exercises, 219
        suggested activities, 219–26
    limitations of, 218–19
    types of clues, 211–15
        symbols, 211–13
        typographic devices, 213–15
Pronunciation symbols, 211–13
Punctuation, 20, 84–86
    apostrophes, 20, 85
    brackets, 85
    capitalization, 86
    colons, 85
    commas, 85
    dashes, 86
    exclamation points, 85
    hyphens, 20, 85
    parentheses, 86
    periods, 20, 85
    question marks, 85
    quotation marks, 85
    virgules, 85

R

Reading, 2–9, 13–14
    dialectical considerations, 7–8
    goal of, 6
    instruction in, 8–9
        comprehension, 9

fluency and study skills, 9
word identification, 9
linguistic process of, 2–4
oral, 6, 7, 11
process of, 6–7
silent, 6–7, 13–14
surface and deep structure, 4–6
verbal communication, 2–4
word calling, 6, 11
Rebus writing, 37
Reduced or weak stress, 160–62
Rhythms of speech, 11
Roots, 107–8, 126, 128
    bound, 107–8
    free, 107–8, 126, 128

S

Secondary stress, 160–63
Segmental phonology, 139–40, 175–76
Segmentation principles, 156–60
Semantic clues, 54–75, 230
    advantages of, 66
    basis for, 63–65
    defined, 54–55
    how they work, 61–63
    lesson materials, 68–75
        exercises, 68–70
        suggested activities, 70–75
    limitations of, 67–68
    types of clues, 55–61
        explicit, 58–61
        implicit, 55–58
    with syntactic clues, 54–55
Semantic information, 4–6, 54–55
Semantic meaning, 4–5
Semantic units, 54
Sentence patterns, 78–79
Sight vocabulary, development of, 33
Sight words, 12
Silent consonant combinations, 188–89
Silent reading, 6–7, 13–14
Slang terminology, 65
Specialized vocabularies, 65
Spelling patterns, 158–60
Stress, 84, 152, 160–63
Structure word markers, 82–83
    adjective and adverb, 83
    clause, 83